Sustainability in Industry 5.0

This book emphasizes the need for data pre-processing, classification and prediction, cluster analysis, mining multimedia, and advanced Machine Learning techniques for scientific programming in Industry 5.0. This book conveys the following:

- Addresses how the convergence of intelligent systems and 5G wireless systems will solve industrial problems in autonomous robots and self-driving cars.
- Highlights the methods of smart things in collaborative autonomous fleets and platforms for integrating applications across different business and industry domains.
- Discusses important topics such as the Internet of Robotic Things, cloud robotics, and cognitive architecture for cyber-physical robotics.
- Explains image compression and advanced Machine Learning techniques for scientific programming in Industry 5.0.
- Presents a detailed discussion of smart manufacturing techniques, Industrial Internet of Things, and supply chain management in Industry 5.0.

This book is primarily written for graduate students and academic researchers in the fields of industrial engineering, manufacturing engineering, electrical engineering, production engineering, and mechanical engineering.

Computational Methods for Industrial Applications

Series Editor – Bharat Bhushan

In today's world IoT platforms and processes in conjunction with the disruptive block-chain technology and path breaking AI algorithms lay out a sparking and stimulating foundation for sustaining smarter systems. Further computational intelligence (CI) has gained enormous interests from various quarters in order to solve numerous real-world problems and enable intelligent behavior in changing and complex environment. This book series focuses on varied computational methods incorporated within the system with the help of artificial intelligence, learning methods, analytical reasoning and sense making in big data. Aimed at graduate students, academic researchers and professionals, the proposed series will cover the most efficient and innovative technological solutions for industrial applications and sustainable smart societies in order to alter green power management, effect of carbon emissions, air quality metrics, industrial pollution levels, biodiversity and ecology.

Blockchain for Industry 4.0: Emergence, Challenges, and Opportunities
Anoop V.S, Asharaf S, Justin Goldston, and Samson Williams

Intelligent Systems and Machine Learning for Industry: Advancements, Challenges and Practices
P R Anisha, C Kishor Kumar Reddy, Nguyen Gia Nhu, Megha Bhushan, Ashok Kumar, and Marlia Mohd Hanafiah

Sustainability in Industry 5.0: Theory and Applications
Edited by C Kishor Kumar Reddy, P R Anisha, Samiya Khan, Marlia Mohd Hanafiah, Lavanya Pamulaparty, and R Madana Mohana

Sustainability in Industry 5.0
Theory and Applications

Edited by
C. Kishor Kumar Reddy, P. R. Anisha,
Samiya Khan, Marlia Mohd Hanafiah,
Lavanya Pamulaparty, and R Madana Mohana

CRC Press
Taylor & Francis Group
Boca Raton London New York

CRC Press is an imprint of the
Taylor & Francis Group, an **informa** business

First edition published 2024
by CRC Press
2385 NW Executive Center Drive, Suite 320, Boca Raton FL 33431

and by CRC Press
4 Park Square, Milton Park, Abingdon, Oxon, OX14 4RN

CRC Press is an imprint of Taylor & Francis Group, LLC

ISBN: 9781032582016 (hbk)
ISBN: 9781032686219 (pbk)
ISBN: 9781032686363 (ebk)

DOI: 10.1201/9781032686363

Typeset in Times
by codeMantra

Contents

Preface..vii

Editors viii

List of Contributors..x

Chapter 1   From Industry 4.0 to Industry 5.0 1

                Bhavani Rachakatla and Sheshank Mouli Garrepalli

Chapter 2   Assessing the Impact of Industry 5.0 on
                Sustainability Strategies 26

                Praveen Kumar Malik and Arshi Naim

Chapter 3   Digital Industrial Revolution: From Sustainability
                Perspective...39

                Samiya Khan

Chapter 4   Machine Learning for Supply Chain Management
                in Industrial 4.0 Era: A Bibliometric Analytics 49

                Monalisha Pattnaik, Ashirbad Mishra, Aryan Pattnaik,
                and Alipsa Pattnaik

Chapter 5   Transforming Industry 5.0: Real Time Monitoring
                and Decision Making with IIOT 76

                Vijay Arputharaj J and Sanjoy Kumar Pal

Chapter 6   Energy Efficiency and Renewable Energy in Industry 5.0............... 107

                Aihloor Subramanyam Sreelatha, Bandi Pallavi,
                and Sheriff Olalekan Ajala

Chapter 7   A Study of Cloud of Things Enabled Machine
                Learning-Based Smart Health Monitoring System.........................156

                Ayontika Das, Riya Paul, Anindya Nag, and Biva Das

Chapter 8   Lung Cancer Classification Using CNN: Addressing
                Class Imbalance and Model Performance Analysis......................... 177

                Dr L K Suresh Kumar, Dr Humera Shaziya,
                and Ms Raniah Zaheer

Chapter 9   Water Quality Forecasting Using Deep Learning:
                A Study of the Brahmaputra Basin 206

                P R Anisha, Rithika Badam, Vijaya Sindhoori Kaza,
                and Poorvi Reddy Lakkadi

Chapter 10 Multimodal Fusion Techniques for Enhanced Fake News
                Detection: A Robustly Optimized BERT and Vision
                Transformer Approach 230

                Sumaya Abdul Rahman, V Sai Deepa Reddy,
                Aayesha Qureshi, and Srinath Doss

Index...253

Preface

Industry 5.0 integrates intelligent systems and the vital and completely human being strengths of analytical solving, value-adding creativity, and deep consideration of clients, to get better products and efficiency and permit mass personalization. The Industry 5.0 prototype promotes the use of smart sensors, equipment, and devices to enable smart manufacturing works that constantly capture production statistics and records by making use of robots. Advanced intelligent system's techniques facilitate the generation of actionable information by analyzing acquired data to accelerate production efficiency without altering the defined resources. In addition, the capability of intelligent system's techniques to deliver predictive and analytical insights has enabled the identification of complex manufacturing patterns and paved the way for a decision-intelligence guide machine in a diversity of producing errands such as continuous inspection and intelligent, predictive maintenance, great improvement, method optimization, supply chain management, and project scheduling with robotic applications. Even though unique intelligent system's techniques have been utilized in a variety of manufacturing applications in the past, many open questions and challenges remain, ranging from large statistics curation, storage, and technology, records reasoning to permit real-time actionable intelligence and augmented reality (AR), virtual reality (VR) to matters which include element computing and cyber-safety elements of smart manufacturing, smart agriculture, remote sensing, waste-water management, environmental engineering, disaster management, Geographic Information System, and so on.

This book consists of ten chapters, majorly covering concepts, applications, and challenges of Intelligent Internet of Things, Machine Learning, Deep Learning, and Image Processing Techniques in various applications. The first part of this book covers journey from Industry 4.0 to Industry 5.0, Assessing the Impact of Industry 5.0 on Sustainability Strategies, Digital Industrial Revolution: From Sustainability Perspective, Machine Learning for Supply Chain Management in Industrial 4.0 Era: A Bibliometric Analytics, Transforming Industry 5.0: Real-Time Monitoring and Decision-Making with IIOT, and Energy Efficiency and Renewable Energy in Industry 5.0. The second part covers A Study of Cloud of Things Enabled Machine Learning-Based Smart Health Monitoring System, Lung Cancer Classification Using CNN: Addressing Class Imbalance and Model Performance Analysis, Water Quality Forecasting Using Deep Learning: A Study of the Brahmaputra Basin, and Multimodal Fusion Techniques for Enhanced Fake News Detection: A Robustly Optimized BERT and Vision Transformer Approach.

The main focus of this book is to provide insights and complete knowledge of Machine Learning, Deep Learning, and Intelligent Internet of Things, and their integration in various industrial applications. We trust that this book will let readers find innovative ideas that are helpful to their research in various aspects.

Editors

Dr C Kishor Kumar Reddy is currently an Associate Professor in the Department of Computer Science and Engineering, Stanley College of Engineering and Technology for Women, Hyderabad, India. He has more than 10 years of research and teaching experience. He has published more than 50 research papers in national and international conferences, book chapters, and journals indexed by Scopus and others. He is an author for two textbooks and two co-edited books. He acted as the special session chair for Springer FICTA 2020, 2022, SCI 2021, INDIA 2022, and IEEE ICCSEA 2020 conferences. He is the corresponding editor of AMSE 2021 conference, published by IoP Science JPCS. He is a member of ISTE, CSI, IAENG, UACEE, and IACSIT.

Dr P R Anisha, TEDx Speaker, is currently working as Associate Professor in the Department of Computer Science and Engineering, Stanley College of Engineering and Technology for Women, Hyderabad, India. She has nine plus years of teaching experience. She earned her PhD from K L University, Guntur, India. Her areas of interest include Artificial Intelligence, Machine Learning, and Image Processing. She has 35 + research articles published in international conferences and journals. She has co-authored two books titled *Introduction to C* and *C++ programming*. She has acted as the special session chair for international conferences for Springer including INDIA 2019, 2022, SCI 2021, FICTA 2020, 2022 besides the IEEE conference ICCSEA 2020. She is a member of ACM and IAENG professional bodies.

Dr Samiya Khan is an alumna of the University of Delhi, India and completed her PhD in Computer Science from Jamia Millia Islamia, India. Currently, she is a Lecturer in Computer Science at the University of Greenwich, United Kingdom. Previously, she served as a postdoctoral research fellow at the University of Wolverhampton, United Kingdom. She has contributed more than 30 research papers and her publications extend across journal articles and book chapters in high impact publications of international repute. She has also presented her research at reputed international conferences. She has served as Associate Editor of *Scientific India Magazine* and reviewer for many reputed journals and conferences such as *IEEE Transactions on Emerging Trends in Computing and Information Processing and Management*, Elsevier. She is a regular contributor to magazines with many articles published in CSI Communications and Scientific India. Besides this, she has co-edited two books published by reputed publishers such as Springer and Elsevier and is also the author of a textbook titled *Big Data and Analytics*. Dr Khan's expertise spans across data science, Artificial Intelligence, edge computing, and the Internet of Things (IoT) with demonstrated experience in the development of heterogeneous systems. Her research interests include the use of Artificial Intelligence for the development of descriptive, diagnostic, predictive, and prescriptive healthcare applications.

Dr Marlia Mohd Hanafiah is a Professor and Head of the Centre for Tropical Climate Change System, Institute of Climate Change, The National University of Malaysia, Malaysia. Her areas of research expertise include Life Cycle Impact Assessment (LCA) and Environmental Foot printing of Green Materials and Energy, Environmental Engineering, Wastewater Treatment & Water Management, and Green Technology and Sustainability. She has 15 plus years of academic teaching experience and more than 170 publications in reputed journals and online book chapter contributions (indexed by SCI, SCIE, SSCI, Scopus, DBLP). She received research grant and consultation (as project leader and team member) of more than RM 7 million.

Dr Lavanya Pamulaparty has been working as Professor and Head of the Department of Computer Science and Engineering in the Methodist College of Engineering and Technology since 2010. She earned her BE degree in Computer Science and Engineering from KITS, Nagpur University. She earned her MTech in Software Engineering from Jawaharlal Nehru and Technological University (JNTUH), Hyderabad and Doctorate degree from JNTUH, Hyderabad, in the area of Data Mining. She has over 21 years of experience in the field of academic research and technological education. She has published 20 papers in various international and national journals and IEEE international/national conferences and two patents. Her papers are indexed in Scopus and SCI. Her areas of interest include Artificial Intelligence and Machine Learning. She is IEEE, CSI, and ISTE life members. She has organized international conferences including ICPET-2016, 2018, and ICAISC-2022.

Dr R Madana Mohana is a senior member of IEEE and a Professor in the Department of IT at the Chaitanya Bharathi Institute of Technology, Hyderabad, India. He has more than 18 years of teaching experience. He earned his PhD with a Machine Learning specialization. He has published more than 50 research articles in various peer-reviewed journals and conferences. He is a life member of ISTE and fellow of IETE. He has organized various conferences, workshops, and delivered keynote addresses.

Contributors

Dr Sheriff Olalekan Ajala
Research Engineer, Roban Energy
Houston, Texas

Dr P R Anisha
Department of Computer Science and
Engineering
Stanley College of Engineering &
Technology for Women
Hyderabad, India

Vijay Arputharaj J
Department of Computer Science
CHRIST (Deemed to be University)
Bangalore, India

Rithika Badam
Department of Computer Science and
Engineering
Stanley College of Engineering &
Technology for Women
Hyderabad, India

Ayontika Das
Department of Computer Science and
Engineering
Adamas University
Kolkata, India

Biva Das
Pharmacy Discipline
Khulna University
Khulna, Bangladesh

Srinath Doss
Faculty of Engineering & Technology
Botho University
Gaborone, Botswana

Sheshank Mouli Garrepalli
George Herbert Walker School of
Business & Technology
Webster University
San Antonio, Texas

Vijaya Sindhoori Kaza
Department of Computer Science and
Engineering
Stanley College of Engineering &
Technology for Women
Hyderabad, India

Samiya Khan
School of Computing and Mathematical
Sciences
University of Greenwich
London, UK

Dr L. K. Suresh Kumar
Department of Computer Science and
Engineering
Osmania University
Hyderabad, India

Poorvi Reddy Lakkadi
Business Analytics
George Mason University School of
Business
Fairfax County, Virginia

Dr Praveen Kumar Malik
School of Electronics and Electrical
Engineering
Lovely Professional University
Phagwara, India

Ashirbad Mishra
Department of C.S.E., College of
    Engineering
University Park, State College
Pennsylvania, USA

Anindya Nag
Computer Science and Engineering
    Discipline
Khulna University
Khulna, Bangladesh

Arshi Naim
Department of Information Systems
King Khalid University
Abha, Saudi Arabia

Sanjoy Kumar Pal
Department of Biological Sciences
Skyline University
Kano, Nigeria

Bandi Pallavi
Department of Electrical and
    Electronics Engineering
Stanley College of Engineering &
    Technology for Women
Hyderabad, India

Alipsa Pattnaik
Birla School of Applied Sciences
Birla Global University
Bhubaneswar, India

Aryan Pattnaik
Department of Computer Science &
    System Engineering
KIIT University
Bhubaeswar, India

Monalisha Pattnaik
Department of Statistics
Sambalpur University
Burla, India

Riya Paul
Department of Biomedical Engineering
Adamas University
Kolkata, India

Aayesha Qureshi
Department of Computer Science and
    Engineering,
Stanley College of Engineering &
    Technology for Women, Hyderabad
India

Bhavani Rachakatla
Department of Computer Science and
    Engineering
University of North Texas
Denton, Texas

Sumaya Abdul Rahman
Department of Information Technology
Stanley College of Engineering &
    Technology for Women
Hyderabad, India

V. Sai Deepa Reddy
Department of Computer Science and
    Engineering
Stanley College of Engineering &
    Technology for Women
Hyderabad, India

Dr Humera Shaziya
Nizam College
Osmania University
Hyderabad, India

Dr Aihloor Subramanyam Sreelatha
The Faculty of Engineering & Science
Aalborg Energy, Aalborg University
Aalborg, Denmark

Raniah Zaheer
University of Najran
Saudi Arabia

1 From Industry 4.0 to Industry 5.0

Bhavani Rachakatla
University of North Texas

Sheshank Mouli Garrepalli
Webster University

1.1 INTRODUCTION

From using steam power and production mechanization in Industry 1.0; electricity and assembly line production in Industry 2.0; partial automation in Industry 3.0 [1]; information and communication technologies in Industry 4.0, we are now at a phase of transition from Industry 4.0 to Industry 5.0, where human-centricity, sustainability, and resilience are its core elements.

This chapter explores the idea of Industry 5.0 and its role in sustainability. We start with an overview of Industry 4.0 and then discuss the emerging trends that caused the leading to Industry 5.0. Then, we further discuss how Industry 5.0 has emerged, its fundamental principles, and how it addresses the shortcomings of Industry 4.0 and additionally examine the role of sustainability in Industry 5.0 along with exploring specific areas such as resource efficiency, waste reduction, circular economy, and green technologies with a further mention of how sustainability is integrated into Industry 5.0's operations, business model. We will also highlight a few practical applications through case studies, with a final focus on the challenges and prospects of Industry 5.0. Although we will briefly discuss the broader social, economic, and political implications of Industry 5.0, these subjects will not be the main focus of this chapter. Moreover, detailed technical aspects of green technologies or in-depth critique of specific industrial policies will be outside the scope of this chapter.

It is critical to have a communique about the significance of Industry 5.0 as a sustainable framework for business practices. In the coming times, comprehending the connection between newly growing commercial paradigms and sustainability is critical for addressing environmental issues and achieving sustainable goals. This chapter adds to the more significant discussion of sustainability in Industry 5.0 by thoroughly examining theory, concepts, applications, and prospects.

This chapter is designed to facilitate a comprehensive understanding of the transition from Industry 4.0 to Industry 5.0 and the subsequent impact on sustainability. The structure of this chapter is as follows:

Initially, we will establish a foundational understanding of the topic, setting the stage and context for the ensuing exploration. This introduction provides readers with a common point of reference for the subject at hand. Next, we will embark on an

DOI: 10.1201/9781032686363-1

analytical journey from Industry 4.0 to Industry 5.0. This section provides a detailed exposition of Industry 4.0 and examines the shift toward its successor, thereby highlighting the continuum of industrial evolution.

In the third section, we explore the rise of Industry 5.0, unearthing its fundamental principles, and how it seeks to rectify the deficiencies of Industry 4.0. This part aims to offer a nuanced perspective on the industry's future. The fourth section delves into the critical role of sustainability in Industry 5.0. We discuss the alignment of Industry 5.0 with broader sustainability, objectives, and how it incorporates sustainable practices. We will further investigate specific sustainability dimensions such as resource efficiency, waste reduction, circular economy, and the implementation of green technologies.

Following this, the fifth section presents an array of case studies that underscore implementing sustainable solutions in the context of Industry 5.0. These examples serve to bridge the gap between theory and practice.

Our subsequent discussion centers on the challenges and potential of integrating sustainability into Industry 5.0. This section provides a balanced perspective on the impediments and prospects of this integration, offering insights into potential solutions and future developments.

The closing section summarizes the key insights gleaned throughout thischapter and offers a cohesive overview of the intricate interplay between Industry 5.0 and sustainability. This summation aims to encapsulate our journey through this complex topic and to leave readers with a thorough understanding of the subject matter.

This structure offers a complete discussion on "Sustainability in Industry 5.0" by providing a logical path from comprehending the concept of Industry 5.0 to its association with sustainability.

1.2   THE JOURNEY FROM INDUSTRY 4.0 TO INDUSTRY 5.0

1.2.1   OVERVIEW OF INDUSTRY 4.0

Industry 4.0, commonly acknowledged as the Fourth Industrial Revolution, signified a substantial evolution in the industrial sphere by incorporating digital technologies and automation. Unlike its antecedents, driven by steam, electricity, and information technology, Industry 4.0 constitutes a convergence of groundbreaking technologies such as Artificial Intelligence, the Internet of Things, Genetic Engineering, and 3D Printing. This period is distinguished by its amalgamation of digital and physical systems, thus constructing interconnected and intelligent value chains (Figure 1.1).

The main technological catalysts propelling Industry 4.0 encompass:

- **Internet of Things (IoT)**: The advent of IoT allowed physical devices to communicate and exchange data, offering a new stratum of automation and real-time decision-making in industrial processes.
- **Industrial Internet of Things (IIoT)**: The IIoT, a salient aspect of Industry 4.0, involves the integration of industrial machinery with software and sensors to collate, exchange, and analyze data. IIoT enhances operational efficiency, facilitates predictive maintenance, and empowers real-time industry decision-making, setting the stage for increasingly intelligent and autonomous systems.

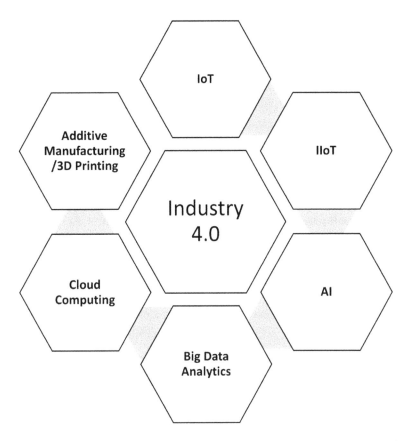

FIGURE 1.1   Key technologies driving Industry 4.0. This diagram illustrates the six key technologies that formed the basis of the Fourth Industrial Revolution.

- **Artificial Intelligence (AI)**: The application of AI and machine learning algorithms fostered the examination and interpretation of the immense volumes of data produced by IoT devices, thus guiding intelligent decision-making processes.
- **Big Data Analytics**: The accumulation and analysis of substantial volumes of data, frequently in real-time, allowed businesses to procure deeper insights into their operations and optimize processes.
- **Cloud Computing**: By capitalizing on cloud technologies, businesses could access and scrutinize data from any location, minimizing the requirement for physical infrastructure and delivering scalable computational resources.
- **Additive Manufacturing/3D Printing**: Often termed as 3D Printing, additive manufacturing represents a revolutionary approach in Industry 4.0, enabling the construction of intricate and customized products layer by layer from digital 3D models. This technology considerably diminishes waste and stimulates on-demand production, contributing to efficiency and sustainability.

Industry 4.0 harbored the conviction in the transformative potential of technology to revolutionize manufacturing and other industrial sectors. A primary objective was to amplify automation and efficiency significantly. This was realized through the establishment of "smart factories," where cyber-physical systems scrutinize the factory's physical processes, make decentralized decisions, and facilitate greater adaptability, resource efficiency, and ergonomics. Additionally, augmenting interconnectivity through the IIoT enabled seamless communication between machines, products, and people—big data and analytics support real-time decision-making and operations optimization, from production to logistics. Furthermore, Industry 4.0 aspired to facilitate a higher degree of product customization under highly flexible mass production conditions. Lastly, advancements in additive manufacturing or 3D Printing were expected to catalyze significant changes in the production process, reducing waste and increasing sustainability.

1.2.2   ACHIEVEMENTS AND SHORTCOMINGS OF INDUSTRY 4.0

1.2.2.1   Achievements of Industry 4.0

Industry 4.0 sparked unprecedented alterations that considerably reshaped the industrial landscape. Key achievements of this era can be categorized as follows:

- **Enhanced Productivity and Efficiency**:Implementing automation and interconnectivity in manufacturing processes significantly boosted productivity and efficiency. Analyzing data in real-time and performing predictive maintenance enabled manufacturers to elevate their quality control and drastically reduce production errors.
- **The emergence of Smart Factories**: The successful deployment of cyber-physical systems and IoT technologies led to the creation of "smart factories." These modern industrial spaces allowed for continuous monitoring and optimization of processes, thereby amplifying the efficiency of production lines, and diminishing resource waste.
- **Facilitation of Mass Customization**: Industry 4.0 technologies, such as flexible and additive manufacturing systems, paved the way for mass customization. This innovation allowed manufacturers to cater to customer-specific needs and preferences on a large scale without compromising efficiency.

1.2.2.2   Shortcomings of Industry 4.0

Despite the groundbreaking transformations, it is critical to acknowledge the challenges that came alongside the transformative strides of Industry 4.0:

- **Cybersecurity and Data Privacy**: The increased reliance on digitalization and connectivity has brought about more pervasive and destructive cybersecurity threats. Additionally, the colossal amounts of data generated, gathered, and analyzed exposed significant data privacy concerns.

- **Investment and Infrastructure Challenges**: The shift to Industry 4.0 necessitated substantial infrastructural investments, presenting a formidable challenge for small and medium-sized enterprises to adapt. The requirement to modernize machinery, systems, and operational procedures posed a significant financial burden.
- **Workforce Impact**: The rise in automation spurred fears of extensive job losses, particularly within roles characterized by routine tasks and lower skill levels. Concurrently, the demand for digital skills surged, creating a workforce skills gap that required urgent attention.
- **Environmental Sustainability Concerns**: While the efficiencies of Industry 4.0 could curtail waste, it also accentuated specific environmental challenges. The considerable energy consumption of data centers and digital devices, alongside the generation of electronic waste, highlighted the urgent need for sustainable practices.
- The above evaluation aims to provide a balanced and realistic perspective on the impact of Industry 4.0, thereby setting a sound foundation for our upcoming discussion on how Industry 5.0 intends to address these identified shortcomings.

1.2.3 THE TRANSITION: EMERGING TRENDS LEADING TO INDUSTRY 5.0

As we move beyond Industry 4.0, we are witnessing the rise of a new industrial age—Industry 5.0.

Several emerging trends drive this transition:

1. **Push for Sustainable Practices**: The shortcomings of Industry 4.0, particularly its environmental sustainability concerns, have ignited a global push for more sustainable practices in the industry. This involves not just cleaner production methods but a rethinking of business models, with a shift toward circular economy concepts.
2. **Human-Centric Designs**: While Industry 4.0 was about automating processes, Industry 5.0 shifted the focus back to the human element. The industry is moving toward human-centric designs where machines and humans collaborate. The emergence of "cobots" or collaborative robots exemplifies this trend, where robots work alongside humans in production, augmenting human capabilities.
3. **Advanced Technologies**: The rise of advanced technologies such as AI and machine learning, digital twins, and edge computing is pivotal in shaping Industry 5.0. These technologies enhance production efficiency and enable more customization, better product development, and predictive maintenance.
4. **Impacts of Global Factors**: Global events like the COVID-19 pandemic have exposed vulnerabilities in our manufacturing and supply chains, accelerating the need for digital transformation. Industry 5.0 technologies can provide greater resilience, allowing for more local production and supply chain diversification.

These trends fundamentally reshape the industrial landscape, signaling the shift from Industry 4.0 to Industry 5.0. The following sections will delve deeper into what Industry 5.0 entails and how it aligns with sustainability goals.

1.3 THE EMERGENCE OF INDUSTRY 5.0

1.3.1 KEY PRINCIPLES OF INDUSTRY 5.0

Since the beginning of the Industrial Revolution, we have witnessed remarkable enhancements, the most significant milestones in human history in the industrial domain. The steam engine was the first monument, but not the last—the setting up of assembly lines to raise the bar for mass production during the Second Industrial Revolution. Digital developments headed the third version of the Industrial Revolution. Computers and the internet reshaped the world in an entirely new way. Concepts such as AI started ruling the roost by enhancing the computer's smartness and working mechanisms. Although Industry 5.0 is the newborn baby, the impact it created on industrial practices and development is unimaginable; a few of the surreal components, like human–robot collaboration, customizations of the robots, the ultimatum of sustainable environmental doings, and human-centric manufacturing are key factors [2,3].

Let us discuss the principles of Industry 5.0 in detail:

1. **Human–Machine collaboration**:

    Industrial robots started replacing human efforts in 1961 when the first animated robot, a mechanical arm, was introduced. However, it was just programmed and encouraged to work alone to function on specific instructions fearing the accidents caused by its inadaptability to sense its surroundings.

    Considering the latest emphasis, BMW, the car manufacturing company, took a step and introduced COBOTS, The collaboration of human Intelligence and experience with robots' robust productivity [4].

    Unlike their ancestors, cobots are designed to work in harmony with humans. Imagine an assembly line where a robotic arm with sensors and precision is lifting and positioning heavy car doors. At the same time, humans work on the intricate installation process with their nimble fingers and years of experience. It is like a perfectly choreographed ballet, where dancers know their steps and complement each other.

    The cobots at BMW are equipped with a myriad of sensors. These sensors constantly monitor the environment and allow the cobots to react in real-time to the humans working alongside them. No longer are the robots confined; they are now partners.

    This has enormous benefits. For one, it drastically reduces the physical strain on human workers. No more backbreaking lifting: the cobots have gotten that covered. Second, it enables higher precision and quality in assembly, as humans can focus on the intricate details without being bogged down by the heavy lifting.

2. Customization and Personalization:

Industry 5.0 heralds a world of customization and technology where one can consume products made in gigantic quantities and get their preference every time, with footwear being at the vanguard of such revolutions—3D Printing crops up as the actor in this revolution.

Imagine this: You do not settle for generic shoe sizes; your feet are measured down to the tiniest details you can have. A few brands like Adidas and Nike have started using 3D Printing in their shoemaking process so that each pair of shoes is as unique as their customers' feet into which it is custom-made.

Here is what makes the high point in 3D Printing. Using state-of-the-art scanning tools, they take many data; foot size, shape, arch, and even how pressure is distributed during movement. They feed this info willy-nilly into the printers.

3D Printing is accelerated by precision and agility. Here they move very carefully on replacing layers of material to craft a shoe that would be more than generic but explicitly customized for the customer whose feet they are custom making them for.

Athletes experience proper momentum on the ground, and individuals with stoop-related conditions get relief from ordinary shoes by switching to funky 3D-printed footwear. As a result, they feel fresher and achieve better results. Lastly, environmental sustainability gets a pat, too, because it is eco-friendly and efficient.

3. Sustainability:

Industry 5.0, the latest phase of industrial evolution, recognizes the imperative significance of sustainability in addressing global challenges. By synergizing sustainability principles with advanced technologies and digitalization, Industry 5.0 aims to drive economic growth while ensuring environmental stewardship and societal well-being.

Alongside these, embracing resource efficiency, waste reduction, and the rise in the use of renewable energy are the main strategies pointed out in Industry 5.0, which in turn help change the environmental impacts and promote future sustainability.

Supposedly, this latest Industry revolution focuses its attention on social equity by promoting ethically driven ways, this has not just been one of the many things that are focused on, but sustainability is one of the fundamental aspects that Industry 5.0 is focusing on; this would result in a harmonious equilibrium of economic advancements, social responsibility, and environmental preservation.

For example, consider Schneider Electric's EcoStruxure, an IoT-based architecture that gathers information on the amount of energy consumed and monitors and analyses it was using sophisticated machine learning and data analytic programs.

4. Human-Centric Manufacturing:

Past, when industries started to install automated belt lines and replace the human workforce, the companies began to receive criticism for treating the employees with the least respect and more like a liability.

A recent study by one of the institutions suggests that the new industrial 5.0 practices have shown tremendous results in productivity, innovation, and user and employee satisfaction. The collaborative work over producing brain-less robots with brain-full humans has led to economic growth and competitiveness.

1.3.2 How Industry 5.0 Addresses the Shortcomings of Industry 4.0

Industry 4.0 has bought remarkable changes and outcomes in the manufacturing industry by utilizing data analysis and automation, yet there are still a few short-comings that should be covered in the next revolution (i.e., Industry 5.0). Integrating human Intelligence and creativity with machines should bring up the equilibrium [5].

1.3.2.1 Association of Human Touch

With the increasing presence of robots replacing human workers in the manufac-turing industry, the challenges of controlling criticism from employee unions and social workers have become more pronounced. Additionally, the battle against losing employment opportunities for human workers has intensified. However, the emer-gence of Industry 5.0 offers promising solutions to these concerns. This latest trend seeks to address the issues by prioritizing increased human involvement in various aspects of manufacturing. Industry 5.0 recognizes the value of human creativity, decision-making abilities, cognition, and emotional Intelligence, which can be lever-aged to enhance machine capabilities that lack these qualities. By integrating human expertise and skills into manufacturing, Industry 5.0 strives to strike a balance that benefits humans and machines. This approach aims to overcome the challenges posed by automation, ensuring that humans remain integral to the industry while augmenting their capabilities with technological advancements.

1.3.2.2 Enhanced Customization

In the Industrial Revolution 4.0, driven by increased production rates and economies of scale, the manufacturing industry was mainly focused on mass production to meet growing demand (and maximize efficiency). However, in the last 3 years, there has been a notable trend of changing priorities among companies that realize the impor-tance of user satisfaction and customization in driving business success. This transi-tion toward enhanced customization has primarily defined the industrial landscape since the beginning of the new century.

It is now recognized across businesses how vital customer experience has become for them to thrive in the market today. With increased competition and consumers attaining increasing expectations and preferences, firms must provide personalized and tailored products during order execution to attract and retain customers. The Industrial Revolution has duly responded to this shift, emphasizing customization much more.

Advanced technologies continue to play an essential role in facilitating enhanced customization. Additive manufacturing, commonly known as 3D Printing, has revolutionized the conventional production process allowing manufacturers to develop highly customized goods. Through 3D Printing, manufacturers can adapt their manufacturing processes to produce unique and personalized products in response to individual customers' specific needs and preferences.

In addition, digitalization and data-driven approaches have put forward the wheels for enhanced customization. By gathering and analyzing information derived from customers' channel transactions, companies can collect valuable insights that lend themselves to developing customized products that meet the unique requirements set by each customer.

Moreover, advancements made regarding automation and robotics have contributed substantially to sustaining growth in customized outcomes. Though still challenged by diverse kinds of product groups, manufacturers integrating robotic systems on their production lines need more flexibility and agility of flexible and agile capabilities provided by these systems. These systems can readily adhere to different specifications frequently without sacrificing levels of quality or speed of production. Thus, effective customization without compromising overall productivity and speed becomes achievable.

1.3.2.3   Sustainable Production Process

Industry 4.0 signified a notable change in the manufacturing paradigm by integrating digital technologies, automation, and data exchange. However, it is widely recognized that this development should have put more effort into sustainability. As the world becomes more aware of the pressing environmental issues, a new response has emerged: Industry 5.0. This approach prioritizes eco-friendly production, offering a promising solution to our environmental concerns.

Real-time monitoring is vital to Sustainable Production Processes in Industry 5.0. Through the integration of sensors, IoT devices, and advanced analytics, manufacturers can gain exceptional visibility into their operations. Real-time monitoring helps manufacturers track and optimize resource consumption, identifies any inefficiencies in material usage, and also assists in making data-driven decisions if something is degrading the environment. Whether its watching energy being used, water depletion, or even raw materials usage, this proactive approach empowers manufacturers to remove waste and increase overall resource efficiency.

Waste reduction is yet another essential aspect of sustainable production in Industry 5.0. Companies can significantly reduce waste generation throughout the production cycle by implementing intelligent manufacturing concepts such as lean manufacturing principles and circular economy strategy. Advanced automation and robotics help control material usage precisely, minimizing scrap and improving yield rates. Moreover, integrating closed-loop systems facilitates the recovery and reuse of valuable resources, reducing waste sent to landfills.

Energy optimization is another critical driver for sustainability in Industry 5.0. With rising prices of energy and environmental connotations related to greenhouse gases emitted, manufacturers spend increasing attention on energy-efficient processes for producing their outputs. Smart grids, energy management systems, and predictive analytics allow companies to measure and manage energy consumption in real time. At the same time, by identifying energy-intensive processes and implementing energy-saving measures, manufacturers try to minimize their carbon footprint and contribute to a more sustainable future.

Industry 5.0 also advocates stakeholder interaction as a means of sustainable production practices. Based on partnerships with suppliers, customers, and other industry players, manufacturers can exchange best practices, develop innovative solutions, and create a shared vision concerning sustainable manufacturing. Collaboration across the supply chain helps eco-friendly initiatives like sourcing sustainable materials, reducing transportation emissions using reduced pollutants, and designing recyclable products [6].

1.3.2.4 Holistic Decision-Making

Data-driven decision-making became a focus as companies realized that just using data for decisions was insufficient. The value of information started to be appreciated, and it came to the limelight that a purely quantitative approach does have its limits. Industry 5.0 recognizes the need for an interactive process with human judgment and data-driven insights woven into one tapestry.

While analysis of patterns, trends, and correlations helps in understanding and making better choices, there is a holistic dimension that data only captures partially. Humans bring intuitive judgments—based on experience and domain expertise— required to make contextually sufficient decisions. This way, Industry 5.0 balances putting forward data alongside human review and creating synergy.

One aspect of holistic decision-making in Industry 5.0 has recognized limitations and biases inherent in data. Data-driven decisions can be influenced by some types of incomplete or even biased sets of data like extrapolations or algorithms either alone or together, depending upon the situation. Human judgment then looks at it with a fine-tooth comb to designate any mitigating actions against these limitations since they obfuscate the true nature of things. Human insufficiency introduces a qualitative dimension that complements quantitative insights derived from data analysis.

Human judgment particularly comes in handy when complex decision-making scenarios crop up where data may not suffice to provide clear-cut answers. Grasping several factors involved in demanding situations makes humans a preferred option, as several problems cannot be quantified permanently. Humans help in identifying and mitigating those limitations of data sets through the use of critical evaluation of the same, sometimes called evidentiary assistance. The means of identifying include sources, considering pros vs. cons (human beings are our best judge), and understanding one's potential implications beyond collective understanding while objectively analyzing data sets.

Hence, Industry 5.0 continually encourages interdisciplinary approaches and collaboration to facilitate holistic decision-making. By combining diverse expertise and perspective accessibility across organizations, more comprehensive decisions can be made leveraging collective Intelligence amidst teams. Cross-functional teams integrate individuals of multiple backgrounds, skill bases, and age ranges; each adding their expertise toward a group view hence the well-rounded decision. Potential Conflicting Factors such as human time constraints restrict the scope of dealing with humans by encompassing complementary facets regarding decision-making objectives. Such multidisciplinary composite views add depth and nuances vital for decision-making processes.

Furthermore, support for continuous learning alongside adaptation has been encouraged continuously in Industry 5.0. Continuous Processes the industry considers three distinct life phases as primary developmental stages, namely (Figure 1.2):

1. Preparatory Stage (Assessment, planning, execution)
2. Growth Stage (Comprehensive growth through adapting, restructuring)
3. Maturity Stage (Continuous process innovation and development)

1.4 THE ROLE OF SUSTAINABILITY IN INDUSTRY 5.0

1.4.1 ALIGNING INDUSTRY 5.0 WITH SUSTAINABILITY GOALS

As the global industrial landscape evolves from Industry 4.0 to Industry 5.0, synchronizing industrial development with sustainability objectives becomes increasingly crucial. Industry 5.0 principles and technologies offer a chance to balance economic growth with environmental protection.

The United Nations has delineated 17 Sustainable Development Goals (SDGs) as a comprehensive roadmap to realize a superior and sustainable future for humanity and the planet by 2030. Many of these goals align seamlessly with the intentions of Industry 5.0, which emphasizes resilient, human-centric processes. These include SDG 7 (Affordable and Clean Energy), SDG 8 (Decent Work and Economic Growth), SDG 9 (Industry, Innovation, and Infrastructure), SDG 12 (Responsible Consumption and Production), and SDG 13 (Climate Action) [7]. Industry 5.0, focusing on sustainable processes and a human-centric approach, contributes significantly to these goals.

Equipped with technologies for energy efficiency, renewables, storage, and autonomy, along with AI and individualized human–machine collaboration (i.e., cobots), the human-centric approach of Industry 5.0 resonates profoundly with the SDGs [5]. It aims to improve working conditions and facilitate economic growth, all while keeping the welfare of the workforce in mind.

The ethos of a sustainable industry is echoed by corporations such as Huawei, Nike, JetBlue, and Hilton Hotels. For instance, Nike's "Move to Zero" mission, aiming for zero waste and zero carbon while increasing the use of recycled materials in their products, aligns perfectly with SDG 12. Similarly, JetBlue, recognizing the significant carbon emissions from air transport, is working toward carbon neutrality by exploring renewable jet fuel options, aligning itself with SDG 13. Huawei's initiative, TECH4ALL, supports digitally disenfranchised populations, increasing digital inclusion for individuals with disabilities and refugees, aligning with SDG 9.

With a focus on technologies that drive sustainable industrial development, aligning Industry 5.0 with sustainability goals offers a clear path toward a sustainable, inclusive, and resilient future. The following section will delve into one of the main ways Industry 5.0 aligns with sustainability goals by exploring the notion of improved resource efficiency.

Industry 4.0

"The rise of automation, data exchange, and manufacturing technologies."

"Milestone 1: Recognition of environmental sustainability concerns and the need for cleaner production methods."

"Milestone 2: Rise of collaborative robots and human-machine collaboration."

"Milestone 3: Adoption of advanced technologies for improved efficiency, customization, and predictive maintenance."

"Milestone 4: Global events prompting digital transformation for resilience in manufacturing and supply chains."

Industry 5.0: "Arrival of Industry 5.0, focused on sustainability, human-centric design, and resilient industrial systems."

FIGURE 1.2   Key milestones in the transition from Industry 4.0 to Industry 5.0.

1.4.2 RESOURCE EFFICIENCY

Resource efficiency assumes a pivotal role in the progressive realm of Industry 5.0, facilitating corporations to optimize their utilization of resources while mitigating their overall environmental footprint. The European Commission defines resource efficiency as developing strategies to encourage the effective and efficient management of natural resources. This implies employing the earth's finite resources sustainably while attenuating environmental impacts. Within an industrial context, this translates to practices that foster the judicious use of energy, material, and human resources in manufacturing processes.

Industry 5.0 has ushered in various avant-garde technologies, including AI, big data analytics, digital twins, and collaborative robotics. When judiciously applied, these technologies can substantially augment resource efficiency within manufacturing processes. For example, integrating AI and IoT sensor data into predictive maintenance facilitates optimal equipment utilization, significantly reducing resource wastage.

About half a century ago, Siemens initiated measures for environmental preservation by establishing an environmental protection department. Since then, they have undertaken numerous initiatives to safeguard the environment and are committed to a 20% reduction of emissions in their supply chain by 2030. They are striving toward a carbon-neutral supply chain by 2050. Furthermore, they aspire to make more significant strides toward a circular economy.

The Siemens Amberg Electronics plant in Germany, widely recognized as a highly automated and digitally advanced factory, is an exemplary instance of resource efficiency. By 2030, this state-of-the-art production facility is slated to become carbon neutral.

This ambitious endeavor has been made feasible through the deployment of digital twins. A digital twin is a mechanical replica of a physical entity, ranging from a circuit board to an entire production plant [8]. Mathematical models are used to analyze the present condition of electrical, heating, and cooling systems. Collaborating with on-site experts facilitates identifying opportunities for energy savings and process improvements. The simulation analysis unveils instances where heating and cooling systems counteract each other, a phenomenon that may have otherwise gone unnoticed. This analysis further illuminates the significant role of detailed knowledge of plant and product specifications in creating a high-quality digital twin.

In its quest for sustainability, the Siemens plant in Amberg has made considerable strides toward decarbonization. As of the fiscal year 2018/2019, this facility accounted for approximately 6.8 tons of CO_2 emissions. Subsequently, the management has embarked on a precise trajectory to carbon neutrality, primarily focusing on enhancing the plant's carbon footprint through individual, cost-effective measures involving strategic, operational optimization and transitioning to green, carbon-neutral energy procurement.

As the project progresses, a comprehensive and agile approach is being adopted, continually adapting to evolving external conditions. This strategy includes installing photovoltaic systems on substantial portions of the plant's roof space. Though this will not further diminish the carbon footprint, it is anticipated to result in significant cost savings and increased autonomy in the power supply.

A vital component of this ambitious plan is the eventual substitution of gas heating with an efficient heat pump system integrated with the cooling system for maximum efficiency. However, the complete removal of gas is not viable due to its necessity in operating annealing furnaces for metal part treatment. The long-term strategy encompasses transitioning from natural gas to biomethane, with investigations underway to replace natural gas with hydrogen.

The plant is projected to achieve complete carbon neutrality by 2030. Significantly, this goal is expected to be accomplished without purchasing emission certificates for flexibility, symbolizing a self-sustaining, sustainable operation.

Improving resource efficiency can yield substantial implications beyond the confines of the factory floor. By reducing waste and curtailing resource use, corporations can experience significant cost savings, bolstering their financial performance. Concurrently, it facilitates contributions toward environmental sustainability, aligning with global objectives like the UN's SDGs. Amid consumers' and regulators' escalating demand for sustainable practices, enhancing resource efficiency can bolster a company's competitiveness.

Minimizing waste and maximizing resource efficiency improves a company's financial performance and benefits the environment. With the advent of the "circular economy," there is even more significant potential for corporations to devise innovative strategies for waste management. This period represents an exhilarating juncture for sustainability.

1.4.3 WASTE REDUCTION AND CIRCULAR ECONOMY

Traditionally, a linear economy adheres to the paradigm of "take-make-dispose," which implies that raw materials are procured and converted into utilized products until discarded as waste. Contrastingly, in a circular economy, these raw material cycles are closed and require more than mere recycling; it necessitates a paradigm shift in how value is created and preserved, how sustainable production is implemented, and which business models are utilized.

The circular economy is anchored in three fundamental principles: (a) Eliminating waste and pollution, (b) Circulation of products and materials at their highest value, and (c) Regeneration of nature. These principles are realized as follows:

By shifting our perspective, waste can be regarded as a design flaw. In a circular economy, it is a prerequisite for any design that materials are reincorporated into the economy at the end of their use. Consequently, the linear "take-make-waste" system is transformed into a circular one. Numerous products could be circulated by being maintained, shared, reused, repaired, refurbished, remanufactured, and recycled as a final recourse. Food and other biodegradable materials that are safe to return to nature can regenerate the land, fueling the production of new food and materials. Through an emphasis on design, the concept of waste can be eradicated.

There are several methodologies by which products and materials can be maintained in circulation. It is beneficial to consider two primary cycles: technical and biological. In the technological cycle, products are reused, repaired, remanufactured, and recycled. In the natural process, biodegradable materials are reintroduced to the earth through composting and anaerobic digestion.

A shift in focus from extraction to regeneration is paramount. Instead of persistently degrading nature, we build natural capital. We deploy farming practices that allow wildlife to rebuild soils, increase biodiversity, and return biological materials to the earth. Most of these materials are lost after use, and the land used to grow them is depleted of nutrients. By transitioning to a regenerative model, we begin to emulate natural systems. In nature, waste is non-existent[9]. The circular economy concept can be integrated into Industry 5.0 to improve supply chain efficiency and reduce waste. This involves minimizing material waste, improving supply management processes, and utilizing AI and additive manufacturing to enable personalized production. The communication, research, and automation capabilities of Industry 4.0 can support circular design in Industry 5.0. The onus is now on companies to take the lead in implementing these practices to pave the way toward a more sustainable future.

Industry 5.0 employs advanced technologies such as the IoT and AI to optimize resource use and reduce waste. Real-time monitoring and management of resource usage and waste generation are enabled through these technologies. This facilitates efficient resource utilization; maintenance needs prediction, and prevention of unnecessary waste by companies.

Digital twins, virtual representations of physical products or systems, further refine this process by allowing simulation and testing without using physical resources. This lets companies virtually perfect their product designs and manufacturing processes, minimizing waste generation during production.

Siemens is a prime example of a company that utilizes digital twin technology in its electric motor production. By digitally simulating and optimizing the motor's performance before it is physically produced, Siemens can significantly reduce material usage and production waste, thus meeting circular economy objectives. Embracing Industry 5.0 technologies facilitates a transition from a linear to a circular production model, where resources are used more efficiently, and waste is minimized.

1.4.4 GREEN TECHNOLOGIES

Green technology, colloquially referred to as "Greentech," denotes a category of environmentally friendly technology based on its production process or supply chain. Four primary objectives underpin these technologies: waste reduction, materials management, pollution prevention, and product enhancement [10].

Waste Reduction strategies and practices aim to alleviate the strain on the environment and waste management systems by curbing the volume of waste generated. In this context, waste reduction serves as a critical goal.

Materials Management pertains to the strategic planning, control, and efficient utilization of materials from acquisition to disposal. The emphasis here is on enhancing manufacturing process efficiency and minimizing waste.

Pollution Prevention involves designing, operating, and modifying industrial processes to curtail or eliminate the discharge of detrimental substances into the environment.

Product Enhancement seeks to effect improvements or modifications to a product's design, performance, or features with a strong focus on sustainability. This can manifest as the creation of energy-efficient products or the usage of environmentally friendly materials.

Green technologies occupy a vital role within Industry 5.0. Corporations are curtailing their carbon footprint by consuming less energy while executing more work by employing energy-efficient machinery. Moreover, renewable energy sources such as solar and wind power are experiencing escalating popularity, with companies like Siemens Gamesa spearheading the charge in integrating wind energy into their processes.

Carbon Capture and Storage (CCS) represents another critical green technology. This mechanism captures carbon dioxide emissions at their origin and sequesters them underground, thus mitigating climate change and reducing CO_2 emissions.

These green technologies contribute to a more sustainable industrial process and yield considerable long-term cost savings. Energy-efficient machinery and renewable energy sources can dramatically reduce energy costs, and corporations can remain compliant with environmental regulations, thereby circumventing potential penalties.

In conclusion, incorporating green technologies in Industry 5.0 balances technological progression and environmental stewardship. As we transition into this new epoch of industry, the prominence of these technologies will continue to escalate.

1.4.5 THE INTEGRATION OF SUSTAINABILITY AND INDUSTRY 5.0

As Industry 5.0 continues its developmental trajectory, integrating sustainability principles into its core architecture is increasingly gaining importance. The amalgamation of such regulations with cutting-edge technology offers profound prospects for stimulating growth that is both sustainable and environmentally considerate.

Multiple methodologies can be adapted to weave sustainability into the fabric of Industry 5.0. One such approach involves enterprises transforming their existing models to prioritize resource efficiency and longevity over producing disposable goods. It has been observed that a growing number of organizations recognize sustainability as a strategic imperative, and implementing new standards and regulations facilitates embedding sustainable practices within industrial operations.

Incorporating sustainability into Industry 5.0 offers numerous advantages. Not only does it contribute to cost efficiencies, but it also aids in enhancing brand reputation and unlocking novel market opportunities. Furthermore, this integration has the potential to catalyze positive repercussions for environmental preservation, social equity, and economic prosperity. However, the pathway to this integration is full of challenges. These range from technical impediments and the requirement for significant capital investment to inherent resistance to change within specific organizations.

Guaranteeing the sustainable evolution of Industry 5.0 necessitates a continuous commitment and concentrated effort. It is incumbent upon businesses and policymakers to join forces to forge a regulatory environment that is supportive and encourages sustainable innovation. Moreover, a steadfast commitment to research and development is crucial to augment the technological capabilities intrinsic to Industry 5.0, thereby advancing sustainability across all industry dimensions (Figure 1.3).

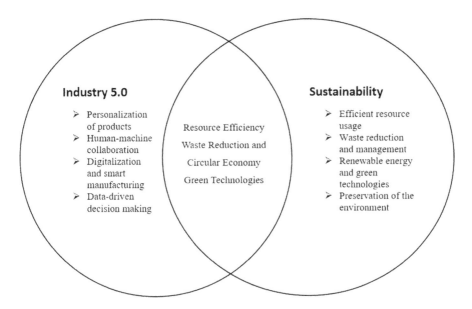

FIGURE 1.3   Alignment of Industry 5.0 with sustainable development.

1.5   CHALLENGES AND FUTURE PROSPECTS IN THE TRANSITION TO INDUSTRY 5.0

1.5.1   CHALLENGES

Transitioning to Industry 5.0 is a journey that requires an in-depth rethinking of existing processes, strategies, and organizational culture. What makes this revolution so powerful is the cornerstone of change, which involves business management in sustainability. Changing these processes to accommodate sustainable practices requires a better understanding of how a company's operations affect the environment, energy use, and carbon footprint. It also implies buying into advanced techniques for real-time tracking and monitoring of machinery operation, fabrication process waste generation, and efficiency of GHG emission. This transition will likely be challenging from both perspectives—resources needed and deadlines set by organizations to shift their enterprises toward forming part of the principles related to a circular economy in terms of development, birth, and death cycle.

The enhanced customization and associated challenges would have to be another prerequisite for initiating the journey. Its principal attributes to the need for businesses to adopt mass customization against mass production, taking things up a notch against flexibility across production lines. Understanding individual customer requirements lies at its base, requiring practical data analysis and collection systems. Implementing such a system might be aided by financial outlays like investments in technology equipment needed to bolster the system. However, there are other concerns around privacy and security of data too. Personnel of the organization would need a training session or two on how to handle and harness the proceeds of the effort effectively, implying one more layer of intricacy in implementing the concept.

Finally, integrating holistic decision-making, i.e., augmentation based on a blend of data dictated-driven insight coupled with human judgment or wisdom, must be considered an insignificant challenge. While 4.0 introduced segments to varying forms of analytics—predictability and knowledge-based—the expedition to 5.0 requires them to gain incense to study human intuition and expertise rather than surrendering all decisions to predefined formulas or machines performing automated tasks. Human groups would examine their lapses during the initiation of the 4.0 transformation when they took heads for granted and chartered over learning curve limits. Also, exceptionally, managers treated workforce operatives as stooges (Figure 1.4).

Technology Infrastructure: Technology plays an inherent role in the transition to Industry 5.0, and an organization's current technological infrastructure needs to be critically examined and evaluated against this new paradigm. The IoT is one such technology that underpins Industry 5.0 and enables real-time data collection and exchange among interconnected devices. Transitioning to an IoT-enabled infrastructure initially appears simple, with clear measures and scope. Indeed, the suitability and adaptability of the existing machinery and devices for such IoT integration need due diligence as they see fit or adapt to any changes brought along IoTs. This inevitably involves a potential overhaul of hardware components while demanding an obligatory upgrade of the software system governing these cumbersome devices. Moreover, setting up the infrastructure for secure transmittal and reception of real-time data on day-to-day operations to ensure no potential threat from cyberspace can always be connected to transitioning to Industry 5.0.

Another essential element in Industry 5.0 will be AI, which brings about predictive capabilities regarding decision-making processes across diverse industrial floor

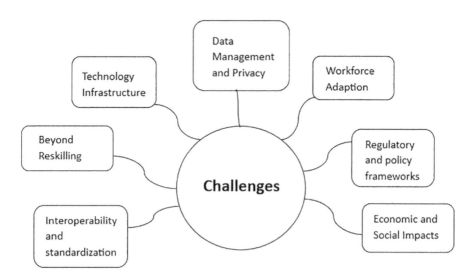

FIGURE 1.4   Key challenges impeding Industry 5.0 evolution.

settings. Adoption of AI, however, empowers not only cost-effective but also trumps all understanding based on common base principles. Thus, it entails taking the time to understand each form of AI—from machine learning through various natural language processing applications and deep learning—to their implications and future use cases in a particular organizational context. Integrating said forms of AI into already established infrastructure would invariably involve specific technical expertise and the ability to make strategic decisions based on insights generated by them. Lastly, just like transitioning toward Industry 5.0 necessitates organizational readiness along several dimensions ranging from organizational cognition to execution integrity, maintaining and managing AI systems, too, requires crucial considerations related to said infrastructural investment.

Data Management and Privacy: One of the fundamental characteristics of Industry 5.0 is the ability to process and orchestrate vast quantities of data. Data comes from many sources, including IoT sensors placed in various machines, devices used in logistics and supply chains, and customer interactions through multiple platforms. This influx of Big Data, often called data volumes, brings about several challenges regarding storage and management. The volume, velocity, and variety of data generated by Enterprise systems are not always handled well by traditional storage organizations. Thus, organizations must explore and invest in advanced data storage solutions, such as cloud-based services and high-capacity data centers. On the other hand, an efficient strategy regarding data management needs to be implemented so that data can be readily accessed, updated, and processed.

Besides storage and management, processing data generated in an Industry 5.0 scenario forms another significant challenge. An organization will determine the value of the data to be collected based on its capacity to analyze and interpret it effectively. Enabled by advanced analytics and AI technology, these tools come into play here, allowing businesses to extract valuable insights from vast pools of raw data. However, deploying and utilizing these tools require definite technical skills and expertise. Therefore, companies might need to invest in training for existing staff or even recruit new talent with the requisite skills. Besides, real-time data processing to enable instant decisions can call for considerable computational resources duly deployed, which also require further investment in high-performance computing (HPC) systems.

The third significant challenge related to the data-centric nature of Industry 5.0 is associated with the extent of data security risks presented. More connected devices increase the vulnerability scale and the risk of cyber threats and breaches; thus, ensuring dedicated data privacy and security is not merely a technological challenge but is legal and ethical. Organizations must stay abreast with and fulfill protection regulations concerning statutes enacted in different venues around the globe. It is challenging for multinational establishments where strengthening data protection measures to guard against criminal activities becomes necessary. Strong cybersecurity structures must be embodied within the mandate for safeguarding sensitive information, with firewalls forming an integral part of a comprehensive plan for regular patching with computer virus scanning. Furthermore, fostering a culture of keeping data private at all levels is also advisable considering how massive enterprise entities become digitally hardened.

Workforce Adaption: As the transition toward Industry 5.0 takes place, it introduces advanced technologies that need appropriate skill sets to function effectively. Given the progressive nature of these technologies, the workforce needs to be skilled or reskilled to meet the demands of this new industrial environment. One of the significant exigencies concerning reskilling the workforce is determining specific skills required in the Industry 5.0 context. This entails technical abilities like data analytics, IoT, AI, and robotics proficiency and soft skills such as critical thinking, problem-solving, adaptability, and collaboration. Considering the pace of technological advancement, it is also essential to have an eye on future skill requirements to prepare the workforce for emerging technologies and processes.

Once requisite skills have been pinpointed, organizations seek to create effective training programs. The said process is far from becoming effortless. Organizations must customize their training programs to cater to a diverse workforce from varied technological literacy levels. This might entail online courses, workshops, and hands-on training sessions. Further, organizations are tasked to ensure that these training programs have flexibility built into them to accommodate new technological advancements, along with anticipating the recommendation for future skill requirements. A learning note can also act as a key, through continual technological evolution, employees require constant upskilling and reskilling.

Creating a culture of adaptability or assimilation is another challenge that organizations transitioning to Industry 5.0 are looking at. Employees must be comfortable with change, readily learn, and continually do new things about technologies and processes. This requires strong leadership and communication by the organization. Leaders should communicate benefits clearly and effectively to let their employees feel valued and involved in the process so that they eagerly participate in the project with gusto, hence, are ready to take full advantage of its benefits. A culture of adaptability also entails organizations being obliged to support their employees during the transition, where giving resources for learning and vice versa, which ranges from allowing time for training, extends down to emotional support given to those who find themselves trying even in challenging situations.

Regulatory and Policy Frameworks: With the advent of Industry 5.0, governments and regulatory bodies face many new challenges and hurdles. In this regard, data privacy issues rank high in government considerations. With Industry 5.0 relying heavily on collecting, storing, and processing vast amounts of data, privacy concerns come first. To respond to these data privacy implications, governments must ensure adequate formulation and enactment of robust data privacy laws that protect individual and organizational information while protecting the data flow necessary for Industry 5.0 operations. Such rules must account for global data flows, particularly in multinational companies' scenarios. This makes international cooperation and harmonization of data privacy regulations imperative to facilitate the responsible transfer and use of data across borders.

For cybersecurity, another crucial consideration comes in place with the burgeoning interconnectivity of devices and systems. With these growing risk factors also rolling out attacks and breaches of many kinds, governments, and regulatory bodies are responsible for brainstorming and putting together rigid cybersecurity standards to protect sensitive data and critical infrastructure from cyber-attacks and breach risks. These standards must be adaptable given that technologies are rapidly growing in both professions involved in Industry 5.0—i.e., technologies shaping emerging digital products and services and cyber threat mechanisms. Alongside these technological developments, intellectual property rights in an Industry 5.0 context carry their unique questions about ownership and rights over data, algorithms, and automated systems coming to the forefront. Upping the intellectual property frameworks for compliance will be crucial for regulators when updating them.

Beyond such practical considerations, the ethical implications of advanced technologies in Industry 5.0 algorithmically raise similar questions regarding job displacement, decision autonomy, and accountability regarding the use or deployment of AI and robotics. Bemused by their increasing capabilities, they often lead to ethical quandaries related to potential job displacement, decision autonomies, and accountability. Developing guidelines that chart the ethical use of these technologies while still charting innovation is indeed complicated but essential. The societal implications of these technologies, notably the digital divide and their impact on privacy rights, require specific contemplation here, given their significance to society. The shift toward Industry 5.0 presents overly complex regulatory landscapes that demonstrate a challenge for proactive and considerate government actions.

Economic and Social Impacts: Economic and social implications of the shift to Industry 5.0 are far-reaching, with potential job displacement standing as one of the most salient concerns. With the heightened desire for innovation and improved levels of automation, specific roles, routine tasks, could soon see machines partially or fully stepping into the shoes of laborers engaged in them. This displacement of workers could prompt an economic meltdown for affected workers and worsen social inequalities. On the other hand, not just will Industry 5.0 be seen as creating new jobs that require skills specific to operating and maintaining advanced technologies but a vital challenge starting up in the industry; the government's challenge is how they plan on managing this transition so that the incumbent workers displaced from traditional roles can successfully shift down their digital footprints to become successful entrepreneurs in more sophisticated operations.

Addressing job displacement entails a comprehensive strategy south of training programs, including reskilling and upskilling. Industry and educational institutions require developing curricula and training programs that equip workers with the skills needed to Operate and Maintain Industries 5.0 landscape. This might entail proficiency in data analytics, robotics, and AI capacity, like problem-solving and adapting abilities. The process should be continuous, although the speed of technological innovations keeps thwarting that same effort. And besides, governments have a pivotal role to play given the investment in employee training and their immense effect on people seeking further education and training programs.

Beyond Reskilling: Job transition support another key component lost between reskilling and upskilling businesses frequently highlight three options when it comes to helping employees prepare for their roles in any organization: career counseling, job matching services, financial support during the transition period (which applies to small firms since they don't have enough resources to deal with providing all workplace benefits). These options go beyond preparation—they enrich self-concepts with helpful information on earnings growth over different wage profiles, help employees through intermittent redundancies by providing retraining possibilities.

Interoperability and Standardization: The vision of a hyper-connected industrial environment in Industry 5.0 depends on the successful interoperation of many systems, devices, and technologies that could be sourced from many vendors and manufacturers with their proprietary methods and protocols. This diversity offers an overarching set of options that render interoperability an imposing but alluring challenge. In this case, interoperability brings about the ability of systems and devices to exchange and use information effortlessly. Achieving this requires compatibility alone at the hardware level but more so at the data formats, communication protocols, and interfaces.

Thus, the interoperability challenge affirms to be neither simply technical nor only strategic. On the one hand, it necessitates increased efficiency and productivity gains that Industry 5.0 promises; on the other, seamless communication and collaboration between such juxtaposed systems, devices, and organizations. For instance, a minor incompatibility can disrupt production when the IoT sensor is used in a factory setting. More significant works encountering a need for these sensor-factory connections will see lesser collaboration between different players in the supply chain, reducing the overall efficiency and competitiveness of the industry. Shreds of evidence are overwhelming in this regard because despite several strategies that have been attempted over several decades for the advancement of the industry, not all together could be implemented. For automation to become a reality for all enterprise companies, a comprehensive strategy that addresses interoperability needs should be developed by leveraging available resources across different stakeholders.

One of those key strategies to address the interoperability challenge is the strata of industry standards and protocols. Measures ensure that regardless of the staggering number of systems and devices, internal and external to any organization, there is a common language or protocol that all of them adhere to whereby the proper manner and ease of interaction takes place. These standards must be flexible and scalable, keeping in view or resonating with the pace at which technology evolutions occur today. Besides this, they should cater to various aspects of Industry 5.0 (e.g., data exchange, cybersecurity, ethical guidelines). Developing these standards would play upon close collaborations among industry players, including regulators and standard-setting organizations, to maximize common goals in establishing them. Interoperability and standardization are critical aspects that affix urgent focus for realizing automation for all enterprise companies.

1.5.2 Prospects

The transition to Industry 5.0 offers affluent opportunities for the future of manufacturing and beyond. Organizations embrace sustainable production processes, enhanced customization, and holistic decision-making as they move toward Industry 5.0. Several exciting prospects emerge:

1. **Sustainable Development**: The focus on sustainability in Industry 5.0 integrates environmental considerations into production processes. This aspect captures efforts to reduce waste, maximize resource usage, and minimize environmental impacts. The more environmentally friendly and resource-efficient economy promoted by the transition to Industry 5.0 is a potential contributor toward a greener future.

2. **Enhanced Customer Experience**: With the emphasis on customized products and experiences through Industry 5.0, customers get highly personalized products and services. The capability to tailor services or products to individual requirements enhances customer satisfaction and loyalty. Companies can grow more profound customer relationships through co-creation, interactive platforms, and data-driven insights, improving customer experience and escalating brand value.

3. **Innovation and Agility**: Establishing continuous learning, adaptation, and innovation culture using tools such as project accelerators and visualization techniques emphasizing the merging of biology and information technologies has attracted organizations that adopt Industry 5.0 and foster an environment conducive to creativity and experimentation (Treacy, 2016). Highly automated systems interpret natural languages, autonomous robots perform physical activities, and much more render traditional jobs obsolete, offering avenues for career transformations and job market shifts.

4. **Economic Growth and Competitiveness**: The adoption of Industry 5.0 may lead to the transformation of jobs and shifts in the labor markets. Leveraging advanced varieties of technology such as AI, robotics, and automation along with more efficient production processes provides avenues for productivity improvement, lower costs, and improved market shares. The enhanced customization and personalized experience boost customer satisfaction and loyalty, increasing customer demand and creating sustainable business growth and market expansion.

5. **Job Evolution and New Opportunities**:Separate from the job transformations induced by adopting Industry 5.0, new opportunities will be created in some organizational infrastructure equipment connected to these tasks. As work gets automated and most menial responsibilities are eliminated, employees are ready to focus on higher-valued activities like inventing, designing various products, solving problems unique to various industries, and many more. Upskilling and reskilling become mass movements as there is a vast base of experts ready to freely share their different skill sets coordinated by industry collaboration hubs.

6. **Collaborative Ecosystems**:By facilitating knowledge exchange and co-innovation across industries, academia, and government sectors, collaborative ecosystems ease knowledge-sharing and co-development hence providing economies of scale thus increases technological advancements. Spreading innovations globally simultaneously fosters cross-industry innovativeness, thus driving revolutionary solutions collectively benefiting everyone.

7. **Global Connectivity and Digital Transformation**: In this global connectivity, real-time monitoring and streamlined decision-making across
geographically displaced locations facilitate smooth collaborations and
co-marketing, resulting in a highly competitive advantage (Global ABI
Research, 2011). Laddered arrays of use cases whose interdependencies
reduce uncertainties, thus improving performance acceleration.

1.6 CONCLUSION

The progression from Industry 4.0 to Industry 5.0 symbolizes a noteworthy milestone in the evolution of industrial processes and technologies. Industry 5.0 brings
forth an era that acknowledges and actively addresses the shortcomings associated
with its predecessor, particularly concerning sustainability, resilience, and human-
focused design.

The promise of Industry 5.0 is one of harmonious collaboration, where the
potency of human intellect and creativity merges seamlessly with the rigorous efficiency of machines. Consider the synergy of advanced technological paradigms such
as AI, the IoT, and collaborative robots or "cobots." These elements combined under
the umbrella of Industry 5.0 serve to enhance productivity, foster innovation, and
improve overall user satisfaction.

Moreover, Industry 5.0 is acutely aware of its responsibility toward the environment. By advocating eco-friendly production, efficient resource management, and
waste reduction, Industry 5.0 propels industrial practices closer to global sustainability objectives. As evidence of this shift, we can look toward established corporations
like Adidas and Nike, which have already integrated technologies like 3D Printing
for streamlined, custom manufacturing.

Aligned with the United Nations'SDGs, Industry 5.0 encourages businesses to
participate in our collective effort toward sustainability. Major corporations, including Siemens, Nike, JetBlue, and Hilton Hotels, have initiated programs that embody
the principles of Industry 5.0. These include strategies focused on environmental
conservation, energy efficiency, and carbon neutrality. Green technologies, therefore, become instrumental in this transition, facilitating the reduction of waste and
improvement of materials management.

Nonetheless, the transition to Industry 5.0 is laden with challenges like any significant evolution. These challenges range from a comprehensive understanding of
a company's operational footprint and environmental impacts to substantial infrastructure investments supporting real-time data collection and interconnected device
communication. One must recognize the significant data security risks that must be
managed.

Governments and regulatory authorities must maintain data privacy and cybersecurity standards. Furthermore, ethical concerns about job displacement, decision
autonomy, and accountability are brought to the fore, necessitating a comprehensive
set of guidelines to govern the ethical use of these technologies while still fostering
an environment conducive to innovation.

In conclusion, Industry 5.0 represents a vast expanse of opportunities. It promises enhanced customer experiences, improved productivity, cost reductions, and

expanded market shares. The potential transformations to the job market, increased knowledge exchange, and cross-sector co-innovation will revolutionize industries, academia, and government sectors. Hence, Industry 5.0 signifies a critical industrial shift and emerges as a driving force for sustainable, human-centric growth.

REFERENCES

[1] Shqair, Maram I., and Safwan A. Altarazi. "Evaluating the Status of SMEs in Jordan with Respect to Industry 4.0: A Pilot Study." *Logistics*, vol. 6, no. 4, 2022, 69. https://doi.org/10.3390/logistics6040069.

[2] Huang, Sihan, et al. "Industry 5.0 and Society 5.0-Comparison, Complementation and Co-Evolution." *Journal of Manufacturing Systems*, vol. 64, 2022, 424–428. https://doi.org/10.1016/j.jmsy.2022.07.010.

[3] Ivanov, Dmitry. "The Industry 5.0 Framework: Viability-based Integration of the Resilience, Sustainability, and Human-centricity Perspectives." *International Journal of Production Research, Taylor and Francis*, 2022, 1–13. https://doi.org/10.1080/00207543.2022.2118892.

[4] Matheson, Eloise, et al. "Human-Robot Collaboration in Manufacturing Applications: A Review." *Robotics*, vol. 8, no. 4, 2019, 100. https://doi.org/10.3390/robotics8040100.

[5] Xu, Xun, et al. "Industry 4.0 and Industry 5.0-Inception, Conception and Perception." *Journal of Manufacturing Systems*, vol. 61, no. 1, 2021, 530–535. https://doi.org/10.1016/j.jmsy.2021.10.006.

[6] Grabowska, Sandra, et al. "Industry 5.0: Improving Humanization and Sustainability of Industry 4.0." *Scientometrics*, 2022. https://doi.org/10.1007/s11192-022-04370-1.

[7] Nunes, Ana Raquel, et al. "The Importance of an Integrating Framework for Achieving the Sustainable Development Goals: The Example of Health and Well-Being." *BMJ Global Health*, vol. 1, no. 3, 2016. https://doi.org/10.1136/bmjgh-2016-000068.

[8] López Martínez, Patricia, et al. "A Big Data-Centric Architecture Metamodel for Industry 4.0." *Future Generation Computer Systems*, vol. 125, 2021, 263–284. https://doi.org/10.1016/j.future.2021.06.020.

[9] Building a Circular Economy: 24-7 Teamworks, 2022, 24-7teamworks.com/building-a-circular-economy/.

[10] Vallero, Daniel, and Chris Brasier. *Sustainable Design*, 2008, https://doi.org/10.1002/9780470259603.

2 Assessing the Impact of Industry 5.0 on Sustainability Strategies

Praveen Kumar Malik
Lovely Professional University

Arshi Naim
King Khalid University

2.1 INTRODUCTION TO SUSTAINABILITY IN INDUSTRY 5.0

The fifth iteration of the industrial revolution is known as Industry 5.0, and its primary focus is on the application of intelligent and digital technology to improve operational efficacy, lower operating expenses, and achieve sustainability objectives. It is an essential element of the so-called Fourth Industrial Revolution, also known as Industry 4.0 referring to the current trend toward the digital transformation of various industries. The interconnection of digital technologies, such as the Internet of Things (IoT), artificial intelligence (AI), machine learning (ML), and robotics, is one of the defining characteristics of the fifth generation of the manufacturing industry, known as Industry 5.0. This connectivity makes it possible to automate operations and to gather, analyze, and respond to data in real time. It also enables the automation of processes. Industry 5.0 presents businesses with the possibility of developing new products and services, cutting down on waste, and making their operations more environmentally friendly by capitalizing on the power of digital technology. Industry 5.0 places a significant emphasis on environmental responsibility [1]. Businesses are able to lower the amount of energy they use, enhance their efficiency, and make greater strides toward achieving environmental sustainability if they harness the potential of digital technology.

Analytics that are data-driven can help businesses optimize their supply chains and lower the negative impact they have on the environment. For instance, businesses can utilize ML algorithms to perform data analysis on their records and locate prospective avenues for lowering their carbon footprint. In addition, businesses can utilize predictive analytics to anticipate and plan for probable dangers and to develop solutions that are sustainable. Additionally, businesses are able to incorporate environmentally friendly practices into their operations while using Industry 5.0. Businesses are able to track the environmental impact of their operations and discover areas in which they can make improvements with the help of

DOI: 10.1201/9781032686363-2

digital technologies [2]. In addition, businesses may evaluate their environmental performance with the use of digital technologies and pinpoint areas in which they can make improvements. In addition, businesses can use digital technology to track their progress and ensure that they are fulfilling their sustainability objectives in order to ensure that they are meeting their goals. As more people want environmentally friendly goods and services, businesses have no choice but to concentrate their efforts on developing environmentally friendly alternatives [3]. The arrival of Industry 5.0 presents businesses with the chance to develop environmentally friendly, cost-effective, and time-saving solutions, all of which will allow them to boost their profits and lessen their negative influence on the environment. Businesses are able to develop more environmentally friendly products by harnessing the power of digital technology. These products can help businesses cut their energy use, enhance their efficiency, and step up their commitment to protecting the environment as shown in Figure 2.1.

- Sustainability in Industry 5.0 is a word that has been coined to describe the movement that has been taking place in the manufacturing industry toward a more environmentally conscious method of conducting business.
- The integration of industrial technologies and practices that lower their impact on the environment and raise their operational efficiency is the primary emphasis of this approach.

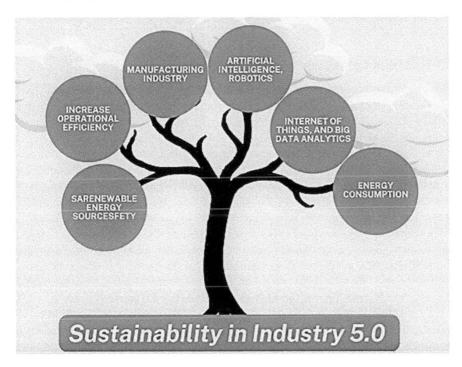

FIGURE 2.1   Sustainability and its uses in different industries.

- It brings together some of the most cutting-edge technology, including AI, robots, the IoT, and big data analytics.
- An environment in which machines, systems, and processes are connected to one another and are able to monitor, evaluate, and improve their own performance is referred to as Industry 5.0.
- It is a significant step in lowering overall energy consumption, as well as reducing waste and emissions, while simultaneously raising levels of efficiency and production.
- The concept of Industry 5.0 also includes the establishment of a circular economy, in which goods are developed with an awareness of their impact on the environment and are fabricated from resources that can be replenished.
- This involves the utilization of renewable energy sources in the production process, such as solar, wind, and hydropower.
- It also incorporates the utilization of green chemistry and 3D Printing in order to cut down on the consumption of hazardous materials, extend the lifespan of products, and cut down on waste.
- In addition to this, it entails the implementation of environmentally friendly technology to cut down on the quantity of energy that is used, such as smart grids and energy storage.
- Reducing the usage of poisonous and hazardous materials while simultaneously increasing the utilization of renewable materials is another focus of the Industry 5.0 initiative.
- As a final step, it entails the implementation of sophisticated analytics and optimization strategies in order to maximize efficiency and minimize waste.

2.1.1 MAJOR CONTRIBUTIONS OF THE CHAPTER

This chapter "Assessing the Impact of Industry 5.0 on Sustainability Strategies" provides some important new insights. It begins with a thorough introduction to Industry 5.0's fundamental concepts, technologies, drivers, and prospective effects. Second, it examines how Industry 5.0 may help achieve sustainability objectives like minimizing harm to the environment, maximizing efficiency with few resources, and broadening social justice. Third, it pinpoints the obstacles and openings that must be exploited to fully achieve the sustainable potential of Industry 5.0. The discussion of this chapter indicate that Industry 5.0 may make a sizable impact on environmental protection. Examples of such cutting-edge technology include AI, robots, and the IoT, all of which have the potential to boost resource efficiency, cut down on emissions, and inspire innovative approaches to doing business that are more environmentally friendly. However, thischapter also highlights a few problems that should be fixed, such as the need for new skills and training, the possibility of job displacement, and the necessity of ensuring that the advantages of Industry 5.0 are shared fairly.

In sum, this chapter is a great introduction to the sustainable possibilities of Industry 5.0. This timely contribution can aid corporations, governments, and other interested parties in becoming ready for the opportunities and threats of the next stage of industrial development.

Some of thischapter's contributions are as follows:

1. It defines Industry 5.0 in a way that is both simple and concise.
2. It reveals the primary technological forces behind Industry 5.0.
3. Potential contributions of Industry 5.0 to sustainability objectives are discussed.
4. It lays out the obstacles and openings that must be conquered if the sustainability benefits of Industry 5.0 are to be fully realized.

This chapter is a great starting point for research on the long-term effects of Industry 5.0. It's a great resource for companies, governments, and anyone else trying to get ready for the opportunities and threats of the next phase of industrial development.

2.2 EVOLUTION OF INDUSTRY 4.0 AND THE EMERGENCE OF INDUSTRY 5.0

Industry 4.0 is a term that was coined to describe the current trend of automation and data interchange in modern manufacturing technology. It is also known as the fourth industrial revolution. It is the merging of traditional manufacturing processes with digital technologies such as the IoT, AI, and cyber-physical systems (CPS). Traditional manufacturing techniques are still used. This industrial revolution has been at the vanguard of the digital transformation of many different industries, thereby ushering in a new era of mass customization and intelligent production. The technologies of the Fourth Industrial Revolution are intended to boost production while simultaneously lowering prices and improving product quality. In addition to this, one of their goals is to improve the effectiveness and adaptability of production processes while simultaneously working toward a more sustainable and environmentally friendly approach. As a result of this, they are helping to pave the way toward an atmosphere in the workplace that is more automated, connected, and secure. The implementation of Industry 4.0 has had a considerable effect on the processes that are used in the operation of organizations as well as the production of goods and services. It has made possible the quick and effective capture of data, which can then be used to enhance both the efficiency of manufacturing operations and the quality of service provided to customers. In addition to this, it has made it possible for businesses to offer goods and services that are more individualized and specific [4].

The advent of Industry 5.0 marks the beginning of the fifth industrial revolution, and it is anticipated that this revolution will bring about even more significant shifts in the manner in which enterprises function. It will bring the digital and real worlds closer together in a way that is more seamless than it has ever been before [5]. The IoT, AI, robotics, virtual reality (VR), augmented reality (AR), blockchain, and quantum computing will be among the most important aspects of Industry 5.0. These technologies will make it possible for organizations to make decisions that are better informed, to generate higher customer engagement, and to get fresh insights into the behavior of their customers. In addition to this, they will make it possible for businesses to build products and services that are more inventive, all while lowering costs and enhancing efficiency. In addition to this, there will be a greater emphasis placed on environmentally friendly practices and ethical manufacturing in Industry 5.0. Businesses will be able to verify that they are not participating in any immoral or environmentally harmful actions by tracing the origins of the products they use, which will be made possible by the implementation of new technologies like as blockchain [6].

This will help businesses to lessen their impact on the environment while simultaneously satisfying the growing demand for more environmentally friendly production processes. In general, the arrival of Industry 5.0 will present companies with the chance to become more flexible, innovative, and productive in their operations. They will be able to develop a deeper comprehension of the requirements of their target audience, as well as become more environmentally responsible and ethical in the conduct of their business. In the end, it will contribute to the creation of a connected and safe environment in the workplace, as well as increased productivity and cost savings [7].

2.3 BENEFITS OF SUSTAINABILITY IN INDUSTRY 5.0

The most recent development in industrial automation is known as Industry 5.0, and it combines the capabilities of ML, robots, AI, and the IoT to improve the total productivity of manufacturing operations, as well as to lower costs and improve overall efficiency. The paradigm of Industry 4.0 has advanced to the next level thanks to this development. In the following paragraphs, we will go over the many reasons why Industry 5.0 should prioritize environmental responsibility [8]. The concept of sustainability refers to the practice of ensuring that the consumption of resources in the present does not have an adverse effect on the ability of future generations to gain access to and make use of these resources. It is becoming more and more crucial for companies to include environmentally responsible business practices into their day-to-day operations as shown in Figure 2.2. The following are some of the advantages of practicing sustainability in Industry 5.0 [6]:

1. Businesses have the potential to gain better efficacy in their operations by incorporating environmentally responsible practices into their manufacturing processes. It is possible to achieve this goal through the optimization of energy use as well as the use of production methods that are more efficient. In addition, the utilization of renewable energy sources such as solar and wind can lessen the quantity of energy that is consumed, which in turn results in a decrease in the expenses that are incurred to maintain operations.

2. Decreased Amount of Waste Produced Businesses that use environmentally friendly business practices are better able to cut down on the amount of waste they generate. This can be accomplished by employing production processes that are more efficient, as well as cutting down on the amount of packaging that is utilized. In addition, in order to cut waste even more, businesses can consider investing in recycling and composting initiatives.

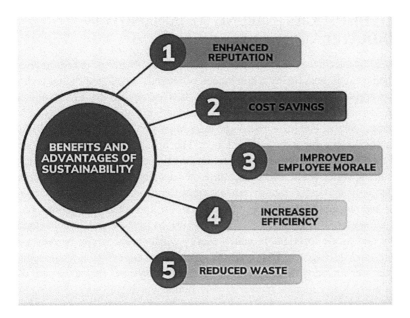

FIGURE 2.2 Benefits and advantages of sustainability in Industry 5.0.

3. An Increase in the Morale of Employees as businesses start to apply sustainable practices, employees will have a greater chance of believing that the work they do has a beneficial impact on the environment. This will lead to an improvement in the morale of employees. This has the potential to lead to higher levels of motivation and engagement among workers, which in turn has the potential to lead to enhanced performance.

4. **Improved Reputation:** Customers are becoming more interested in purchasing from businesses that are dedicated to environmental responsibility. Companies have the opportunity to distinguish themselves from their rivals and develop a great reputation if they make a commitment to implementing environmentally friendly practices. This has the potential to result in greater sales as well as enhanced client loyalty.

5. **Cost Savings:** The implementation of environmentally friendly practices can, over the course of time, result in cost savings. This goal can be accomplished by cutting down on usage of both energy and resources, as well as trash production. In addition, businesses may be eligible to get tax breaks and other benefits from the government if they demonstrate a commitment to environmental responsibility.

In the current era of Industry 5.0, sustainability is becoming an increasingly crucial factor for companies to consider. Businesses that adopt sustainable practices have the potential to realize a number of benefits, including higher efficiency, decreased waste, enhanced reputation, improved staff morale, and cost savings. At the end of the day, sustainability is an investment that has the potential to benefit businesses over the long term.

2.4 TECHNOLOGIES ENABLING SUSTAINABILITY IN INDUSTRY 5.0

Industry 5.0 is a term that has been used to refer to the subsequent industrial revolution that is being made possible by a confluence of recently developed digital technology and novel approaches to the creation of goods. It is anticipated that this revolution will result in considerable gains in the efficacy, productivity, and sustainability of several industrial processes. The IoT is one of the most important technologies that will enable sustainability in the Industry 5.0 revolution. The IoT is a network of interconnected devices that are able to collect and share data with one another as well as with other systems in the wider world. Businesses have the capacity to get important insights into their operations and make data-driven decisions that lead to increased efficiency, cost savings, and sustainability if they integrate the IoT into their production processes. Connected sensors, for instance, can be put to use to monitor energy consumption in real time and locate locations in which energy consumption might be reduced. The term "artificial intelligence" (AI) refers to one of the most essential technologies that is enabling sustainability in Industry 5.0. The usage of systems that are powered by AI makes it possible to automate industrial procedures, which eliminates the requirement for labor performed by hand and leads to lower levels of both emissions and energy consumption [9]. AI may also be used to analyze data from linked sensors and detect patterns in that data. These patterns can then be utilized to improve the efficiency of production processes and make them more environmentally friendly.

Another type of technology that is contributing to the realization of sustainability in the Industry 5.0 era is advanced analytics. Advanced analytics can provide useful insights by evaluating enormous amounts of data coming from connected devices. These insights have the potential to be used to improve industrial processes and cut down on energy consumption. For instance, predictive analytics can be used to forecast the demand for items and then alter production accordingly. This eliminates the requirement for unnecessary overproduction, which in turn reduces the amount of energy that is consumed. Finally, cloud computing enables sustainability in Industry 5.0 by giving enterprises access to on-demand computing resources, which in turn makes Industry 5.0 more competitive. Businesses can lower their requirement for physical infrastructure and, as a result, their overall energy usage by utilizing cloud computing to their advantage. In addition, cloud-based apps can be utilized to improve both the efficiency of manufacturing processes and their impact on the environment. The IoT, AI, Advanced Analytics, and Cloud Computing are some of the emerging digital technologies that are making Industry 5.0 possible. Businesses are able to obtain useful insights into their operations, automate production processes, and optimize production processes by employing these technologies. This allows businesses to lower their consumption of energy and enhance their sustainability.

2.5 ORGANIZATIONAL CHALLENGES OF IMPLEMENTING SUSTAINABILITY IN INDUSTRY 5.0

Industry 5.0 is a term that refers to the use of modern digital technologies, such as AI, the IoT, robotics, and AR, to boost efficiencies, productivity, and sustainability in the manufacturing sector. In order for enterprises to successfully adopt sustainability in

Industry 5.0, they will need to tackle a wide range of organizational difficulties. The first obstacle is that the company's culture does not adequately emphasize the significance of being environmentally responsible. There is a widespread lack of awareness among businesses regarding the significance of sustainability and the potential for this concept to cut costs and boost revenues. To be successful in overcoming this obstacle, businesses need to develop a culture of sustainability, in which sustainability is regarded as an essential component of their business practices. This can be accomplished by ensuring that all employees are aware of the advantages of sustainability and that they are incentivized to work toward achieving it. The necessity of organizational alignment is the second hurdle that must be overcome. In order for businesses to successfully transition to Industry 5.0, it is essential for them to have goals, plans, and procedures that are all in sync with one another. This indicates that all of the divisions within the organization need to collaborate in order to achieve the same goals, and that the company should be able to react rapidly and appropriately to changes in the external environment [10].

The third obstacle is the necessity of making the required expenditures in various forms of technology. In order for enterprises to successfully implement sustainability in Industry 5.0, they need to be willing to invest in the technologies that are required. Investing in sensors, analytics, and automation, in addition to the infrastructure required to support these technologies, is one example of what this could entail as shown in Figure 2.3. The necessity of ensuring appropriate governance and control constitutes the fourth problem. As organizations make their way toward Industry

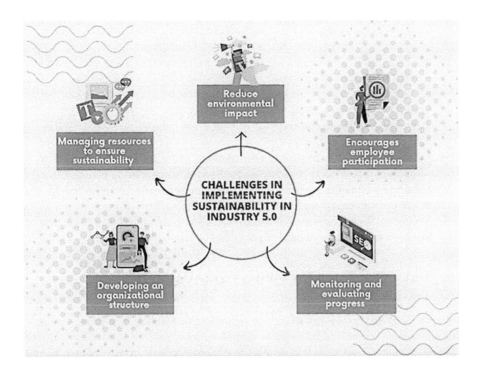

FIGURE 2.3   Challenges in implementing sustainability in Industry 5.0.

5.0, it is imperative for them to ensure that their activities are being monitored and controlled in the appropriate manner. This indicates that enterprises need to have crystal clear policies and procedures in place in order to guarantee that all data is managed correctly and that technology is used in a responsible manner. Additionally, businesses have a responsibility to make certain that their staff members are adequately informed and instructed regarding the significance of environmental stewardship. This necessitates the provision of training and instruction on the various facets of sustainability, including its advantages and how it can be applied in the workplace.

Implementing sustainability in Industry 5.0 presents organizations with a variety of organizational challenges, such as a lack of awareness in the corporate culture, the need for organizational alignment, the need to make the necessary investments in technology, the need to ensure proper governance and control, and the need to train and educate employees on the importance of sustainability. In addition, implementing sustainability in Industry 5.0 presents organizations with a variety of organizational challenges. In order for enterprises to be successful in overcoming these hurdles, they need to establish a culture that prioritizes sustainability, ensure that the organization is aligned, make the appropriate investments in technology, ensure that correct governance and control are in place, and give education and training on the significance of sustainability [11].

- Creating a hierarchical organizational structure that is able to effectively include various aspects of environmental stewardship.
- Developing an efficient plan for the management of resources in order to guarantee that sustainability objectives will be reached.
- Creating a culture that supports activities to improve environmental sustainability and encourages the engagement of staff members.
- Making certain that the aims of the organization with regard to sustainability are reflected in its policies.
- Making modifications to practices and technologies in order to lessen their impact on the environment.
- Providing training to employees so that they may comprehend sustainability norms and act accordingly.
- Establishing reliable procedures for tracking and assessing the manner in which progress is being made toward achieving sustainability goals.
- Making investments in research and development in order to discover original answers to the issues posed by sustainability.
- Managing the expectations of stakeholders and presenting the success that has been made on sustainability projects.

2.6   DEVELOPING SUSTAINABILITY STRATEGIES FOR INDUSTRY 5.0

The term "Industry 5.0" refers to the use of modern technology to automate the production process, as well as to gather and analyze data, with the goals of increasing customer happiness, decreasing operating expenses, and improving overall productivity. The development of AI and the IoT have both contributed to the realization of this possibility. The push toward Industry 5.0 is putting pressure on businesses to lessen their impact on the environment and become more environmentally responsible. In order to accomplish this, businesses will need to devise sustainability strategies that are comprehensive enough to include all aspects of their operations. An analysis of the operations you are now doing should be the first thing you do when formulating a strategy for sustainability. This involves gaining an awareness of the areas in which energy, water, and other resources are being utilized, as well as locating any potential dangers or opportunities for enhancement. Collecting data, performing analysis, and conducting interviews with stakeholders are all viable methods for carrying out this study. The next thing that you need to do is determine your objectives and devise a plan to achieve them. This will need taking into consideration the effects of a number of different technological developments, such as the utilization of renewable energy sources, the implementation of circular economic principles, and the implementation of digital solutions to reduce waste. Additionally, businesses need to take into account the opportunities and dangers presented by each technology, in addition to the expenses associated with using each one [12].

Businesses should design a plan for how they intend to put their sustainability goals into action. This road map ought to include milestones, timeframes, and key performance indicators (KPIs) to monitor progress. In addition to that, it must to include training and communication plans in order to guarantee that workers are aware of the changes and how they can support them. Monitoring the progress of sustainability plans on a regular basis and making necessary adjustments should be done by businesses in order to increase the likelihood that these strategies will be effective. Additionally, they should solicit comments from stakeholders and include those individuals in the decision-making process. This will help to guarantee that the plans are effectively implemented and that they are aligned with the values of the organization. The creation and execution of an all-encompassing sustainability strategy enables businesses to lessen their negative impact on the environment while simultaneously improving their efficacy, competitiveness, and level of customer happiness. They will be in an advantageous position for success in Industry 5.0 as a result of this.

2.7 REAL-WORLD APPLICATIONS OF SUSTAINABILITY IN INDUSTRY 5.0

Industry 5.0 places a significant emphasis, as do all other industries, on the principle of sustainability. The fifth iteration of the industrial revolution is referred to as "Industry 5.0," and it will be defined by the employment of cutting-edge technology like AI and robotics, in addition to the IoT and Big Data. These technologies are revolutionizing the management of manufacturing and other types of industrial processes, making it possible to achieve higher levels of both precision and efficiency. Nevertheless, it is essential that these advancements be accomplished in a manner that is environmentally responsible. Efficiency in energy use is one method by which the principles of sustainability are being integrated into Industry 5.0. The ability to cut expenses while simultaneously lowering carbon emissions is one of the primary reasons why energy efficiency should be a priority for every sector.

AI and predictive analytics are two tools that companies participating in Industry 5.0 can employ to improve their ability to monitor and control energy consumption. For instance, AI-driven predictive maintenance can help to discover possible problems before they arise, and AI-driven energy optimization can help to optimize energy use by reducing wasteful energy use. Utilizing non-conventional or naturally occurring sources of energy is just another method by which sustainability is being included into Industry 5.0. Industrial processes are able to be powered by a variety of renewable energy sources, including solar and wind power. These alternative energy sources are not only more environmentally friendly than more traditional sources of energy, but they are also becoming more economical. Businesses participating in Industry 5.0 have the opportunity to lower their carbon footprint and advance their sustainability objectives by utilizing renewable energy sources. Thirdly, businesses participating in Industry 5.0 are incorporating environmentally friendly materials into their manufacturing processes. Manufacturing can have a negative influence on the surrounding environment; however, this impact can be mitigated by making use of sustainable materials, which can also assist to enhance production efficiencies. For instance, businesses are increasingly making use of recycled materials and bioplastics in the manufacturing processes they employ. This contributes to the reduction of the quantity of trash that is created, as well as the amount of energy and resources that are utilized in the production process. At long last, businesses participating in Industry 5.0 have begun implementing environmentally conscious policies and procedures inside their supply chains. This involves lowering the amount of trash produced by packaging, employing environmentally friendly transportation techniques, and ensuring that suppliers are adhering to ethical standards. These techniques help to make certain that the entire supply chain is more environmentally friendly and resource-conserving [13]. Sustainability plays a significant role in the overall vision of Industry 5.0. Energy efficiency, the usage of renewable energy sources, and the utilization of sustainable materials are just some of the strategies that businesses are using to make their operations as environmentally friendly as they possibly can be. Companies may ensure that their operations are more environmentally friendly, cost-effective, and efficient if they follow these procedures and make the necessary changes.

2.8   CONCLUSION

It is possible that Industry 5.0 will usher in a new era of sustainability initiatives and lead to the creation of a global economy that is more sustainable and equitable. Industry 5.0 is giving the necessary tools to construct production and consumption models that are smarter, more efficient, and more sustainable. These tools are made possible through the utilization of modern digital technology, predictive analytics, and AI. In addition, the greater connectivity and automation that are made possible by Industry 5.0 have the potential to contribute to the reduction of waste and the enhancement of the efficacy of the production processes. Companies are able to devise and put into action sustainability strategies that are more all-encompassing and efficient when they make use of the power offered by Industry 5.0.

2.9 FUTURE OUTLOOK

Uncertainty surrounds both the future of Industry 5.0 and the effect it will have on sustainability plans. Despite this, it is highly likely that the potential impact on sustainability initiatives will expand as a greater number of firms adopt this technology. In addition, the potential for the technology to be used in approaches that promote environmental sustainability is set to grow as it advances and becomes more prevalent. The ultimate key to the success of Industry 5.0 and the influence it will have on sustainability initiatives will be the degree to which businesses are willing to invest in and deploy the necessary technology. Industry 5.0 has the potential to assist businesses in accomplishing their sustainability objectives and fostering the development of a global economy that is more sustainable and equitable if the appropriate investments and implementations are made.

REFERENCES

[1] D. K. Jain, Y. Li, M. J. Er, Q. Xin, D. Gupta and K. Shankar, "Enabling Unmanned Aerial Vehicle Borne Secure Communication With Classification Framework for Industry 5.0," *IEEE Transactions on Industrial Informatics*, vol. 18, no. 8, 5477–5484, 2022. doi: 10.1109/TII.2021.3125732.

[2] Alojaiman, B. "Technological Modernizations in the Industry 5.0 Era: A Descriptive Analysis and Future Research Directions," *Processes*, 11, 1318, 2023. doi: 10.3390/pr11051318.

[3] K. Bakon, T. Holczinger, Z. Süle, S. Jaskó and J. Abonyi, "Scheduling Under Uncertainty for Industry 4.0 and 5.0," *IEEE Access*, vol. 10, 74977–75017, 2022. doi: 10.1109/ACCESS.2022.3191426.

[4] Kim, S.; Ha, T. "Influential Variables and Causal Relations Impact on Innovative Performance and Sustainable Growth of SMEs in Aspect of Industry 4.0 and Digital Transformation," *Sustainability*, 15, 7310, 2023. doi: 10.3390/su15097310.

[5] S. Ghosh, T. Dagiuklas, M. Iqbal and X. Wang, "A Cognitive Routing Framework for Reliable Communication in IoT for Industry 5.0," *IEEE Transactions on Industrial Informatics*, vol. 18, no. 8, 5446–5457, 2022. doi: 10.1109/TII.2022.3141403.

[6] P. R. Anisha, C. Kishor Kumar Reddy, Nhu Gia Nguyen, Megha Bhushan, Ashok Kumar, and Marlia Mohd Hanafiah, *Intelligent Systems and Machine Learning for Industry Advancements, Challenges, and Practices*, CRC Press, Taylor and Francis, 2022.

[7] W. U. Khan, A. Ihsan, T. N. Nguyen, Z. Ali and M. A. Javed, "NOMA-Enabled Backscatter Communications for Green Transportation in Automotive-Industry 5.0," *IEEE Transactions on Industrial Informatics*, vol. 18, no. 11, 7862–7874, 2022. doi: 10.1109/TII.2022.3161029.

[8] A. Verma et al., "Blockchain for Industry 5.0: Vision, Opportunities, Key Enablers, and Future Directions," *IEEE Access*, vol. 10, 69160–69199, 2022. doi: 10.1109/ACCESS.2022.3186892.

[9] H. R. Chi, C. K. Wu, N. -F. Huang, K. -F. Tsang and A. Radwan, "A Survey of Network Automation for Industrial Internet-of-Things Toward Industry 5.0," *IEEE Transactions on Industrial Informatics*, vol. 19, no. 2, 2065–2077, 2023. doi: 10.1109/TII.2022.3215231.

[10] T. -A. Tran, T. Ruppert, G. Eigner and J. Abonyi, "Retrofitting-Based Development of Brownfield Industry 4.0 and Industry 5.0 Solutions," *IEEE Access*, vol. 10, 64348–64374, 2022. doi: 10.1109/ACCESS.2022.3182491.

[11] M. Sverko, T. G. Grbac and M. Mikuc, "SCADA Systems with Focus on Continuous Manufacturing and Steel Industry: A Survey on Architectures, Standards, Challenges and Industry 5.0," *IEEE Access*, vol. 10, 109395–109430, 2022. doi: 10.1109/ACCESS.2022.3211288.

[12] P. Fraga-Lamas, J. Varela-Barbeito and T. M. Fernández-Caramés, "Next Generation Auto-Identification and Traceability Technologies for Industry 5.0: A Methodology and Practical Use Case for the Shipbuilding Industry," *IEEE Access*, vol. 9, 140700–140730, 2021. doi: 10.1109/ACCESS.2021.3119775.

[13] L. Zong, F. H. Memon, X. Li, H. Wang and K. Dev, "End-to-End Transmission Control for Cross-Regional Industrial Internet of Things in Industry 5.0," *IEEE Transactions on Industrial Informatics*, vol. 18, no. 6, 4215–4223, 2022. doi: 10.1109/TII.2021.3133885.

3 Digital Industrial Revolution

From Sustainability Perspective

Samiya Khan
University of Greenwich

3.1 INTRODUCTION

The digital industrial revolution has transformed the conventional industrial sector by incorporating state-of-the-art technologies to improve the efficacy of the overall system [1]. A range of technologies have been used for making organizations digitally empowered, which include Internet of Things (IoT), Artificial Intelligence (AI), robotics, cloud computing and many others. Digital adoption aims to empower manufacturers so that they can manufacture products with greater efficacy, higher productivity and in a cost-effective manner [2]. Besides this, the digital industrial revolution has given rise to new business models such as digital supply chain management [3] and on-demand manufacturing [4]. Thus, digital industrial revolutions do not just transform the way in which organizations operate, but they also create opportunities for growth.

However, before moving on to the digital industrial revolution, it is important to mention that chronological progression of the industrial revolutions to comprehend evolution and inclusion of digital technologies in the industrial sector [5]. The first industrial revolution or Industry 1.0 occurred in the 1800s and marked the beginning of mechanized production, allowing manufacturers to mass produce. Although Industry 1.0 is usually associated with the invention of the steam engine, some of the important characteristics of this industrial revolution also included the introduction of water and steam power. The next industrial revolution, Industry 2.0, came about in the 1900s, and marked the introduction of assembly line and electricity. Therefore, developments during this industrial revolution allowed faster and larger scale mass production. It was around this time that computers were also introduced to the masses and their usage for automation was being explored. Industry 3.0 of the 1960s observed the emergence of computers and the development of one of the most disruptive technologies of the modern age, the Internet. This allowed process automation, introduction of the first digital technologies for industry such as CAD/CAM, and the emergence of the first robotic systems for industrial use.

DOI: 10.1201/9781032686363-3

Over the last decade, rapid advancements in technology and its adoption in the commercial sector have been witnessed. Industry 4.0 [6], which is also referred to as the first digital industrial revolution, happened in the 2010s, majorly supported by the emergence of some pathbreaking technologies such as big data, AI and IoT [7]. This digital industrial revolution transformed the concept of a factory by introducing smart factories [8]. In less than a decade of the fourth industrial revolution, researchers proposed the next generation of digital industrial revolution in the form of Industry 5.0. Taking the use of existing state-of-the-art technologies, a step further, this generation incorporates cyber-physical systems, Industrial Internet of Things (IIoT) and autonomous robots to Industry 4.0 technologies [9]. Industry 5.0 has played an instrumental role in maturing the concept of smart factories.

This chapter aims to investigate the evolution of digital industrial revolution from Industry 4.0 to Industry 5.0, as the technological developments swiftly move forward. The rest of this chapter is organized in the following manner: Sections 3.2 and 3.3 elaborate on the differences between Industry 4.0 and Industry 5.0, focusing on analyzing the evolution process from the former to the latter, exploring their enabling technologies and applications. Section 3.4 discusses the social, economic, and environmental impact of Industry 5.0. Finally, Section 3.5 synopsizes the key findings of this chapter.

3.2   EVOLUTION, CONTRASTS, AND ENABLING TECHNOLOGIES

Industry 4.0 is a revolution in the domain of data exchange and automation for the manufacturing industry. Some of the enabling technologies include IoT, cyber-physical systems and cloud. The vision of Industry 4.0 centers on the concept of smart factory where machines can facilitate real-time communication with other machines and humans, allowing a flexible, productive, and efficient process flow [10]. In other words, a smart factory is a modular structure that uses cyber-physical systems to monitor physical processes and creates a virtual copy of the system to enable decentralized decision-making.

Industry 5.0 is the successor of Industry 4.0, which evolves the existing framework and focuses on the inclusion of technologies such as robotics and AI in the manufacturing process. As a result, factories will be able to efficiently produce products of high quality. In addition to robotics and AI, Industry 5.0 also focuses on development of other enabling technologies such as quantum computing, future networks such as 6G and beyond, and blockchain [11]. These technologies are expected to make the production processes safer, efficient, and transparent.

Development of new materials using nanotechnology, biotechnology and 3D Printing [12] can also potentially aid in creating sustainable and cost-effective products, and thus should also be included in the list of enabling technologies for Industry 5.0. In entirety, Industry 5.0 can be viewed as the future of manufacturing. It is the fusion of physical, biological, and digital technologies [12], with the objective to achieve higher levels of optimization and automation in the manufacturing industry. Additionally, it will create new opportunities for businesses to use data-driven insights and create value out of the same.

Some of the key differences between Industry 4.0 and Industry 5.0 lie in their objectives and their use of their enabling technologies. For instance, Industry 4.0

focuses on data exchange and automation for optimizing production processes and uses AI and machine learning for the same. On the other hand, Industry 5.0 focuses on the automation of the entire value chains and integrates AI, IoT, and robotics to develop new and efficient business models. It can be said that Industry 4.0 is based on cyber-physical systems [13], whereas Industry 5.0 is based on cognitive systems [14].

Industry 5.0 uses a range of enabling technologies to support its vision. It uses cyber-physical systems, cloud computing, IoT and cognitive computing to develop an efficient automated industrial system. The task of further automating and optimizing industrial processes is accomplished using machine learning and AI. Augmented and virtual realities are used for improving customer experience and providing real-time analysis. The security and privacy aspect of the system are handled using distributed ledger technology and edge computing. Finally, to monitor and control industrial operations, digital twins are used, which create digital replicas of processes and physical assets. Figure 3.1 illustrates the range of technologies used for enabling digital industrial revolutions.

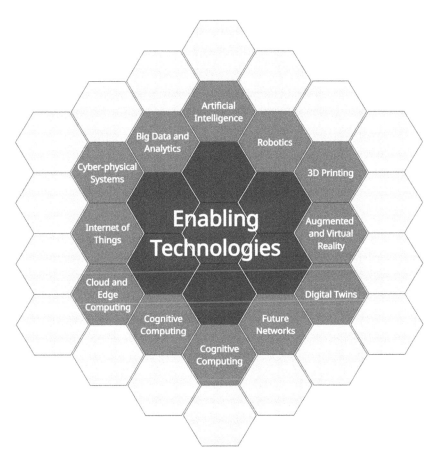

FIGURE 3.1 Enabling technologies for Industry 4.0 and Industry 5.0.

3.3 GENERIC AND SECTOR-SPECIFIC APPLICATIONS

Industry 4.0 deals with the integration of physical and digital technologies in the industrial ecosystem. As mentioned previously, Industry 4.0 makes use of advanced technologies such as AI, IoT, robotics and cloud computing to transform business operations. Key objectives of Industry 4.0 are to incorporate data-driven analytics and automation in traditional business processes to increase productivity, improve efficiency and reduce costs. Based on these objectives, key classes of Industry 4.0 applications include automation [15], data analysis [16], connectivity [17], cybersecurity [18], and extended reality [19]. Businesses typically include repetitive tasks and processes. Thus, automation applications do not just free a resource and time for more complex tasks, but it also improves process or task-level accuracy. One of the most important facets of Industry 4.0 is data-driven insights and decision making, so that businesses can make informed decisions and develop strategies for improving efficiency and reducing costs.

To achieve the objectives, it is critical for systems to connect and communicate with each other and their administrators. Therefore, applications that allow real-time data sharing and analysis and facilitate remote monitoring and control of the system also fall under Industry 4.0 umbrella. With increased connectivity and remote access and control, comes a greater threat and need for cybersecurity. Therefore, applications that implement sophisticated security measures to help businesses in keeping their data and systems safe are also a part of this application domain. Finally, Industry 4.0 has also explored the possibility of overlaying digital information onto the physical world to help workers and staff to improve productivity and make better decisions.

Many examples of Industry 4.0 applications can be found in sectors such as the automotive, retail and agriculture industry, among others. These examples are detailed in Table 3.1. It is important to state that applications of Industry 4.0 are not restricted to these sectors and applications. This table is just a glimpse of some of the sectors and applications.

Industry 5.0 aims to integrate advanced technologies such as IoT, AI, robotics, 3D Printing, and many others, into the manufacturing process. The adoption of these technologies is expected to transform the way in which products are designed, manufactured, and delivered to the customers [26]. One of the most crucial domains of Industry 5.0 applications is the usage of machine learning and AI for automation of production processes. Repetitive tasks such as assembly, painting, and welding can be done by AI-driven robots to improve efficiency and reduce costs [27]. Any potential problems in the systems can also be predicted using data-driven analysis to ensure timely action is taken to avoid any losses [28].

Another class of Industry 5.0 applications is the use of IoT devices for monitoring and control of production processes. Machines can be tracked with the help of sensors to detect and predict potential issues. This will not only optimize production, but it will also reduce the downtime of production due to machine failure and repair. 3D Printing has proven to be an extremely useful technology when it comes to production of complex machine components and parts in a cost and time effective manner [14]. Some examples of sector-specific applications of Industry 5.0 are described in

TABLE 3.1

Sector-Specific Applications of Industry 4.0

Sector	Application Area	Example
Automotive sector [20]	• Automated production processes. • Maintain quality control • Reduce costs	Assembly and manufacturing of parts is carried out by machines, which can be monitored with the help of sensors to predict any failures and reduce downtime.
Energy sector [21]	• Monitor and control energy production and consumption	IoT sensors can be used to acquire real-time data about energy usage and pattern analysis of this data can be used to develop strategies to improve energy efficiency.
Healthcare [22]	• Improve patient care. • Reduce costs	Wearable sensors can be used for patients within or outside the hospital premises to monitor vital parameters to predict any short-term or long-term critical scenario.
Agriculture [23]	• Improve crop yields. • Reduce costs	IoT sensors can be used to monitor soil conditions and provide real-time data on crop health) This data can then be used to optimize irrigation and fertilizer use, resulting in higher crop yields.
Retail [24]	• Increase efficiency. • Improve customer service. • Reduce costs	IoT sensors can be used to track customer behavior in stores, allowing retailers to better understand customer needs and preferences. This data can then be used to improve customer service and optimize product placement.
Logistics [25]	• Improve efficiency. • Reduce costs	IoT sensors can be used to track the location of goods in transit, allowing for more efficient delivery routes. This data can then be used to optimize delivery times and reduce costs.

Table 3.2. It is important to state that applications of Industry 5.0 are not restricted to these sectors and applications. This table is just a glimpse of some of the sectors and applications.

The applications of these technologies in Industry 5.0 are open to innovation and exploration. Additionally, new materials such as graphene are being used for making stronger and lighter components [32] and new processes such as additive manufacturing [33] are being used to improve the accuracy and precision with which complex parts are created. Therefore, in contrast to Industry 4.0, Industry 5.0 is not just optimizing existing production processes, it is driving the development of new production processes and materials.

3.4   SUSTAINABILITY AND IMPACT

One of the key components of Industry 5.0 is sustainability and it focuses on development of technologies that are environmentally and economically beneficial.

TABLE 3.2

Roles and Responsibilities of Passive Stakeholders

Sector	Application Area	Example
Manufacturing [14]	Improve efficiency and accuracy of manufacturing processes	• Automation and robotics are being used to reduce labor costs and increase production speed. • IoT sensors are being used to monitor and control production processes. • AI is being used to optimize production schedules and reduce waste.
Healthcare [29]	Improve the quality of healthcare services	• AI and machine learning are being used to diagnose and treat patients more accurately and quickly. • IoT sensors are being used to monitor patient health and provide real-time data to healthcare professionals.
Logistics [30]	Improve the efficiency of logistics operations	• Automation and robotics are being used to reduce labor costs and increase production speed. • IoT sensors are being used to monitor and control the movement of goods. • AI is being used to optimize delivery routes and reduce delivery times.
Retail [31]	Improve the customer experience in retail stores	• AI and machine learning are being used to personalize product recommendations and provide more accurate product information. • IoT sensors are being used to track customer movements and provide real-time analytics to store owners.
Agriculture [31]	Improve the efficiency of agricultural operations	• Automation and robotics are being used to reduce labor costs and increase production speed. • IoT sensors are being used to monitor and control crop growth. • AI is being used to optimize crop yields and reduce waste.

Thus, domain development includes energy efficiency, use of renewable energy sources and development of smart manufacturing processes that reduce carbon emissions and waste. Besides this, the use of data-driven insights to anticipate customer needs and optimize production processes catalyzes the development of sustainable supply chains [31] and uses the principles of circular economy to reduce waste [34] and enhance resource efficiency.

3.4.1 ECONOMIC PERSPECTIVE

Industry 5.0 majorly focuses on developing an efficient and sustainable industrial environment. This revolution is expected to have a significant economic impact [35], which will lead to increased sustainability in the sector. The economic implications of using advanced technologies such as 3D Printing, robotics and AI are expected to reduce production and process costs by reducing waste and increasing efficiency. The increased profitability and productivity for businesses will create more jobs and result in higher wages. Additionally, the use of these technologies will allow businesses to develop new services and products, creating new opportunities for growth and expansion.

3.4.2 SOCIAL PERSPECTIVE

Industry 5.0 is expected to bring about a new era of data exchange, automation, and manufacturing technologies. The concept and its applications are expected to have significant social impact. One of the foremost impacts is the creation of employment and economic opportunities [36]. Increased and intelligent automation will reduce the need for labor in these jobs. Jobs in areas such as data analytics and AI are expected to increase. Staff employed for these jobs can be upskilled to take on more innovative and creative role such as monitoring and management of these automated systems. Skilled jobs will lead to enhanced wages, which will reduce inequality. This will additionally have an impact on working conditions and the quality of life of the employed staff. The reduction in the need for labor in repetitive tasks will also reduce the associated energy costs and carbon emissions, reducing pollution in the long-term and improving the environment.

3.4.3 ENVIRONMENTAL PERSPECTIVE

The use of advanced technologies such as AI, IoT and 3D Printing will reduce energy consumption and emissions, which will lead to a more efficient and sustainable industrial environment. For instance, the use of AI will optimize processes, reducing energy consumption. Moreover, IoT sensors can be used to monitor consumption patterns and develop control strategies for reducing energy consumption. Technologies such as 3D Printing will reduce the need for raw materials. As a result, Industry 5.0 will also reduce waste [37]. Industry 5.0 can help reduce emissions by enabling companies to switch to renewable energy sources and reduce their carbon footprint [38]. Lastly, Industry 5.0 can help businesses keep track of their environmental performance, which will enable them to identify areas of improvement and make more sustainable and impactful decisions.

The increased levels of intelligent automation for repetitive tasks will reduce the need for labor for these jobs. As a result, there will be lesser workplace injuries and improved working conditions [39]. Moreover, the staff employed for these jobs can be upskilled to handle system monitoring jobs. Therefore, the use of these technologies will allow businesses to develop sustainable services and products, with reduced environmental impact.

3.5 CONCLUSION

This chapter describes the journey of the industrial sector through multiple industrial revolutions, particularly Industry 4.0 and Industry 5.0. Industry 4.0 is characterized by the integration of technologies such as cyber-physical systems, AI and IoT into the industrial sector to automate and optimize production processes. On the other hand, Industry 5.0 is characterized by the integration of technologies such as AI and robotics in the manufacturing sector with the vision to not just optimize processes, but also revolutionize the way in which products are designed, manufactured, and delivered to the customers.

The impact of Industry 5.0 is expected to be far-reaching with increased efficacy, cost-effectiveness, and improved product quality. Besides this, it is also expected to catalyze development of new services and products, with higher safety of workplaces, reduced negative impact on the environment, reduced emissions, and higher economic benefits for businesses. As ongoing research continues to advance this field, it is expected to evolve, mature, and become more sophisticated with time. Therefore, smart factories of the future will include autonomous management of production processes and integrate advanced analytics to make production more efficient and cost-effective.

This next generation of industrial revolution will integrate digital, biological, and physical systems to create a new wave of innovation and invention for transforming the way businesses operate and manage the product lifecycle. Evidently, the potential areas of innovation are vast, and businesses are already exploring new business models, products, and services to leverage the power of Industry 5.0. With the right investments in research and development, Industry 5.0 could revolutionize the way businesses operate and create entirely new markets.

REFERENCES

[1] Milojevic, Milos, and Franck Nassah. "Digital industrial revolution with predictive maintenance." In *Are European Businesses Ready to Streamline Their Operations and Reach Higher Levels of Efficiency* (2018). https://www.ge.com/digital/sites/default/files/download_assets/PAC_Predictive_Maintenance_GE_Digital_Executive_Summary_2018_1.pdf

[2] Rüßmann, Michael, Markus Lorenz, Philipp Gerbert, Manuela Waldner, Jan Justus, Pascal Engel, and Michael Harnisch. "Industry 4.0: The future of productivity and growth in manufacturing industries." *Boston Consulting Group* 9, 1 (2015): 54–89.

[3] Agrawal, Prakash, and Rakesh Narain. "Digital supply chain management: An overview." *IOP Conference Series: Materials Science and Engineering* 455, 1 (2018), 012074.

[4] Lu, Yuqian, and Xun Xu. "Cloud-based manufacturing equipment and big data analytics to enable on-demand manufacturing services." *Robotics and Computer-Integrated Manufacturing* 57 (2019): 92–102.

[5] Yavari, Farzad, and Nazanin Pilevari. "Industry revolutions development from Industry 1.0 to Industry 5.0 in manufacturing." *Journal of Industrial Strategic Management* 5, 2 (2020): 44–63.

[6] Ghobakhloo, Morteza. "Industry 4.0, digitization, and opportunities for sustainability." *Journal of Cleaner Production* 252 (2020): 119869.

[7] Chiarini, Andrea. "Industry 4.0 technologies in the manufacturing sector: Are we sure they are all relevant for environmental performance." *Business Strategy and the Environment* 30, 7 (2021): 3194–3207.

[8] Chen, Baotong, Jiafu Wan, Lei Shu, Peng Li, Mithun Mukherjee, and Boxing Yin. "Smart factory of industry 4.0: Key technologies, application case, and challenges." *IEEE Access* 6 (2017): 6505–6519.

[9] Elangovan, Uthayan. *Industry 5.0: The Future of the Industrial Economy.* Boca Raton, FL, CRC Press (2021).

[10] Gorecky, Dominic, Mathias Schmitt, Matthias Loskyll, and Detlef Zühlke. "Human-machine-interaction in the industry 4.0 era." In *2014 12th IEEE International Conference on Industrial Informatics (INDIN)*, 289–294, Porto Alegre, IEEE (2014).

[11] Basu, Deborsi, Uttam Ghosh, and Raja Datta. "6G for industry 5.0 and smart CPS: A journey from challenging hindrance to opportunistic future." In 2022 IEEE Silchar Subsection Conference (SILCON), 1–6. Silchar, IEEE (2022).

[12] Mitchell, John, and David Guile. "Fusion skills and industry 5.0: Conceptions and challenges." In *Insights into Global Engineering Education after the Birth of Industry 5.0*, Edited by Montaha Bouezzeddine, Rijeka, IntechOpen (2022).

[13] Jazdi, Nasser. "Cyber physical systems in the context of industry 4.0." In *2014 IEEE International Conference on Automation, Quality and Testing, Robotics*, 1–4. Cluj-Napoca, IEEE (2014).

[14] Maddikunta, Praveen Kumar Reddy, Quoc-Viet Pham, B. Prabadevi, Natarajan Deepa, Kapal Dev, Thippa Reddy Gadekallu, Rukhsana Ruby, and Madhusanka Liyanage. "Industry 5.0: A survey on enabling technologies and potential applications." *Journal of Industrial Information Integration* 26 (2022): 100257.

[15] Tyagi, Amit Kumar, Terrance Frederick Fernandez, Shashvi Mishra, and Shabnam Kumari. "Intelligent automation systems at the core of industry 4.0." In International Conference on *Intelligent Systems Design and Applications*, pp. 1–18. Cham, Springer International Publishing (2020).

[16] Sharma, Abhilasha, and Harsh Pandey. "Big data and analytics in industry 4.0." *A Roadmap to Industry 4.0: Smart production, Sharp Business and Sustainable Development* (2020): 57–72.

[17] Zheng, Ting, Marco Ardolino, Andrea Bacchetti, and Marco Perona. "The applications of industry 4.0 technologies in manufacturing context: A systematic literature review." *International Journal of Production Research* 59, 6 (2021): 1922–1954.

[18] Culot, Giovanna, Fabio Fattori, Matteo Podrecca, and Marco Sartor. "Addressing industry 4.0 cybersecurity challenges." *IEEE Engineering Management Review* 47, 3 (2019): 79–86.

[19] Damiani, Lorenzo, Melissa Demartini, Guido Guizzi, Roberto Revetria, and Flavio Tonelli. "Augmented and virtual reality applications in industrial systems: A qualitative review towards the industry 4.0 era." *IFAC-PapersOnLine* 51, 11 (2018): 624–630.

[20] Ghosh, Raj Krishan, Anindya Banerjee, Prasenjit Aich, Deborsi Basu, and Uttam Ghosh. "Intelligent IoT for automotive industry 4.0: Challenges, opportunities, and future trends." *Intelligent Internet of Things for Healthcare and Industry.* Edited by Uttam Ghosh, Chinmay Chakraborty, Lalit Garg, and Gautam Srivastava, pp. 327–352. Cham, Springer (2022).

[21] Alarcón, Mariano, Fernando Manuel Martínez-García, and Félix Cesáreo Gómez de León Hijes. "Energy and maintenance management systems in the context of industry 4.0. Implementation in a real case." *Renewable and Sustainable Energy Reviews* 142 (2021): 110841.

[22] Paul, Shuva, Muhtasim Riffat, Abrar Yasir, Mir Nusrat Mahim, Bushra Yasmin Sharnali, Intisar Tahmid Naheen, Akhlaqur Rahman, and Ambarish Kulkarni. "Industry 4.0 applications for medical/healthcare services." *Journal of Sensor and Actuator Networks* 10, 3 (2021): 43.

[23] Liu, Ye, Xiaoyuan Ma, Lei Shu, Gerhard Petrus Hancke, and Adnan M. Abu-Mahfouz. "From industry 4.0 to agriculture 4.0: Current status, enabling technologies, and research challenges." *IEEE Transactions on Industrial Informatics* 17, 6 (2020): 4322–4334.

[24] Har, Loh Li, Umi Kartini Rashid, Lee Te Chuan, Seah Choon Sen, and Loh Yin Xia. "Revolution of retail industry: From perspective of retail 1.0 to 4.0." *Procedia Computer Science* 200 (2022): 1615–1625.

[25] Efthymiou, Orestis K., and Stavros T. Ponis. "Industry 4.0 technologies and their impact in contemporary logistics: A systematic literature review." *Sustainability* 13, 21 (2021): 11643.

[26] Xian, Wei, Kan Yu, Fengling Han, Le Fang, Dehua He, and Qing-Long Han. "Advanced manufacturing in industry 5.0: A survey of key enabling technologies and future trends." *IEEE Transactions on Industrial Informatics* (2023): 1–15. https://ieeexplore.ieee.org/abstract/document/10121632?casa_token=Tx2yleSBygkAAAAA:1NpfBZpy6QlF_5pOYB2KalfJDdNmNvH2Tk45bHumrK8MOtWV_HJuMQSQboJ2Fws3hZ8x5AFgYK6p

[27] Tiwari, Saurabh, Prakash Chandra Bahuguna, and Jason Walker. "Industry 5.0: A macroperspective approach." In *Handbook of Research on Innovative Management Using AI in Industry 5.0*, 59–73. IGI Global, Hershey, PA (2022).

[28] van Oudenhoven, Bas, Philippe Van de Calseyde, Rob Basten, and Evangelia Demerouti. "Predictive maintenance for industry 5.0: Behavioral inquiries from a work system perspective." *International Journal of Production Research 61, 22* (2022): 7846–7865.

[29] Gomathi, L., Anand Kumar Mishra, and Amit Kumar Tyagi. "Industry 5.0 for healthcare 5.0: Opportunities, challenges and future research possibilities." In 2023 7th International Conference on Trends in Electronics and Informatics (ICOEI), 204–213. Tirunelveli, IEEE (2023).

[30] Jafari, Niloofar, Mohammad Azarian, and Hao Yu. "Moving from industry 4.0 to industry 5.0: What are the implications for smart logistics?" *Logistics* 6, 2 (2022): 26.

[31] Leng, Jiewu, Weinan Sha, Baicun Wang, Pai Zheng, Cunbo Zhuang, Qiang Liu, Thorsten Wuest, Dimitris Mourtzis, and Lihui Wang. "Industry 5.0: Prospect and retrospect." *Journal of Manufacturing Systems* 65 (2022): 279–295.

[32] Banholzer, Volker M. "From "Industry 4.0 "to "Society 5.0 "and "Industry 5.0 ": Value-and mission-oriented policies." *Technological and Social Innovations-Aspects of Systemic Transformation*. IKOM WP Vol. 3, No. 2/2022. Nürnberg, Technische Hochschule Nürnberg Georg Simon Ohm (2022).

[33] Ivanov, Dmitry. "The industry 5.0 framework: Viability-based integration of the resilience, sustainability, and human-centricity perspectives." *International Journal of Production Research* 61, 5 (2023): 1683–1695 (2022).

[34] Atif, Sehrish. "Analyzing the alignment between circular economy and industry 4.0 nexus with industry 5.0 era: An integrative systematic literature review." *Sustainable Development* 31, 4 (2023): 2155–2175.

[35] Leong, Yoong Kit, Jian Hong Tan, Kit Wayne Chew, and Pau Loke Show. "Significance of industry 5.0." In *The Prospect of Industry 5.0 in Biomanufacturing*, Edited By Pau Loke Show, Kit Wayne Chew, and Tau Chuan Ling, 95–114. Boca Raton, FL, CRC Press (2021).

[36] Huang, Sihan, Baicun Wang, Xingyu Li, Pai Zheng, Dimitris Mourtzis, and Lihui Wang. "Industry 5.0 and society 5.0-comparison, complementation and co-evolution." *Journal of manufacturing systems* 64 (2022): 424–428.

[37] Fazal, Nadia, Abid Haleem, Shashi Bahl, Mohd Javaid, and Devaki Nandan. "Digital management systems in manufacturing using industry 5.0 technologies." In Advancement in Materials, Manufacturing and Energy Engineering, Vol. II: Select Proceedings of ICAMME 2021, 221–234. Singapore, Springer Nature Singapore (2022).

[38] Singh, Talwinder, Davinder Singh, Chandan Deep Singh, and Kanwaljit Singh. "Industry 5.0." *Factories of the Future: Technological Advancements in the Manufacturing Industry,* Edited By Chandan Deep Singh and Harleen Kaur, 21–45.. Scrivener Publishing LLC (2023).

[39] Mekkunnel, F., 2019. Industry 5.0: Man-machine revolution (Doctoral dissertation, Wien).

4 Machine Learning for Supply Chain Management in Industrial 4.0 Era
A Bibliometric Analytics

Monalisha Pattnaik
Sambalpur University

Ashirbad Mishra
The Pennsylvania State University

Aryan Pattnaik
KIIT University

Alipsa Pattnaik
Birla Global University

4.1 INTRODUCTION

Management of supply chain of businesses is imperative to optimize their operations and enhance efficiency (Pal & Yasar, 2023). The error in the processes in the operations need to minimized and the shift from one process to another needs to be smooth. This streaming of processes in the Industry 4.0 era is achieved through digitization and automation. Historically issues in operations have been examined manually and static fixes have been applied. Machine learning offers unique opportunities to harness the power of data, make intelligent decisions, and drive transformative outcomes in the supply chain domain (Bansal et al., 2022, Henrique et al., 2019, Jaquart et al., 2021, 2022). It can be used to model processes so that errors can be determined automatically, fixes are recommended briskly and even operations can be re-structured for the dynamic landscape. In some cases, learning algorithms require minimal domain expertise since data logs/flow charts can be harnessed to perform the tasks. Leveraging machine learning algorithms and models can make each process more efficient and accurate, quality checks more cost effective, improve forecasting accuracy, and mitigate risks. This can provide competitive edge to modern supply chains in the 4.0 era (Hajoary, 2023, Bigliardi et al., 2023, Pandey et al., 2023, Govindan & Arampatzis, 2023).

In this present paper, an overview of extensive research on applications of ML in SCM and industry 4.0 is discussed. By applying six different extensive analyses of the existing literatures, some significant and critical points in the advancement of literature are identified. Related to the present research topics a chronological and productive analysis of is presented as a first analysis. Rest of the four different analyses are based on co-authorship, co-citation, citation and bibliographic coupling analytics to discuss how the applications of ML in SCM and industry 4.0 investigations has been deliberated in many technical and scientific journals (Dias Lopes et al., 2023). The final approach identifies different research topics on the keywords like machine learning, supply chain management and industry 4.0 using VOSviewer software package. The most broadly used keywords are selected and then analysed significantly through three different analyses like network, overlay and density.

The present article is structured as follows: Section 4.2 explains about the research parameters using keywords and adoption of methodology to present analysis. In Section 4.3, different bibliometric analytic methods and the results are discussed and explained. Finally, in conclusion all the results are explained in Section 4.4 provided to the researcher to classify realistic gaps in accessible literature and focus to the original research path in the light of the keywords namely ML, SCM and industry 4.0 (De Groot, 2012).

4.2   RESEARCH PARAMETERS AND METHODOLOGY

The data is extracted from WoS database on 29 May 2023. By considering all publications given by search, 8,227 relevant articles were collected. The search criteria are explained as follows:

The key terms are presented by the Boolean expressions, "Machine Learning and Supply Chain Management or Industry 4.0". The data collected by the search were first exported into text format and then subsequently, the data was prepared for import into the software package VOSviewer for required analysis purpose (Pattnaik, 2023).

In this chapter, six different analyses are conducted namely chronological and productivity, co-authorship, co-citation, citation, bibliographic coupling, keyword and co-occurrence analyses. All these analyses are utilized the network visualizations but only keyword and co-occurrence analyses are utilized all the three visualizations like network, overlay and density. Chronological and productivity, co-authorship, co-citation, citation, bibliographic coupling, keyword and co-occurrence analyses are discussed in Sections 4.3.1–4.3.6, respectively (Van Eck and Waltman, 2010, Bevilacqua et al., 2019). All the above bibliometric maps restrain items like papers, journals, authors, organizations, countries, keywords and links.

4.3   RESULTS AND ANALYSIS

The results of chronological and productivity analyses are presented which are directly extracted from WoS database website.

4.3.1 CHRONOLOGICAL AND PRODUCTIVITY ANALYSIS

The results of trend analysis like chronological and productivity are presented from Figures 4.1 to 4.8. Figure 4.1 represents the chronological evolution of the number of publications related to the three terms like applications of ML in SCM/industry 4.0. It is observed that ML techniques applied in SCM or Industry 4.0 have an exponential growth in the last few decades. Consequently, as shown in Figure 4.1, the scientific output related to the application of all the three key terms has resulted dramatic growth especially after 2020 whereas in 2015 it is only 19 out of 8,313 articles. Furthermore, 7,580 articles have been published in just the last 5 years. Figure 4.2 shows the total number of published articles in the line of research in different WoS categories. Maximum articles are published in engineering stream and computer science stream. Figure 4.3 represents the total number of citations in different major topics of analysis. Figure 4.4 represents the total number of article published by different authors. Figures 4.5–4.8 represent the total number of published articles in the line of different document types, affiliations, publication types and publishers, respectively. In Figure 4.5, the contribution of total number of publications as articles, review articles, early access and editorial materials are 6,912, 1,037, 517 and 248 out of 8,313 articles. Similarly from Figure 4.8 it is observed that, the total number of publications

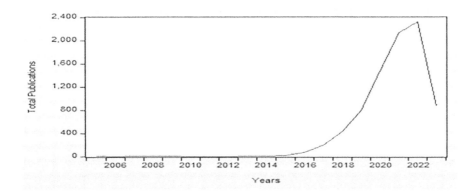

FIGURE 4.1 Timeline of the number of publications.

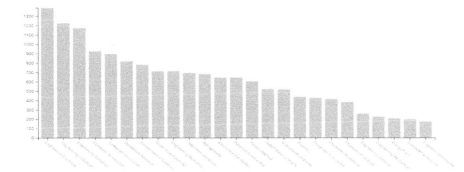

FIGURE 4.2 WoS categories of the number of publications.

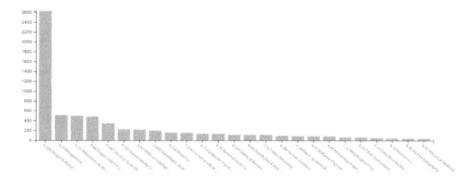

FIGURE 4.3   Topic of the number of citations.

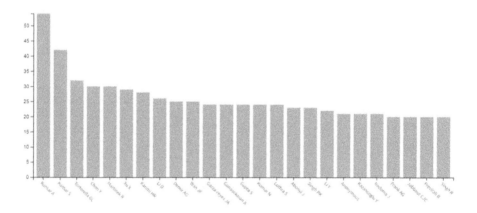

FIGURE 4.4   Authors of the number of publications.

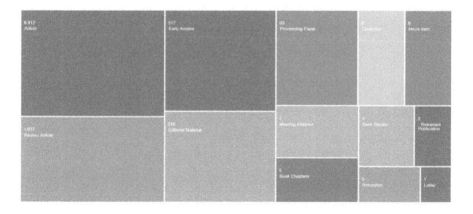

FIGURE 4.5   Document type of the number of publications.

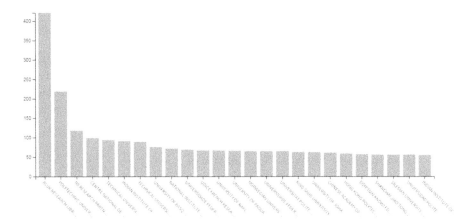

FIGURE 4.6 Affiliation of the number of publications.

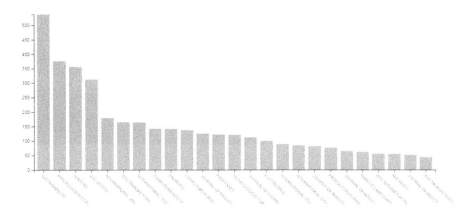

FIGURE 4.7 Publication title of the number of publications.

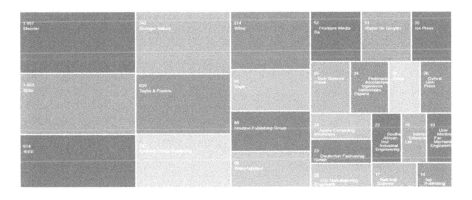

FIGURE 4.8 Publisher of the number of publications.

out of 8,313 is 1,957 published in Elsevier, whereas 1,953 published in MDPI, 914 published in IEEE, 743 published in Springer, 639 published in Taylor & Francis and 392 published in Emerald group of publishing.

In Section 4.3.2, three type network visualizations of co-authorship are discussed. In Section 4.3.3, two types of co-citation network visualization, in Sections 4.3.4 and 4.3.5 five and four type of citation and bibliographic coupling network visualizations are discussed, respectively. All types of visualizations like network, overlay and density are discussed in Section 4.3.6 for keywords and co-occurrence analysis.

4.3.2   CO-AUTHORSHIP NETWORK VISUALIZATIONS

The author network map of co-authorship is shown in Figure 4.9 and Table 4.1. The least number of documents and citations of an author were put to 3 and 3, respectively.

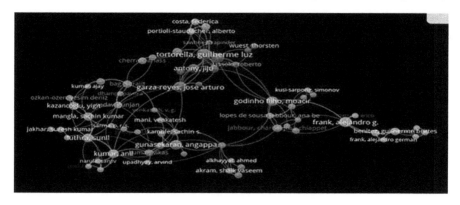

FIGURE 4.9   Co-authorship authors network map.

TABLE 4.1
Top 15 Co-Authorship Authors Occurrences (Fractional Counting)

Sl. No.	Authors	Document	Total Link Strength	Citation
1	Xu, Xun	10	8	2,161
2	Ivanov, Dunitry	11	8	1,826
3	Li, Ling	7	3	1,818
4	Xu, Lida	7	1	1,774
5	Ayala, Nestor Fabian	5	5	1,685
6	Zhong, Ray, Y	5	5	1,679
7	Li, Di	7	7	1,614
8	Wang, Shiyong	6	6	1,577
9	Wan, Jiau	5	6	1,546
10	Frank, Alegandra German	3	3	1,471
11	Gunasekaran, Angappa	10	7	1,421
12	Dolgui, Alexandre	8	7	1,341
13	Ghobakhloo, Morteza	12	10	1,298
14	Voigt, Kai-ingo	9	9	1,198
15	Sokolov, Boris	5	5	1,052

Out of the 5,932 authors, 316 met the threshold. So this network map has 316, 9, 154 and 130 are authors, clusters, links and TLS, respectively. "Ivanov, Dunitry", "Xu, Xun" and "Li, Ling" are the top three documents with 11, 10 and 7 number of documents published, respectively.

Figure 4.10 and Table 4.2 present the co-authorship country network map. The least number of documents and citations of a country were put to 3 and 3, respectively. Out of the 102 countries, 77 met the threshold for analysis purpose. So this network map has 77, 10, 775 and 1,046.5 are countries, clusters, links and TLS,

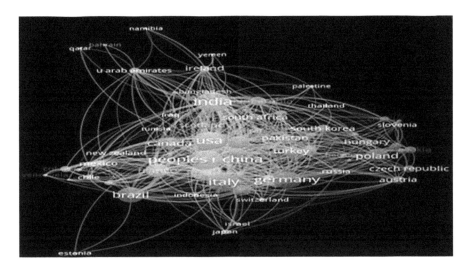

FIGURE 4.10 Co-authorship countries network map.

TABLE 4.2
Top 15 Co-Authorship Countries Occurrences

Sl. No.	Country	Cluster	Link	Total Link Strength	Documents	Citation
1	USA	6	48	143	199	11,199
2	Germany	1	44	102	172	10,290
3	England	3	53	143	177	9,447
4	China	9	46	134	229	8,807
5	Italy	8	52	107	222	8,503
6	Brazil	8	31	84	142	8,490
7	India	6	57	159	235	7,595
8	France	4	42	87	108	7,151
9	Spain	4	49	75	178	3,251
10	Sweden	2	26	30	39	2,594
11	Canada	7	38	55	79	2,542
12	New Zealand	9	12	13	15	2,524
13	Australia	5	51	71	92	2,201
14	Turkey	2	31	30	62	2,070
15	Portugal	8	28	33	70	1,887

respectively. Top three countries are "United States of America", "Germany" and "England" with 11,199, 10,290 and 9,447 citations, respectively.

4.3.3 CO-CITATION NETWORK VISUALIZATIONS

The co-citation source/journal network visualization is shown in Figure 4.11 and Table 4.3. The least number of citations of a co-citation journal network map was set to ten. Out of 30,615 sources, 1,421 met the threshold and 1,000 are the most relevant sources.

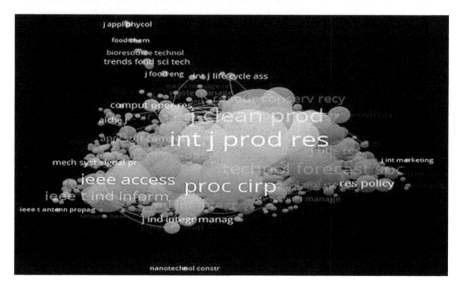

FIGURE 4.11   Source co-citation network map.

TABLE 4.3
Top 15 Co-Citation Source Occurrences

Sl. No.	Source	Cluster	Link	Total Link Strength	Citation
1	Int Jour Prod Res	4	996	3,959.35	4,370
2	Jour Clean Prod	5	996	3,011.40	3,487
3	Int Jour Prod Eco	4	995	2,768.60	2,978
4	Proc Cirp	3	991	2,416.66	2,589
5	Sustainability	5	997	2,238.68	2,434
6	Technol Forecast Soc	1	989	1,804.99	1,943
7	Comput Ind	3	994	1,747.11	1,814
8	Procedia Manufact	3	990	1,580.44	1,659
9	IEEE Acc	2	979	1,416.57	1,531
10	Comput Ind Eng	4	988	1,387.81	1,451
11	Prod Planning Cont	4	975	1,321.84	1,406
12	Jour Manuf Tech Mgmt	1	964	1,088.69	1,135
13	Int Jour Adv Manuf	3	978	1,076.08	1,145
14	Jour Manuf Sys	3	983	996.67	1,040
15	IEEE Transc Ind Info	2	949	977.12	1,106

So this map has 1,000 sources, 7 clusters, 231,735 links and 45,529.27 TLS. Hence, the top three journals are *International Journal of Production Research*, *Journal of Cleaner Production* and *International Journal of Production Economics* with 4,370, 3,487 and 2,978 citations, respectively, using co-citation source network visualization.

In Figure 4.12 and Table 4.4, the co-citation author network map is shown. The least number of citations of co-citation map was put to ten. Out of the 58,003 authors, 1,811 met the threshold and 1,000 authors are most relevant for analysis. So this

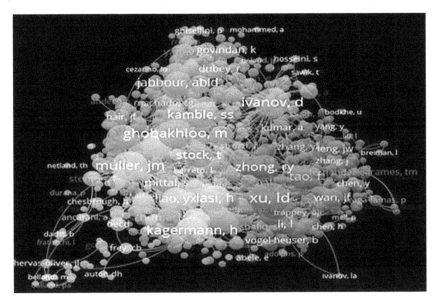

FIGURE 4.12   Author co-citation network map.

TABLE 4.4
Top 15 Co-citation Author Occurrences

Sl. No.	Authors	Cluster	Link	Total Link Strength	Citation
1	Xu, Id	1	986	474.38	504
2	Muller, Jm	4	959	420.69	430
3	Ghobakhloo, M	2	975	419.61	428
4	Ivanov, D	2	950	374.80	426
5	Kagermann, H	4	963	356.29	362
6	Lasi, H	4	983	342.32	344
7	Tortorella, Gl	5	918	312.94	326
8	Zhong, Ry	1	953	310.41	316
9	Frank, Ag	4	955	306.56	309
10	Herman, M	1	926	284.16	302
11	Tao, F	2	959	291.12	296
12	Kamble, SS	2	959	290.18	294
13	Stock, T	3	955	281.13	283
14	Iee, J	1	943	277.31	283
15	Lu, Y	1	954	265.85	271

network visualization has 1,000, 6, 225,169 and 20,888.65 authors, clusters, links and TLS. Top three authors are "Xu, Id", "Muller, JM" and "Ghobakhloo, M." with 504, 430 and 428 citations, respectively.

4.3.4 Visualizations for Citation Network

The citation network map, in which the citations of the items like documents, journals, author, organizations, and countries, is determined based on sharing the number of documents is discussed in this section. In Table 4.5, top 15 citations of documents, journals, author, organizations, and countries are presented. The document citation network visualization is shown in Figure 4.13. The least number of article citations

TABLE 4.5
Top 15 Document Citations (Fractional Counting)

Sl. No.	Document	Cluster	Link	Citation
1	Lasi (2014)	18	225	2,012
2	Xu (2018)	3	170	1,268
3	Zhong (2017)	14	106	1,092
4	Liao (2017)	12	172	888
5	Frank (2019)	6	144	866
6	Lu (2017)	7	100	813
7	Hofmann (2017)	26	124	747
8	Wang (2016)	10	87	682
9	Dalenogare (2018)	23	126	675
10	Oztemel (2020)	77	77	639
11	Ivanov (2019)	4	47	619
12	Thuy Duong Pesterreich (2016)	8	103	585
13	Ghobakhloo (2018)	2	107	508
14	Lopes De Sousa Jabbour (2018)	1	95	490
15	Kamble (2018)	11	105	488

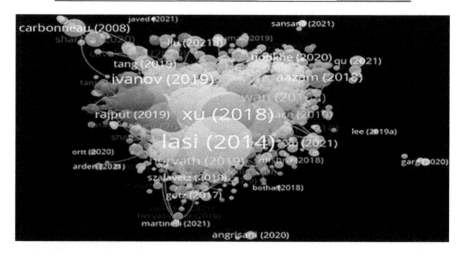

FIGURE 4.13   Citation documents network map.

was set to ten. Out of 2,001 documents, 971 met the threshold. By selecting the greatest TLS, it has 921, 28 and 7,789 documents, clusters and links, respectively. Top three documents are Lasi (2014), Xu (2018) and Zhong (2017) with 2,012, 1,268 and 1,092 citations, respectively. The journal citation network map shown in Figure 4.14 and Table 4.6 where 3 and 3 are set as the least number of articles and citation of a journal, respectively. Out of 430 sources, 140 met the threshold. Using the greatest TLS, it has 137, 14, 2,095 and 10,786 journals, clusters, links and TLS, respectively. Top three journals are *International Journal of Production Research, International Journal of Production Economics* and *Sustainability* with 7,018, 4,151 and 4,024

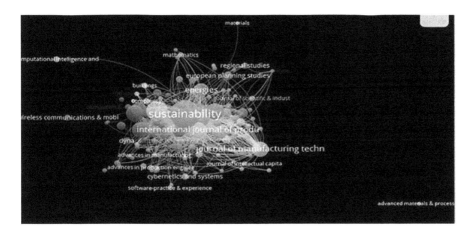

FIGURE 4.14 Citation sources network map.

TABLE 4.6
Top 15 Journal Citations (Fractional Counting)

Sl. No.	Journal	Cluster	Link	Total Link Strength	Document	Citation
1	*Int Jour of Prod Res*	4	119	1,778	52	7,018
2	*Int Jour Prod Econ*	4	104	1,260	33	4,151
3	*Sustainability*	5	112	2,094	156	4,024
4	*Technol Forest Soc Change*	8	97	1,412	56	3,832
5	*Comput Indust*	5	107	1,012	49	3,814
6	*Jour Cleaner Prod*	2	91	1,345	49	2,987
7	*Jour Manf Technol Mgmt*	11	90	1,057	47	2,337
8	*Comput Indust Eng*	2	98	765	42	2,089
9	*IEEE Acc*	1	77	407	54	1,905
10	*Prod Planning Control*	7	83	771	35	1,650
11	*Process Safety Envt Prod*	5	78	458	8	1,559
12	*IEEE Trans*	1	43	111	39	1,497
13	*Jour Indu Infra Int*	1	69	305	14	1,479
14	*Jour Intel Manuf*	1	63	210	13	1,267
15	*Jour Mgmt Factor Syst*	6	64	286	22	1,154

citations, respectively. The author citation network map is shown in Figure 4.15 and
Table 4.7 where 3 and 3 are set as the least number of articles and citation of an
author, respectively. Out of the 5,932 authors, 316 met the threshold. Selecting the
greatest TLS it produces 315, 12, 181 and 66 authors, clusters, links and TLS, respectively. Top three authors are "Xu, Xun", "Ivanov, Dmitry" and "Li, Ling" with 2,161,

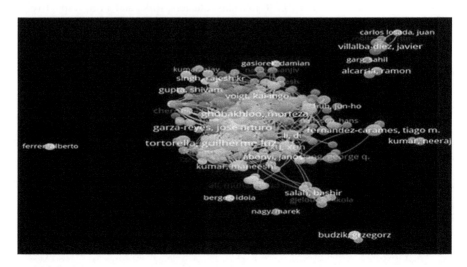

FIGURE 4.15   Citation authors network map.

TABLE 4.7
Top 15 Author Citations (Fractional Counting)

Sl. No.	Author	Cluster	Link	Total Link Strength	Document	Citation
1	Xu, Xun	4	174	362	10	2,161
2	Ivanov, Dmitry	8	127	344	11	1,827
3	Li, Ling	3	182	387	7	1,826
4	Xu, Li Da	3	163	360	7	1,818
5	ayala, Nestor Fabian	9	188	679	5	1,774
6	Zhong, Ray Y	4	154	296	5	1,685
7	Li, Di	3	109	87	7	1,679
8	Wong, Shiyong	3	108	273	6	1,614
9	Wan, Jiafu	3	105	249	5	1,577
10	Frank, Alejandrao German	9	173	526	3	1,546
11	Gunasekaran, Angappa	7	177	563	10	1,471
12	Dolgui, Alexandre	8	116	299	8	1,421
13	Ghobakhloo, Morteza	7	231	912	12	1,341
14	Voigt, Kai Ingo	6	159	541	9	1,298
15	Sokolov, Boris	8	104	234	5	1,198

1,827 and 1,826 citations, respectively. In Figure 4.16 and Table 4.8 the organization citation network visualization is presented where 3 and 3 are set as the least number of articles and citation of an author, respectively. Out of the 2,359 organizations, 459 met the threshold. So it creates 459, 11, 18,370 and 31,726 organizations, clusters,

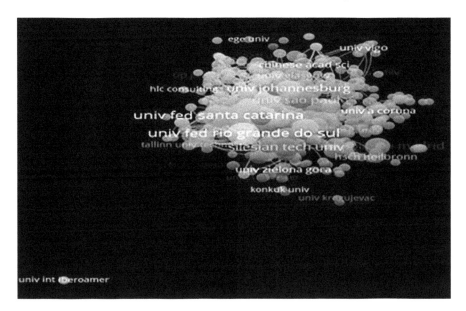

FIGURE 4.16   Citation organizations network map.

TABLE 4.8
Top 15 Organization Citations (Fractional Counting)

Sl. No.	Organization	Cluster	Link	Total Link Strength	Document	Citation
1	Univ fedrio grande do sul	11	335	1,788	31	2,601
2	Old dominion univ	2	302	730	14	2,376
3	Univ Auckland	3	274	568	10	2,376
4	Univ Stuttgart	3	271	565	6	2,048
5	Berlin school econ & law	8	190	485	11	1,770
6	Univ fed santa catarina	7	295	1,413	32	1,641
7	Friedrich Alexander univ etclangen	1	242	729	12	1,341
8	Lulea univ techno	2	133	216	5	1,319
9	Natl inst ind eng nitie	4	97	731	9	1,307
10	Politeen Milan	7	250	793	27	1,299
11	Univ Minnesota	5	246	432	3	1,276
12	Montpellier business	4	240	556	10	1,264
13	Univ Kentucky	3	237	381	4	1,188
14	Univ hormozgan	11	258	635	4	1,103
15	Univ derby	4	263	663	15	1,084

links and TLS, respectively. Top three organizations are "Univ Fedrio Grande Do Sul", "Old Dominion Univ" and "Univ Auckland" with 2,601, 2,376 and 2,376 organizations of citations, respectively. The country citation network map is shown in Figure 4.17 and Table 4.9. Here, 3 and 3 are set as the least number of articles and citations of a country, respectively. Out of 102 countries, 77 met the threshold. So this

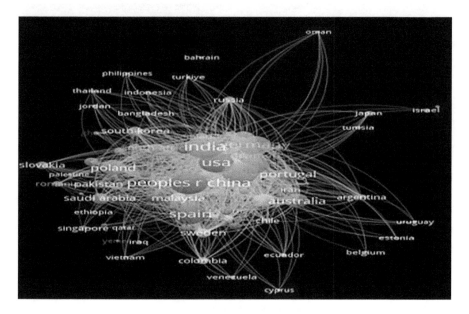

FIGURE 4.17   Citation countries network map.

TABLE 4.9
Top 15 Country Citations (Binary Counting)

Sl. No.	Country	Cluster	Link	Total Link Strength	Document	Citation
1	USA	1	74	6,280	199	11,199
2	Germany	5	75	4,658	172	10,290
3	England	4	75	6,002	177	9,447
4	China	1	73	4,401	229	8,807
5	Italy	3	75	6,069	222	8,503
6	Brazil	3	75	6,250	142	8,490
7	India	5	75	6,813	235	7,595
8	France	6	75	4,638	108	7,151
9	Spain	1	69	2,237	178	3,251
10	Sweden	4	72	1,637	39	2,594
11	Canada	4	72	2,033	79	2,542
12	New Zealand	1	65	799	15	2,524
13	Australia	3	73	2,468	92	2,201
14	Turkey	1	70	1,564	62	2,070
15	Portugal	3	68	1,720	70	1,887

network visualization has 77, 7, 2,044 and 43,006 countries, clusters, links and TLS, respectively. Top three countries are "United States of America", "Germany" and "England" with 11,199, 10,290 and 9,447 cited number of documents, respectively.

4.3.5 Visualizations of Bibliographic Coupling Network

It deals with the network of bibliographic coupling visualization, in which the inter linkage of the items like articles, journals, organizations, and countries is studied based on contribution of the number of references. Tables 4.10–4.12 show the top 15 bibliographic coupled of the above four items, respectively. The bibliographic document coupling network map is shown in Figure 4.18. The least number of citations of an article was fixed to ten. Out of the 2,001 documents, 971 met the threshold. So it produces 971 documents and 13 clusters. Top three documents are "Lasi (2014)", "Xu (2018)" and "Zhong (2017)" with 2,012, 1,268 and 1,092 citations, respectively. The bibliographic journal coupling visualization map is shown in Figure 4.19 and Table 4.10. The least number of articles and journal citation were fixed to 3 and 3, respectively. Out of the 430 documents, 140 met the threshold. So it creates 140 journals. *Sustainability, Technological Foresting and Social Changes* and *International Journal of Production Research* are the top three journals with 156, 56 and 52 documents shared, respectively. The bibliographic organization coupling network map is shown in Figure 4.20 and Table 4.11. The least number of articles and an author citation for a density map were fixed to 3 and 3, respectively. Out of the 2,359 organizations, 459 met the threshold. So it has 459, 8, 96,082 and 2,168,337 organizations, clusters, links and TLS, respectively. Top three organizations are "Univ Fed Santa Catarina", "Univ Fed Rio Grande De Sul" and "Politeen Milan" with 32, 31 and 27 articles shared, respectively. The bibliographic country coupling network map is

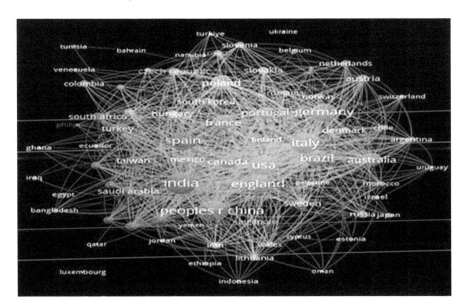

FIGURE 4.18   Bibliographic coupling country network map.

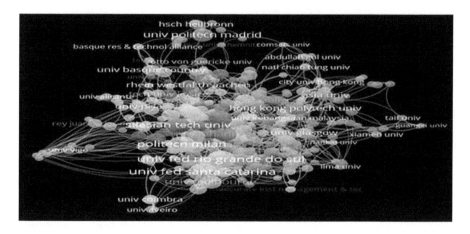

FIGURE 4.19 Bibliographic coupling organization network map.

TABLE 4.10
Top 15 Bibliographic Coupled Documents and Journals

Sl. No.	Bibliographic Coupled Document	Year	Citation	Bibliographic Coupled Journal	Document	Citation
1	Lasi	2014	2,012	*Sustainability*	156	4,024
2	Xu	2017	1,268	*Technol Forest Soc Change*	56	3,832
3	Zhong	2017	1,092	*Inter Jour Prod Res*	52	7,018
4	Liao	2019	888	*Jour Cleaner Prod*	49	2,987
5	Frank	2017	866	*Jour Manufact Tech Mgmt*	47	2,334
6	Lu	2017	813	*Comp Indust Eng*	42	2,089
7	Hofman	2016	747	*Prod Planning Control*	35	1,650
8	Wang	2018	682	*Appl Sci Basel*	78	956
9	Dalenogare	2020	675	*Inter Jour Prod Econ*	33	4,151
10	Oztemel	2019	639	*Comput Indust*	49	3,814
11	Ivavon	2016	619	*IEEE Acc*	54	1,905
12	Thy Duong Oesterreich	2018	585	*Sensors*	52	905
13	Ghobakhloo	2018	508	*Energies*	34	415
14	Lopesdesousa Jabbour	2018	490	*Processes*	34	427
15	Kamble	2018	488	*Inter Jour Comp Integ Manufact*	22	264

FIGURE 4.20 Bibliographic coupling source network map.

TABLE 4.11

Top 15 Bibliographic Coupled Organizations

Sl. No.	Organization	Citation	Total Link Strength	Document
1	Univ Fed Santa Catarina	1,641	103,629	32
2	Univ Fedrio Grande Do Sul	2,601	103,661	31
3	Politeen Milan	1,299	57,538	27
4	Silesian Tech Univ	330	43,353	23
5	King Saud Univ	701	19,131	22
6	Univ Johannesburg	774	37,818	19
7	Univ Melbourne	171	58,456	18
8	Univ Politeen Madrid	230	10,135	18
9	Hong Kong Polytech Univ	892	17,145	17
10	Univ Sao Paulo	456	27,607	16
11	Univ Politein Valencia	156	18,087	16
12	Tech Univ Munich	538	37,796	15
13	Univ Derby	1,084	37,450	15
14	Old Dominion Univ	2,376	25,559	14
15	Free Univ Bozen Bolzano	990	49,437	13

shown in Figure 4.21 and Table 4.12. The least number of articles and a country citation in the network visualization were fixed to 3 and 3, respectively. Out of the 102 countries, 77 met the threshold. So it produces 77, 8, 2,910 and 2,977,681 countries, clusters, links and TLS. Top three countries are "India", "China" and "Italy" with sharing 235, 229 and 222 documents, respectively.

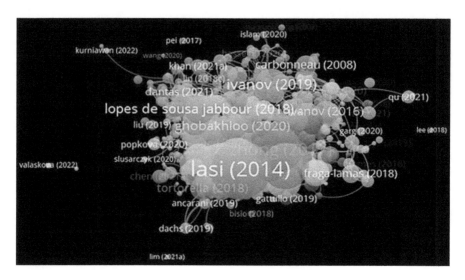

FIGURE 4.21   Bibliographic coupling author network map.

TABLE 4.12
Top 15 Bibliographic Coupled Countries

Sl. No.	Country	Cluster	Link	Total Link Strength	Document
1	India	1	76	482,031	235
2	China	8	76	2,572,256	229
3	Italy	2	76	439,491	222
4	US	7	76	372,843	199
5	Spain	1	76	201,688	178
6	England	3	76	368,482	177
7	Germany	2	76	254,304	172
8	Brazil	3	76	391,946	142
9	Poland	4	76	175,887	113
10	France	5	76	254,016	108
11	Australia	2	76	221,111	92
12	Canada	3	76	146,449	79
13	Portugal	7	76	134,955	70
14	Turkey	1	76	122,198	62
15	Malaysia	1	76	111,125	57

4.3.6   Keywords Co-occurrence Network and Density Visualizations

This part of the study explains detailed about the keywords co-occurrence bibliometric analyses namely network, overlay and density. All the above three maps were created analyzed using 8,227 documents. Keyword co-occurrence network visualization studies the relatedness of the keywords. It is determined through the repeated occurrence of the keywords in the number of documents. The strength of the links indicates the number of publications in which two keywords occur together. These three maps are presented in Figures 4.22–4.24, respectively. By applying binary counting principle, the least number of occurrences of a keyword were put to ten in order to get relevant result. In order to obtain an optimal replacement between readability and comprehensiveness of bibliometric visualizations, this option has been adopted. In Tables 4.13–4.15, the results of each of the bibliometric maps, respectively, are exemplified. The recent keywords are listed in Table 4.15. So in the recent keyword overlay map presents 574, 5, 59,117 and 37,463 keywords, clusters, links and TLS, respectively. "COVID", "Pandemic" and "Alignment" are three top recent keywords

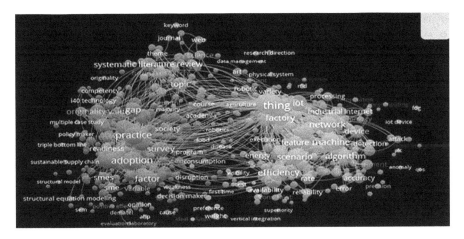

FIGURE 4.22 Keyword network map.

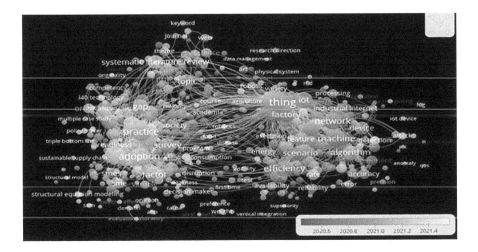

FIGURE 4.23 Keyword overlay map.

FIGURE 4.24   Keyword density map.

TABLE 4.13
Top 15 Keywords Network Map

Sl. No.	All Keywords	Cluster	Link	Total Link Strength	Occurrences
1	Thing	2	549	5,041	354
2	Internet	2	543	4,674	330
3	Adoption	1	525	2,991	244
4	Relationship	1	486	2,688	229
5	Practice	1	507	2,630	223
6	Machine	2	461	2,423	208
7	Sustainability	1	494	2,515	202
8	Factor	1	495	2,258	197
9	Network	2	467	2,506	197
10	Efficiency	2	499	2,356	190
11	IoT	2	479	2,684	181
12	Factory	2	465	1,884	165
13	Scenario	2	447	1,808	161
14	Survey	1	474	2,008	159
15	Algorithm	2	399	1,742	154

TABLE 4.14

Keywords Overlay Map

Sl. No.	Red		Green		Blue		Yellow & and Violet	
	Keyword	Occurrence	Keyword	Occurrence	Keyword	Occurrence	Keyword	Occurrence
1	AHP	17	AI	167	3D Printing	30	Block chain technology	26
2	Statistical analysis	14	Block chain	79	Content analysis	31	Sensitivity analysis	17
3	Smart technology	13	Classification	50	Data mining	19	Big data analysis	16
4	Regression analysis	13	Cloud computing	10	Digitalization	11		
5	Multi criteria decision	15	Communication technology	60	Big data analysis	45		
6	Disruptive technology	12	Decision tree	12	Discriminant analysis	35		
7	Digital technology	87	Data analytic	21	Text mining	10		
8	SEM	17	Deep learning	27				
9	I 40 technology	31	Genetic algorithm	17				
10	Simulation	92	IoT	181				
11			Machine learning	122				
12			Neural network	45				
13			Wireless sensor network	11				
14	Factor	1	495	2,258		197		2,021.1

TABLE 4.15

Top 15 Recent Keywords Occurrences Overlay Map

Sl. No.	Keyword	Cluster	Link	Total Link Strength	Occurrences	Published Year
1	COVID	1	264	547	40	2021.7
2	Pandemic	1	234	431	33	2021.9
3	Alignment	1	131	190	18	2020.6
4	Digital solution	1	126	158	13	2021.4
5	Hierarchy	1	173	253	17	2021.3
6	I 40 technology	1	210	413	31	2021.8
7	SEM	1	189	391	28	2021.7
8	Robotics	5	152	235	18	2021.5
9	Big data analysis	5	143	226	16	2021.5
10	Block chain technology	5	185	359	26	2021.2
11	Sensitivity analysis	4	156	241	17	2020.9
12	IoT	2	479	2,684	181	2020.8
13	Algorithm	2	399	1,742	154	2020.9
14	Adoption	1	525	2,991	244	2021.1

in Table 4.15 with 40, 33 and 18 occurrences and published in the recent years "2,021.7", "2,021.9" and "2,021.6", respectively.

In the network visualization of co-occurrence, the relatedness of the incidence of keywords like author and all keywords are studied which is included on the repetitions times of co-occurrence in the keywords they have shared. Top 15 all and author keywords co-occurrences, respectively are presented in Tables 4.16 and 4.17. For co-occurrence network map, the least number of occurrences of the keywords was set to 10 and out of 6,378 keywords, 257 met the threshold. After selecting the greatest TLS of the authors, it has 256, 7, 11,773 and 5,861.5 keywords, clusters, links and TLS, respectively. All the results are presented in Figures 4.25, 4.26 and Table 4.16. At the top of the table "Industry 4", "Industry 4.0" and "Future" are presented with 855, 839 and 625 occurrences of the co-occurrence all keywords network visualization, respectively. Similarly, "Industry 4", "AI" and "Dynamic capabilities" are presented with 855, 34 and 16 occurrences of all keywords are published in the recent years "2,021.4", "2,021.5" and "2,021.6", respectively. In Figures 4.27, 4.28 and Table 4.17 co-occurrence author keywords network and overlay visualizations are shown. The least number of occurrences of author keywords was set to 10. Out of 4,704 keywords, 108 met the threshold. So this map has 108, 8, 1,588 and 1,886.5 author keywords, clusters, links and TLS, respectively. Top three keywords are like "Industry 4", "Industry 4.0" and "Sustainability" with 855, 625 and 138 occurrences for network visualizations, respectively. Similarly, "Industry 4", "Fourth Industrial Revolution" and "Production" are the top three keywords with 855, 70 and 16 occurrences of author keywords and published in the recent years "2,021.4", "2,021.5" and "2,021.6" for overlay visualizations, respectively.

TABLE 4.16
All Keywords Co-Occurrence Network Map

Sl. No.	Keyword	Cluster	Link	Total Link Strength	Occurrence	Keyword	Occurrence	Published Year
1	Industry 4	1	253	819	855	Industry 4	855	2021.4
2	Industry 4.0	1	246	584	839	AI	34	2021.5
3	Future	7	242	358	625	Dynamic capabilities	16	2021.6
4	Management	5	230	304	358	Diffusion	17	2021.5
5	Internet	1	234	303	305	Digitalization	17	2021.7
6	Framework	5	238	294	303	Block chain technology	21	2021.8
7	Bigdata	2	235	265	295	Patterns	13	2021.6
8	Model	4	216	209	265	Industry 5	11	2022.0
9	Challenges	5	220	209	210	Anomaly detection	11	2021.5
10	Implementation	3	207	200	209	Reliability	12	2021.4
11	Systems	3	217	200	200	0 technologies	19	2021.7
12	Sustainability	5	207	198	200	COVID	21	2021.7
13	Performance	3	215	192	198	Economy	21	2021.4
14	Innovation	3	201	185	192	Digital technologies	24	2021.6
15	Technologies	5	220	179	186	Policy	10	2021.8

TABLE 4.17

Author Keywords Co-Occurrence Network Map

Sl. No.	Keyword	Cluster	Link	Total Link Strength	Occurrence	Keyword	Occurrence	Published Year
1	Industry 4	4	104	819	855	Industry 4	855	2021.4
2	Industry 4.0	2	96	449	625	Fourth Industrial Revolution	70	2021.5
3	Sustainability	3	72	137	138	Production	16	2021.6
4	Internet of things	2	75	122	125	Collaboration	10	2021.8
5	Smart grid	8	71	91	93	Technology innovation	12	2021.4
6	Machine learning	6	50	80	102	Sustainable development goals	11	2021.8
7	AI	2	60	79	81	Digitalization	17	2021.8
8	Circular economy	3	42	79	80	I4	11	2021.4
9	Fourth Industrial Revolution	6	59	68	70	AI	10	2021.4
10	Supply chain management	1	49	68	77	Collaboration	10	2021.8
11	Manufacturing	1	69	67	67	Industry 5	14	2022
12	Big data	2	55	65	66	Knowledge management	11	2021.3
13	Cyber physical systems	1	40	36	62	Digitalization	33	2021.3
14	Smart factory	2	51	58	60	Production	16	2021.6
15	Digitalization	4	26	26	58	Digital technologies	21	2021.6

FIGURE 4.25 Co-occurrence all keyword network map.

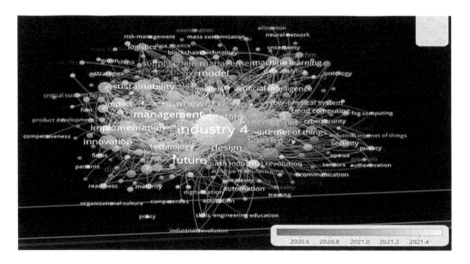

FIGURE 4.26 Co-occurrence all keyword overlay map.

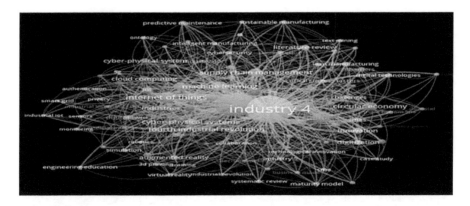

FIGURE 4.27 Co-occurrence author keyword network map.

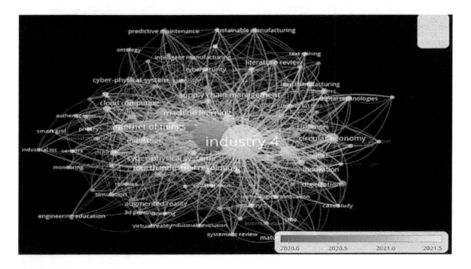

FIGURE 4.28 Co-occurrence author keyword overlay map.

4.4 CONCLUSION

Overview from existing literature on applications of machine learning technique on supply chain management in industrial 4.0 era is presented in this paper. Through VOSviewer software package different types of bibliometric maps are analysed using a large number of datasets (8,227 records). The technique of enabling different bibliometric network maps (Bevilacqua et al., 2019) present to have microscopic and wide-ranging ideas of the up to date of the existing literatures. From this study, the research gaps may be identified for further research scope. From first analysis, the trends of the present topic can be identified directly in Figures 4.1–4.8. Through all the three namely network, overlay and density bibliometric analyses, significant keywords can be identified by the researchers. The authors can identify significant source, journal, author, organization and country globally which contains the applications of machine learning technique in SCM and industry 4.0. Hence, more useful insights in SCM and industry 4.0 can be investigated by using the present methodology with some specific comparisons can be studied as a future research scope.

REFERENCES

Bansal, M., Goyal, A., & Choudhary, A. (2022). Stock market prediction with high accuracy using machine learning techniques. *Procedia Computer Science*, 215, 247–265. https://doi.org/10.1016/j.procs.2022.12.028.

Bevilacqua M., Ciarapica F.E. & Marcucci G. (2019). Supply chain resilience research trends: a literature overview. *IFAC Papers Online*, 52(13) 2821–2826. https://doi.org/10.1016/j.ifacol.2019.11.636.

Bigliardi, B., Bottani, E., Casella, G., Filippelli, S., Petroni, A., Pini, B., & Gianatti, E. (2023). Industry 4.0 and Covid-19: evidence from a case study. *Procedia Computer Science*, 217, 1803–1809. https://doi.org/10.1016/j.procs.2022.12.380.

De Groot, R.J. (2012). In *Virus Taxonomy, Ninth Report of the International Committee on Taxonomy of Viruses*, eds. King, A. M. Q. et al., 806–828. London, UK: Elsevier Academic Press.

Dias Lopes, J., Estevão, J., & Toth-Peter, A. (2023). Industry 4.0, multinationals, and sustainable development: A bibliometric analysis. *Journal of Cleaner Production*, 413. https://doi.org/10.1016/j.jclepro.2023.137381.

Govindan, K., & Arampatzis, G. (2023). A framework to measure readiness and barriers for the implementation of Industry 4.0: A case approach. *Electronic Commerce Research and Applications*, 59. https://doi.org/10.1016/j.elerap.2023.101249.

Hajoary, P.K. (2023). Industry 4.0 maturity and readiness- A case of a steel manufacturing organization. *Procedia Computer Science*, 217, 614–619. https://doi.org/10.1016/j.procs.2022.12.257.

Henrique, B.M., Sobreiro, V.A., & Kimura, H. (2019). Literature review: Machine learning techniques applied to financial market prediction. *Expert Systems with Applications*, 124, 226–251. https://doi.org/10.1016/j.eswa.2019.01.012.

Jaquart, P., Dann, D., & Weinhardt, C. (2021). Short-term bitcoin market prediction via machine learning. *Journal of Finance and Data Science*, 7, 45–66. https://doi.org/10.1016/j.jfds.2021.03.001.

Jaquart, P., Köpke, S., & Weinhardt, C. (2022). Machine learning for cryptocurrency market prediction and trading. *Journal of Finance and Data Science*, 8, 331–352. https://doi.org/10.1016/j.jfds.2022.12.001.

Pal, K., & Yasar, A.U.H. (2023). Internet of things impact on supply chain management. *Procedia Computer Science*, 220, 478–485. https://doi.org/10.1016/j.procs.2023.03.061.

Pandey, V., Sircar, A., Bist, N., Solanki, K., & Yadav, K. (2023). Accelerating the renewable energy sector through Industry 4.0: Optimization opportunities in the digital revolution. *International Journal of Innovation Studies*, 7(2), 171–188. https://doi.org/10.1016/j.ijis.2023.03.003.

Pattnaik, M. (2023). Healthcare management and COVID-19: data-driven bibliometric analytics. *OPSEARCH*, 60, 234–255. https://doi.org/10.1007/s12597-022-00576-2.

Van Eck, N.J. & Waltman, L. (2010). Software survey: VOSviewer, a computer program for bibliometric mapping. *Scientometrics* 84, 523–538. https://doi.org/10.1007/s11192-009-0146-3.

5 Transforming Industry 5.0
Real Time Monitoring and Decision Making with IIOT

Vijay Arputharaj J
CHRIST (Deemed to be University)

Sanjoy Kumar Pal
Skyline University

5.1 INTRODUCTION TO INDUSTRY 5.0: UNLEASHING THE POWER OF IIOT TRANSFORMATION

In the era of Industry 5.0, the convergence of industrial processes with advanced technologies like the Industrial Internet of Things (IIoT) has opened up new avenues for real-time and decision-making in industrial settings. The ability to gather, analyze, and visualize data in real time through interactive dashboards has revolutionized how industries operate, enabling agile responses, improved efficiency, and informed decision-making. The transformative potential of decision-making and real-time monitoring with IIoT dashboards in the framework of Industry 5.0 and its impact on various aspects of industrial operations are briefed along with the answers to the questions listed below:

- What are the key technologies involved in the transformation from Industry 4.0 to Industry 5.0?
- How does IIoT contribute to Industry 5.0?
- What is the significance and impact of real-time monitoring in IIoT?

5.1.1 EMBRACING THE EVOLUTION: INDUSTRY 4.0 TO INDUSTRY 5.0

Both Industry 4.0 and 5.0 represent significant advancements in industrial technologies and the integration of digital systems. Here's an overview of the technologies used in each era:

Industry 4.0, in other words, the 'Fourth Industrial Revolution', brought about the convergence of traditional manufacturing processes with digital technologies [1]. The key technologies used in Industry 4.0 are shown in Figure 5.1.

The Industry 5.0 represents next phase of industrial evolution, emphasizing human-machine collaboration and the integration of intelligent systems. While Industry 5.0 figures upon the technologies of past Industry 4.0, it introduces new elements to

DOI: 10.1201/9781032686363-5

Artificial Intelligence & Machine Learning	Big Data and Analytics	Cloud Computing	Cyber-Physical Systems (CPS)	Internet of Things (IoT)
AI and ML algorithms enable machines to learn, adapt, and make autonomous decisions based on data analysis.	This techniques enable the processing, analysis, and interpretation of large datasets to drive informed decision-making.	Cloud platforms enable access to computing resources, data storage, and analytical tools on-demand, facilitating collaboration and resource optimization.	CPS involves the integration of physical systems with computational elements, allowing for real-time monitoring, control, and automation.	IoT technologies enable the connection of physical devices, machines, and sensors to collect and exchange data.

FIGURE 5.1 Major key components of Industry 4.0.

enhance the humans and machine interaction. Key technologies with recent advancements in Industry 5.0 are shown in Table 5.1.

Edge Computing: As the volume of data generated by IoT devices increases, edge computing allows for data analysis and processing to be performed faster to the source. It decreases latency, enables quick decision-making process, and reduces necessity on cloud-infrastructure. Some of the following examples in Table 5.2 represent significant achievements in the field of edge computing [8] within the context of Industry 5.0.

Additive Manufacturing (3D Printing): Additive manufacturing technologies enable the creation of complex components and products through layer-by-layer construction. This flexible and customizable manufacturing approach offers cost savings, rapid prototyping, and on-demand production capabilities [10].

Sustainable Technologies: Industry 5.0 places a strong emphasis on sustainability and environmentally friendly practices. Technologies in Figure 5.2 such as renewable energy systems, energy-efficient processes, and circular economy principles are incorporated to reduce environmental impact and promote sustainable development [11].

5.2 INDUSTRY 5.0: THE NEXT FRONTIER OF INDUSTRIAL REVOLUTION

Fifth Industrial Revolution (Industry 5.0) is a concept that emphasizes the integration of human intelligence with advanced technologies to produce more collaborative and sustainable industrial environment. The IIoT plays a crucial role in realizing the vision of Industry 5.0 by enabling the seamless connection, communication, and data exchange between machines, systems, and humans in industrial settings. Here are some ways in which IIoT contributes to Industry 5.0 [12].

- **Interconnectivity**: IIoT connects devices, sensors, machines, and systems, enabling real-time data flow for better visibility and control.
- **Data-Driven Insights**: IIoT generates vast data that can be analyzed to optimize processes, improve efficiency, and predict maintenance needs.
- **Smart and Autonomous Systems**: IIoT enables the deployment of connected machines and robots for decentralized decision-making and adaptive production.

TABLE 5.1
Key Technologies and Advancements in Industry 5.0

Key Technology	Advancements	Remarkable Achievement
Human-machine interaction (HMI) in Industry 5.0	Natural Language Processing (NLP) advancements	Significant advancements have been made in NLP, allowing machines to understand and process human language more effectively. This has led to the development of voice-activated assistants like Amazon Alexa and Apple Siri, revolutionizing the way humans interact with machines [2].
	Augmented Reality & Virtual Reality (AR&VR)	AR and VR technologies have been applied to various industries, enabling immersive experiences and enhancing human-machine collaboration. In manufacturing, for example, AR glasses have been used to guide workers through complex assembly processes, improving efficiency and reducing errors [3].
	Gesture recognition and motion tracking	Gesture recognition and motion tracking technologies have advanced, allowing machines to interpret human gestures and movements accurately. This enables intuitive interactions with machines, such as gesture-based controls for devices and robots [4].
	Brain-computer interfaces	BCIs have shown promising advancements, enabling direct communication between the human brain and machines. Researchers have developed systems that allow individuals with paralysis to control robotic limbs or communicate through thought commands [5].
	Emotion recognition and adaptive interfaces	Advancements in emotion recognition technology have allowed machines to recognize and react to social emotions. This enables much personalized with adaptive interfaces that can adjust their behavior based on the user's emotional state, leading to improved user experiences [6].

(Continued)

TABLE 5.1 (*Continued*)
Key Technologies and Advancements in Industry 5.0

Key Technology	Advancements	Remarkable Achievement
Collaborative robotics in Industry 5.0	Universal robots UR5 (2008)	Universal Robots introduced the UR5, a lightweight collaborative robot that was one of the first successful commercially available cobots. It offered easy programming, safety features, and the ability to work together with humans devoid of the need for protective barriers
	KUKA LBR IIWA (2013)	KUKA introduced the LBR IIWA (Intelligent Industrial Work Assistant), which became one of the early collaborative robots capable of human-like sensitivity and dexterity. It enabled safer interactions between humans and robots in industrial environments.
	Rethink robotics Baxter and Sawyer Year: 2012 (Baxter), 2015 (Sawyer)	Rethink Robotics introduced Baxter and later Sawyer, collaborative robots designed for manufacturing and assembly tasks. They featured advanced sensing, adaptable grippers, and intuitive user interfaces, enabling easy programming and human-robot collaboration.
	ABB YuMi (2015)	ABB introduced YuMi, a dual-arm co-operative robot specifically developed for minor parts assembly. It was equipped with vision systems, precise motion control, and advanced safety features, allowing it to work safely alongside humans on intricate assembly tasks.
	Ford's collaborative robots	Ford Motor Company implemented collaborative robots in their manufacturing processes, demonstrating how human-robot collaboration can enhance productivity and efficiency. These robots worked alongside human operators, assisting with tasks such as lifting heavy objects and repetitive assembly operations [7].

TABLE 5.2

Significant Achievements in Industry 5.0 in Edge Computing

Technology	Advancements in Industry 5.0
Fog computing concept	Cisco introduced the concept of fog computing, which later became associated with edge computing. Fog computing aimed to extend cloud computing capabilities to the network's edge, bringing computation, storage, and networking resources closer to the data source.
Microsoft azure IoT edge	Microsoft introduced Azure IoT Edge, a platform that enables the deployment and management of cloud services on edge devices. It allows for data processing and analytics to occur at the edge, improving responsiveness, reducing bandwidth usage, and addressing connectivity challenges.
Siemens' industrial edge	Siemens launched the Industrial Edge platform, which aimed to bring real-time data processing and analytics capabilities to the edge of industrial networks. The platform enabled decentralized computing, reducing latency and enabling faster decision-making in industrial settings.
Edge AI chipsets	Various technology companies, including Intel, NVIDIA, and Qualcomm, have developed specialized edge AI chipsets. These chipsets are designed to provide high-performance AI inference capabilities at the edge, enabling real-time data analysis and decision-making without relying solely on cloud resources.
Edge computing in autonomous vehicles	Edge computing plays a crucial role in enabling real-time processing and decision-making in autonomous vehicles. By bringing computational power closer to the vehicle, edge computing facilitates low-latency data analysis, enhancing safety, and enabling autonomous functionalities [9].

Renewable Energy Sources and Mangement | Smart Grid Technologies | Waste Management and Recycling | Water Conservation Technologies | Intelligent Manufacturing Systems

FIGURE 5.2   Sustainable technologies in Industry 5.0.

- **Collaborative Human-Machine Interaction**: IIoT facilitates interaction through AR and VR, enhancing productivity, safety, and decision-making.
- **Predictive Maintenance and Resource Optimization**: IIoT continuously monitors equipment, predicts failures, minimizes downtime, and optimizes resource utilization.
- **Enhanced Supply Chain management**: IIoT provides real-time visibility and traceability, improving logistics, reducing delays, and enhancing efficiency.

5.2.1   Empowering Industry 5.0: Harnessing the Potential of IIoT

Real-time monitoring in industrial settings offers numerous advantages and has significant implications for various aspects of operations. Here are some advantages and implications of real-time monitoring [13]:

- **Improved Operational Efficiency**: Real-time monitoring enables continuous tracking of critical parameters such as production rates, energy consumption, and equipment performance, allowing for timely identification of inefficiencies and bottlenecks. This facilitates proactive decision-making, resource optimization, and process improvements [14].
- **Enhanced Quality Control**: Real-time monitoring enables the detection of deviations or anomalies in product quality during the manufacturing process. This allows for immediate corrective actions, reducing the risk of producing defective products and improving overall quality control [15].
- **Predictive Maintenance**: Real-time monitoring of equipment and machine data enables the implementation of predictive maintenance strategies. By analyzing real-time sensor data and identifying patterns or anomalies, maintenance activities can be scheduled proactively, minimizing downtime, and reducing maintenance costs [16].
- **Improved Safety and Risk Mitigation**: Real-time monitoring of environmental factors, worker behavior, and equipment conditions enhances safety management. It enables the timely identification of potential hazards, allowing for immediate interventions and reducing the risk of accidents or incidents [17].
- **Data-Driven Decision-Making**: Real-time monitoring provides access to real-time data, empowering decision-makers with accurate and up-to-date information. This enables data-driven decision-making, allowing for agile responses to changing conditions, optimizing processes, and driving continuous improvement [18].

5.2.2   Real-Time Monitoring in Industry 5.0: A Comprehensive Literature Review

Real-time monitoring with IIoT dashboards in Industry 5.0 refers to the use of IIoT technologies [19] and dashboards to collect, analyze, and visualize real-time data for monitoring and decision-making in industrial settings [20]. It combines the connectivity of IIoT devices, sensors, and systems with the power of data analytics and visualization to enable real-time insights, proactive maintenance, and efficient resource management [21].

The following literature surveys provide comprehensive reviews of the current state of research, advancements, challenges, and future directions related to real-time monitoring with IIoT dashboards [22] in the background of Industry 5.0.

The challenges in implementation of IIoT technologies in industrial settings have gained significant momentum over the years [23]. This advancement has allowed for the collection of real-time data from various sensors and devices deployed in

TABLE 5.3

Notable Advancements and Overview of IIoT Technologies

Era	IIoT Technologies
Early stages (2000s–2010s)	During this period, the concept of IIoT began to emerge, highlighting the integration of internet-connected devices and industrial processes.
	Companies and industries started recognizing the potential benefits of deploying IIoT technologies to optimize their operations and improve efficiency.
Growth and expansion (2010s–2020s)	In the early 2010s, the adoption of IIoT technologies started to gain momentum, with industries embracing the concept to enhance their processes.
	Organizations began deploying sensors, devices, and network infrastructure to enable the collection of real-time data from industrial assets.
	The advancements in wireless communication and networking technologies, along with the decreasing cost of sensors, contributed to the wider adoption of IIoT in industrial settings.
Industrial transformation (2020s–Present)	The current period marks a significant shift toward Industry 4.0 and Industry 5.0, where IIoT plays a central role in driving digital transformation.
	The adoption of IIoT technologies enables industries to gather real-time data from machines, equipment, and other assets, providing insights into performance, efficiency, and predictive maintenance.
	The integration of IIoT with cloud computing, edge computing, and data analytics further enhances the capabilities of real-time data collection and analysis in industrial settings.
	Industries across various sectors, including manufacturing, energy, transportation, and healthcare, have embraced IIoT to optimize processes, improve productivity, and reduce operational costs.

industrial environments [24]. The following summary in Table 5.3 provides a detailed overview of the adoption of IIoT in industrial settings, along with notable advancements and their respective years [23–26].

In 2011, the term "Industry 4.0" was introduced, marking the emergence of the Fourth Industrial Revolution. Industry 4.0 is categorized by the incorporation of cyber-physical systems, IoT-related technologies, and data-driven technologies in industrial processes. This advancement has paved the way for the digital transformation of industries, enabling the seamless connection of machines, devices, and systems, and leveraging real-time data analytics to enhance operational efficiency, productivity, and decision-making in industrial settings [27].

The adoption of IIoT in industrial settings has paved the way for real-time monitoring, data-driven decision-making, and the transformation of traditional industries into intelligent, connected ecosystems by using certain IIoT principles, processes and protocols [28]. The continuous advancements in IIoT technologies, along with the increasing availability of scalable solutions, have further accelerated the adoption and integration of IIoT in industrial environments. The adoption of IIoT technologies gained momentum, enabling the collection of real-time data from various sensors and devices deployed in industrial environments [29]. Table 5.4 depicts various industries with its advanced technologies and applications [30].

TABLE 5.4

Various IIoT Advancements in Different Industries

Industry	Advancement	Applications
Manufacturing industry	IIoT technologies enable real-time data collection from sensors embedded in manufacturing equipment, machines, and production lines.	In a manufacturing plant, IIoT sensors installed on production equipment can gather data on parameters such as temperature, pressure, vibration, and energy consumption. This real-time data allows for predictive maintenance, optimized resource allocation, and improved overall equipment effectiveness (OEE).
Energy industry	IIoT facilitates the collection of data from energy infrastructure, enabling real-time monitoring and optimization of energy consumption.	Smart energy grids equipped with IIoT sensors can monitor energy generation, distribution, and consumption. This real-time data enables utilities to identify inefficiencies, optimize energy distribution, and implement demand-response mechanisms for efficient energy management.
Transportation and logistics industry	IIoT enables real-time tracking and monitoring of assets, vehicles, and goods throughout the supply chain.	Connected sensors embedded in vehicles, shipping containers, and warehouses provide real-time visibility into the location, condition, and status of goods. This helps optimize route planning, minimize delivery delays, and enhance supply chain efficiency.
Healthcare industry	IIoT facilitates remote patient monitoring and real-time data collection from medical devices.	Wearable devices and medical sensors connected through the IIoT enable continuous monitoring of vital signs, patient activity, and medication adherence. This real-time data enables healthcare professionals to remotely monitor patients, make timely interventions, and provide personalized care.
Agriculture industry	IIoT technologies allow for precision agriculture and real-time monitoring of crops, soil conditions, and irrigation systems.	IIoT sensors placed in the field collect data on soil moisture, temperature, and nutrient levels. This information is used to optimize irrigation schedules, apply fertilizers precisely, and monitor plant health, leading to improved crop yields and resource efficiency.

(Continued)

TABLE 5.4 (Continued)
Various IIoT Advancements in Different Industries

Industry Technology	Advancement	Description Applications
Wireless protocols (i) Wi-Fi		Enables high-speed wireless communication within a limited range, typically used for local area networking (LAN) applications.
Wireless protocols (ii) Bluetooth		Provides short-range wireless connectivity between devices, commonly used for low-power IoT devices and sensor networks.
Wireless protocols (ii) Zigbee		Designed for low-power, low-data-rate wireless communication over short distances, suitable for IoT applications with a large number of nodes.
Cellular networks 2G, 3G, 4G, and 5G:		Cellular networks offer wide-area coverage and provide reliable connectivity for IoT devices in remote or mobile applications. Each generation offers increased data rates, lower latency, and improved network capacity.
Ethernet		Ethernet is a wired networking technology that allows for high-speed and reliable data transmission over local area networks (LAN) and wide area networks (WAN). It is commonly used for industrial automation and control systems.
LoRaWAN - long range wide area network		LoRaWAN is a low-power wide-area network protocol that provides support to long-range communiqué for IoT system and devices. It is very apt for applications which need higher range with low power consumption, such as smart cities and agricultural monitoring.
MQTT - Message queuing telemetry transport		MQTT is a light weight messaging and transporting protocol intended for efficient and reliable data transfer between devices and servers. It is widely used in IoT applications, including IIoT, where low bandwidth and limited resources are a concern.
Edge computing		Edge computing encompasses analyzing data at network edge which is quite nearer to the data source. It is an alternative to rely only on cloud-based servers. It reduces dormancy, advances decision-making and real-time monitoring process, and reduces bandwidth requirements.
Industrial ethernet protocols		Specific industrial Ethernet protocols, such as Modbus TCP/IP, PROFINET, and EtherNet/IP, are widely used in industrial automation and control systems to enable real-time data exchange and communication between devices and machines.

IIoT dashboards were developed to provide real-time visualization and monitoring of industrial data. These dashboards present key performance indicators (KPIs), analytics, and insights in an easily understandable format, empowering decision-makers with real-time information [26]. IIoT dashboards evolved to incorporate advanced techniques in data analytics, like machine learning and predictive analytics, to derive actionable comprehensions from real-time data. This integration enables proactive decision-making and facilitates predictive maintenance, quality control, and resource optimization [27].

IIoT dashboards saw advancements in terms of user interface design, interactive features, and customizable visualization options. These enhancements improve the user experience, making it easier for operators and decision-makers to understand complex industrial data and take prompt actions [28].

IIoT dashboards started integrating with cloud platforms and edge computing technologies [29]. Cloud integration enables scalable storage, analysis, and remote access to industrial data, while edge computing brings real-time processing and decision-making capabilities closer to the data source [30].

5.3 LEVERAGING IIOT FOR REAL-TIME DATA COLLECTION AND ANALYSIS: CUTTING-EDGE METHODOLOGIES

IIoT for real-time data collection and analysis involves several steps of setting up an industrial IoT dashboard [31]. The general steps involved in the process are shown in Figure 5.3.

5.3.1 DEFINING OBJECTIVES AND UNCOVERING USE CASES FOR IIOT IMPLEMENTATION

Clearly define the objectives and goals of leveraging IIoT for real-time data collection and analysis in specific industrial architecture context [32]. Identify the use cases where real-time data insights can bring the most value and address specific challenges or opportunities.

- **Define Objectives**: Clearly articulate the specific goals and objectives you want to achieve by implementing IIoT for real-time data collection and analysis [33]. These objectives should align with your organization's overall strategic vision and business priorities. Examples of objectives could include improving operational efficiency, enhancing product quality, optimizing maintenance schedules, reducing downtime, increasing safety, or achieving cost savings [34].
- **Identify Use Cases**: Identify and prioritize the specific use cases or scenarios where real-time data analysis can able to provide the maximum significant impact and value. Consider the areas within your industrial processes where real-time insights can drive actionable decisions, optimize performance, or mitigate risks. Examples of use cases could include predictive maintenance, real-time quality control, supply chain optimization, energy management, asset tracking, remote monitoring, or process optimization [35].

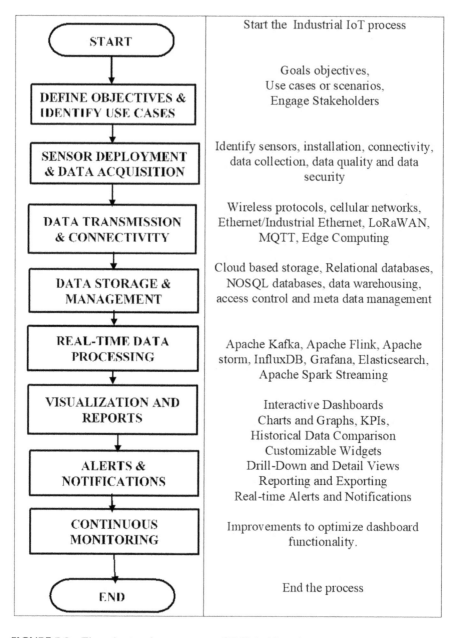

FIGURE 5.3 Flow chart and process note of IIoT dashboards.

- **Assess Feasibility and Impact**: Evaluate the feasibility and potential impact of each identified use case. Consider factors such as the availability of relevant data sources, technological capabilities, infrastructure requirements, resource allocation, and expected return on investment [36]. Prioritize the use cases based on their feasibility, potential benefits, and alignment with your defined objectives.

- **Set Specific and Measurable Goals**: Establish specific, measurable, achievable, relevant, and time-bound (SMART) goals for every identified use case. Define KPIs or metrics that will help track progress and measure the success of implementing IIoT real-time data collection and analysis and consider implications for big data analytics [37]. For example, if the objective is to improve operational efficiency, the goal could be to reduce downtime by 20% within 6 months.
- **Engage Stakeholders**: Involve relevant stakeholders from different departments or functions in the process of defining objectives and identifying use cases. Collaborate with operations teams, data analysts, subject matter experts, and decision-makers to gain insights, gather requirements, and ensure alignment with organizational goals. The Figure 5.4 shows the extended architecture of IIoT layers:

App Layer / IIoT Dashboards

Layer-4: IIoT dashboards, which provide a visual representation of the collected data, are typically part of the Application Layer

Data Management and Analytic Layer

Layer-3: Processing and managing the vast amount of data generated by the IoT devices

Network & Internet Gateway Layer

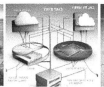

Layer-2: Communication between the devices/sensors in the Sensor and Device/Perception Layer

Sensors and Device Layer

Layer-1: Physical devices or sensors that collect data from the environment or industrial processes

FIGURE 5.4 Layers and architecture of IIoT dashboard.

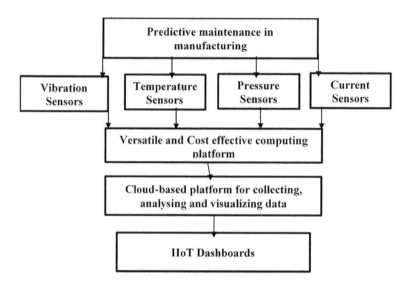

FIGURE 5.5 Block diagram: IIoT dashboard in manufacturing industry.

5.3.2 UNLEASHING THE POWER OF SENSOR DEPLOYMENT AND DATA ACQUISITION IN REAL TIME

Determine the appropriate sensors and devices needed to collect relevant data from industrial assets, machines, or processes. Install and configure the sensors to capture data in real-time and ensure proper connectivity to transmit the collected data.

Sensor deployment and data acquisition play a vital role in IIoT for real-time data collection and analysis. Here's an example of sensor deployment and data acquisition in IIoT for real-time data collection and analysis in manufacturing industry [38,39]:

The above block diagram in Figure 5.5 showcases the block diagram with the following use case in manufacturing industry to perform 'Predictive Maintenance' in manufacturing and primary objective to improve machine uptime and reduce unplanned downtime by implementing predictive maintenance techniques using real-time data [40].

Sensor Deployment and Data Acquisition Process:

- **Identify Critical Sensors**: Determine the specific sensors required to monitor the health and performance of manufacturing machines [41]. For example, vibration sensors, temperature sensors, pressure sensors, or current sensors.
- **Sensor Installation**: Install the identified sensors at strategic locations on the machines to capture relevant data [42]. For instance, place vibration sensors on rotating parts or temperature sensors near critical components.
- **Sensor Connectivity**: Establish connectivity options to ensure seamless data transmission from the sensors to the data storage or analysis platforms. This can be achieved through wired connections, wireless protocols (such as Wi-Fi or Bluetooth), or edge computing devices [42,43].
- **Data Collection and Transmission**: Configure the sensors to collect data at regular intervals or in real-time, depending on the specific requirements.

Enable the sensors to transmit the collected data to a centralized data storage system or cloud-based infrastructure securely [44].

- **Data Validation and Quality Assurance**: Implement data validation mechanisms to ensure the accuracy and reliability of the collected sensor data. Perform regular checks to identify and rectify any inconsistencies or anomalies in the data [45].
- **Time Synchronization**: Ensure that the sensors are synchronized to a common time reference to maintain accurate timestamps for the collected data. This enables proper alignment and correlation of data from different sensors [46].
- **Data Security**: Implement appropriate security measures to protect the sensor data from unauthorized access or tampering. Utilize encryption, access controls, and other security protocols to ensure data integrity and confidentiality [47].
- **Data Integration**: Integrate the sensor data with other relevant data sources, such as maintenance logs, operational data, or historical records, to gain a comprehensive view of the machine's health and performance [48].
- **Scalability Considerations**: Plan for scalability and flexibility in sensor deployment, allowing for easy expansion or reconfiguration as per changing needs or additional machines in the manufacturing environment [49].

By deploying sensors and acquiring data in this manner, manufacturers can continuously collect real-time data from machines, enabling predictive maintenance techniques. This real-time data collection and analysis help identify anomalies, detect early signs of machine failure, and trigger maintenance actions to prevent unplanned downtime and optimize overall equipment performance detailed in Figure 5.6 with Essential Elements of Streaming Sensor Data in IIoT [48–50].

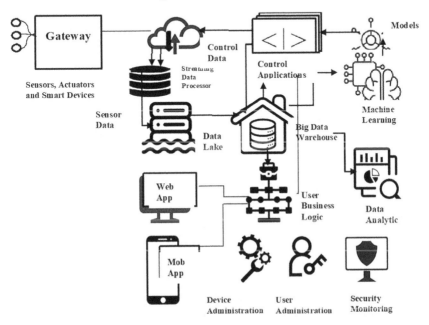

FIGURE 5.6   Essential elements of streaming sensor data in the IIoT.

5.3.3   Seamless Data Transmission and Connectivity in IIoT Landscape

Establish a robust and secure network infrastructure to enable seamless data transmission from the sensors to the data storage or analysis platforms [51]. Ensure reliable connectivity options, such as Wi-Fi, Ethernet, cellular networks, or even edge computing, depending on the specific requirements of the industrial environment [52].

In IIoT, various data transmission and connectivity technologies are utilized to ensure seamless communication between devices, sensors, and systems [53]. Some commonly used technologies in IIoT for data transmission and connectivity are shown in Table 5.5.

TABLE 5.5
IIoT Data Transmission Protocols and Technologies

Technology	Description
Wireless protocols (i) Wi-Fi	Enables high-speed wireless communication within a limited range, typically used for local area networking (LAN) applications.
Wireless protocols (ii) Bluetooth	Provides short-range wireless connectivity between devices, commonly used for low-power IoT devices and sensor networks.
Wireless protocols (ii) Zigbee	Designed for low-power, low-data-rate wireless communication over short distances, suitable for IoT applications with a large number of nodes.
Cellular networks 2G, 3G, 4G, and 5G:	Cellular networks offer wide-area coverage and provide reliable connectivity for IoT devices in remote or mobile applications. Each generation offers increased data rates, lower latency, and improved network capacity.
Ethernet	Ethernet is a wired networking technology that allows for high-speed and reliable data transmission over local area networks (LAN) and wide area networks (WAN). It is commonly used for industrial automation and control systems.
LoRaWAN - long range wide area etwork	LoRaWAN is a low-power wide-area network protocol that provides support to long-range communiqué for IoT system and devices. It is very apt for applications which need higher range with low power consumption, such as smart cities and agricultural monitoring.
MQTT - Message queuing telemetry transport	MQTT is a light weight messaging and transporting protocol intended for efficient and reliable data transfer between devices and servers. It is widely used in IoT applications, including IIoT, where low bandwidth and limited resources are a concern.
Edge computing	Edge computing encompasses analyzing data at network edge which is quite nearer to the data source. It is an alternative to rely only on cloud-based servers. It reduces dormancy, advances decision-making and real-time monitoring process, and reduces bandwidth requirements.
Industrial ethernet protocols	Specific industrial Ethernet protocols, such as Modbus TCP/IP, PROFINET, and EtherNet/IP, are widely used in industrial automation and control systems to enable real-time data exchange and communication between devices and machines.

It is essential to consider that the choice of data transmission and connectivity technology depends on various factors, including the specific use case, communication range, data volume, power consumption requirements, security considerations, and available infrastructure. A combination of these technologies may be used in complex IIoT deployments to ensure reliable and efficient data transmission in industrial settings and novel edge architecture for AI-IoT services deployment [54].

5.3.4 EFFECTIVE DATA STORAGE AND MANAGEMENT STRATEGIES FOR REAL-TIME INSIGHTS

Set up a centralized data storage system or cloud-based infrastructure to securely store the collected real-time data. Implement data management practices, including data cleaning, pre-processing, and data integration from various sources, to ensure data quality and consistency [55].

In IIoT, effective data storage and management are essential for handling the large volumes of data generated by connected devices, sensors, and systems and load-optimized sensor data store for IIoT gateways [56]. Table 5.6 shows detailed key aspects of data storage and management in IIoT.

TABLE 5.6
Key aspects of Data Storage and Management in IIoT

Purpose	Technologies
Data storage infrastructure (Cloud-based storage)	Utilizing cloud platforms such as AWS - Amazon Web Services, Google Cloud Platform or Microsoft Azure, allows for scalable, flexible, and reliable data storage. Cloud storage offers high availability, data redundancy, and easy accessibility from anywhere [57].
Data storage infrastructure (On-premises storage)	Some organizations prefer to maintain their data storage infrastructure on-premises to have complete control over data security, compliance, and latency. This typically involves deploying dedicated servers, storage systems, or data centers [58]
Database Systems (Relational Databases)	Traditional RDBMS - relational database management systems like Oracle, Microsoft SQL Server or MySQL are commonly used for structured data storage in IIoT. They provide ACID (Atomicity, Consistency, Isolation, Durability) compliance and support complex querying capabilities [59].
Database systems (NoSQL databases)	Non-relational databases such as MongoDB, Cassandra, or Apache HBase are suitable for storing unstructured or semi-structured data generated by IIoT devices. NoSQL databases offer scalability, flexibility, and fast data ingestion [59]

(Continued)

TABLE 5.6 (*Continued*)
Key aspects of Data Storage and Management in IIoT

Purpose	Technologies
Time-series data storage	Time-series databases like InfluxDB, Prometheus, or Graphite are designed specifically to handle large volumes of time-stamped data generated by sensors and devices in IIoT applications. They provide efficient storage, retrieval, and analysis of time-series data [60].
Data integration and aggregation (Data integration platforms)	Integration platforms such as Apache Kafka, MQTT brokers, or enterprise service buses (ESBs) enable seamless data aggregation and consolidation from various sources in IIoT deployments. They ensure efficient data flow between connected devices, systems, and applications [61].
Data integration and aggregation (Data warehousing)	Data warehousing solutions like Apache Hadoop, Snowflake, or Google BigQuery enable centralized storage and integration of data from multiple sources, facilitating comprehensive analytics and reporting [62].
Data security and compliance (Data encryption)	Implement encryption techniques to safeguard secured data both in transit and at rest. Encryption safeguards that information remains secure and unreadable to unauthorized parties [63].
Data security and compliance (Access controls)	Utilize role-based access controls (RBAC) and authentication mechanisms to manage data access permissions and ensure data privacy and confidentiality [64]
Data security and compliance(Compliance measures)	Adhere to industry-specific regulations (e.g., GDPR, HIPAA) and implement necessary compliance measures to safeguard data integrity, privacy, and regulatory requirements.
Data lifecycle management(Data retention policies)	Define policies for data retention and archiving based on regulatory requirements, business needs, and data analysis purposes. This ensures efficient storage utilization and compliance [65].
Data lifecycle management(Data backup and recovery)	Implement regular backup procedures to protect against data loss or system failures. Having robust backup and recovery mechanisms is crucial for data resilience and business continuity.
Data governance and metadata management	Data Governance Frameworks: Establish data governance frameworks to define policies, standards, and procedures for data management, quality assurance, and data lifecycle governance.
Metadata management	Maintain metadata repositories to catalog and manage data attributes, data lineage, and data relationships, aiding data discovery and understanding.

Effective data storage and management practices in IIoT ensure the availability, reliability, security, and accessibility of data for real-time analysis, decision-making, and business insights. These practices enable organizations to maximize the potential of their IIoT deployments and derive meaningful value from the collected data. Securing the integrity of big data in IIoT for smart manufacturing is a rapidly expanding and promising area with a futuristic outlook [66].

5.3.5 REAL-TIME DATA PROCESSING AND ANALYSIS: TRANSFORMING DATA INTO ACTIONABLE INSIGHTS

To handle incoming real-time data with minimal delay, it is crucial to employ suitable data processing techniques like stream processing or edge computing [67]. These techniques enable the extraction of valuable insights, identification of patterns, anomalies, or predictive trends through the application of analytics algorithms, machine learning models, or statistical techniques [68,69].

Real-time data processing and analysis within IIoT dashboards provide continuous monitoring, analysis, and decision-making capabilities based on the most up-to-date information. This empowers organizations to optimize operations, improve efficiency, detect anomalies, and proactively address issues, leading to enhanced business outcomes in industrial settings [70].

Real-time data processing and analysis in IIoT dashboards rely on a variety of technologies that address the challenges of real-time data ingestion, processing, and visualization [71]. Some key technologies used in this context listed in Table 5.7.

Some of the following technologies listed in Table 5.8 are widely used in the big data and real-time data processing domains and offer different capabilities for handling streaming data, storing and analyzing time series data, and creating visualizations and dashboards [72].

TABLE 5.7
Technologies for Real-Time Data Processing and Analysis IIoT Dashboards

Technology	Applications
Stream processing	Enables the processing of data in motion, allowing for real-time analysis and decision-making.
Edge computing	Brings data processing capabilities closer to the source, reducing latency and enabling real-time insights at the edge of the network.
Analytics algorithms	Algorithms designed to analyze and extract valuable information from real-time data streams.
Machine learning models	Utilized to detect patterns, anomalies, or predict trends within the real-time data, enabling proactive decision-making.
Statistical techniques	Employed to analyze and interpret real-time data, providing valuable insights and supporting informed decision-making.

TABLE 5.8

Big Data and Real-Time Data Processing Domains in IIoT Dashboards

Technology	Applications
Apache kafka	Kafka [73] is a distributed streaming platform that allows for real-time data ingestion and processing. It enables the collection, storage, and processing of high-volume, high-throughput data streams from multiple sources, making it suitable for real-time data pipelines in IIoT applications.
Apache flink	Flink is a powerful stream processing framework that supports real-time data processing, event time processing, and stateful computations. It provides capabilities for windowing, time-based aggregations, and complex event processing, making it well-suited for real-time analytics in IIoT dashboards [74].
Apache storm	Storm is a distributed stream processing system that enables real-time processing of high-velocity data streams. It provides fault tolerance, scalability, and low-latency processing, making it suitable for real-time analytics and event processing in IIoT applications [75].
InfluxDB	InfluxDB is a time-series database designed for handling large volumes of time-stamped data, making it ideal for storing and retrieving real-time data in IIoT dashboards. It offers high-performance queries, efficient data compression, and retention policies, allowing for real-time analytics and visualization [76].
Grafana	Grafana is an open-source data visualization and monitoring platform that integrates with various data sources, including time-series databases like InfluxDB. It provides customizable dashboards, real-time streaming updates, and a wide range of visualization options, making it popular for visualizing real-time data in IIoT applications [77].
Elasticsearch	Elasticsearch is a distributed search and analytics engine that can be used for real-time data indexing, search, and analysis. It offers near real-time indexing and querying capabilities, making it suitable for storing and retrieving real-time data in IIoT dashboards [78].
Apache spark streaming	Spark Streaming is a real-time stream processing framework that is part of the Apache Spark ecosystem [79]. It provides scalable and fault-tolerant stream processing capabilities, enabling real-time data ingestion, transformation, and analytics in IIoT applications.

These technologies, along with others, provide the necessary tools and frameworks to handle the complexities of real-time data processing and analysis in IIoT dashboards. They enable organizations to extract valuable insights, make informed decisions, and drive real-time actions based on the continuously evolving data from industrial processes and systems.

5.3.6 Visualizing and Reporting Real-Time Insights with Impactful Dashboards

Develop interactive and user-friendly dashboards or visualization tools to present real-time data and analysis results in a comprehensible format. Enable stakeholders, decision-makers, and operators to access and interpret the real-time data through intuitive visualizations, charts, and reports. Visualization and reporting in IIoT dashboards play a critical role in presenting real-time data in a meaningful and easily understandable format [80]. Here are some approaches and techniques for visualization and reporting in IIoT dashboards listed in Table 5.9.

TABLE 5.9
Approaches and Techniques for Visualization and Reporting in IIoT Dashboards

Type	Applications
Interactive dashboards	IIoT dashboards provide interactive visualizations that allow users to explore and interact with the data. Users can zoom in/out, filter data based on criteria, and dynamically adjust the time range to focus on specific periods of interest [81].
Real-time data updates	IIoT dashboards display real-time data updates, ensuring that the visualizations reflect the most current information from the connected devices, sensors, and systems. Real-time updates enable users to monitor changing conditions and make timely decisions [82].
Charts and Graphs	Dashboards often include various types of charts and graphs such as line charts, bar charts, pie charts, scatter plots, and heatmaps. These visual representations allow users to quickly grasp trends, patterns, and correlations in the data [83].
Key performance indicators (KPIs)	IIoT dashboards prominently display key performance indicators relevant to industrial processes. KPIs can include metrics such as machine performance, production rates, energy consumption, quality indicators, and equipment downtime. Clear visual indicators such as gauges, meters, or progress bars help users monitor and track performance against targets [84].
Historical data comparison	IIoT dashboards often provide the capability to compare current real-time data with historical trends and patterns. This allows users to identify anomalies, deviations, or changes in behavior, providing valuable insights for decision-making [85].
Customizable widgets	Dashboards offer customizable widgets that allow users to configure their own views based on their specific needs. Users can select relevant metrics, create personalized visualizations, and arrange the widgets according to their preferences [86].
Drill-down and detail views	IIoT dashboards enable drill-down capabilities to explore more detailed information. Users can click on specific data points or regions of interest to view more granular data, supporting deeper analysis and troubleshooting [87].

(Continued)

TABLE 5.9 (*Continued*)

Approaches and Techniques for Visualization and Reporting in IIoT Dashboards

Type	Applications
Reporting and exporting	IIoT dashboards often include reporting features that allow users to generate and export reports in various formats such as PDF, Excel, or CSV. Reports can summarize key metrics, trends, and insights for sharing with stakeholders or for further analysis [88].
Real-time alerts and notifications	Dashboards can be configured to generate real-time alerts and notifications based on predefined thresholds or critical events. Users can receive alerts via email, SMS, or in-app notifications, ensuring timely response and intervention [89].

Visualization and reporting in IIoT dashboards enhance situational awareness, enable data-driven decision-making, and support performance monitoring in industrial settings. These features empower users to derive insights, identify issues, and take proactive actions based on the real-time data visualizations and reports provided by the dashboards [90].

5.3.7 Instant Alerts and Notifications: Staying Ahead in the Age of IIoT

Implement alert mechanisms and notification systems to trigger immediate actions or alerts based on predefined thresholds, anomalies, or critical events detected from the real-time data. Configure real-time alerts to notify relevant personnel or systems to take proactive measures or initiate automated responses when necessary.

5.3.8 Continuous Monitoring and Optimization: Maximizing Efficiency in Real Time

Establish a feedback loop to continuously monitor and evaluate the effectiveness of the IIoT-enabled real-time data collection and analysis system. Regularly assess the performance, accuracy, and efficiency of the system and make necessary adjustments or improvements to optimize its functionality.

5.4 ENHANCING OPERATIONAL VISIBILITY AND BEST PRACTICES: IMPLEMENTING SUCCESSFUL IIoT DASHBOARDS

Enhancing operational visibility involves leveraging IIoT dashboards to improve understanding and insight into various aspects of industrial operations such as machinery-related faults and energy conception-related faults. This is achieved by capturing and visualizing real-time data from connected devices, sensors, and systems, enabling data-driven decision-making that optimizes performance and drives operational excellence [91].

Data-driven decision-making with IIoT dashboards entails utilizing real-time data collected from industrial processes to gain insights, identify patterns, and make informed decisions [92] for e.g. based on the patterns and insights the business owner can decide about starting or shutting down the plant in a long run. By visualizing this data through intuitive and interactive dashboards, decision-makers can monitor KPIs, track operational metrics, and assess the overall health of their industrial operations [93].

An example of enhancing operational visibility and data-driven decision-making with IIoT dashboards can be observed in the manufacturing industry, specifically in a large automotive manufacturing plant [94,95].

In this industry, IIoT sensors are deployed throughout the production line to capture real-time data on various parameters such as machine performance, equipment health, energy consumption, and quality metrics. This data is transmitted and collected in a centralized IIoT platform, which feeds into a comprehensive dashboard [96].

The IIoT dashboard provides a visual representation of specific KPIs related to the manufacturing process [97]. For example, it displays real-time data on production rates, machine utilization, downtime, and quality metrics like defect rates or rework percentages.

By monitoring these metrics in real time, plant managers and operators gain immediate visibility into the performance and health of the production line. They can identify bottlenecks, diagnose issues, and take proactive measures to optimize operations. For instance, if a machine's performance starts to decline, the dashboard triggers an alert, notifying the responsible personnel to address the issue promptly [98].

The dashboard also enables data analysis and visualization, allowing stakeholders to identify trends, patterns, and correlations. They can track the impact of process changes, evaluate the effectiveness of improvement initiatives, and make data-driven decisions to enhance productivity and quality [98].

Moreover, the IIoT dashboard can support predictive analytics capabilities. By analyzing historical and real-time data, the dashboard can generate predictive models to forecast potential machine failures, optimize maintenance schedules, and minimize downtime [99].

Overall, in the manufacturing industry, the use of IIoT dashboards enhances operational visibility, empowers data-driven decision-making, and enables proactive measures to optimize production, reduce costs, and improve product quality [99,100].

5.4.1 REVOLUTIONIZING CRUDE OIL PRODUCTION WITH IIoT AND EDGE COMPUTING

Ramzey et al. present a framework that leverages IIoT and Edge Computing technologies to enhance operational visibility and enable data-driven decision-making in the crude oil production industry [101].

The framework aims to address the challenges faced in real-time monitoring and controlling of crude oil production processes by utilizing the capabilities of IIoT and

Edge Computing. It establishes a smart monitoring system that collects and analyzes real-time data from various sensors and devices deployed in the production environment [101].

Key points and useful information extracted from the article include:

- **Objective**: The framework's primary objective is to enable real-time monitoring and control of crude oil production processes, allowing operators to make data-driven decisions and optimize production efficiency.
- **IIoT Integration Process**: The framework integrates IIoT technologies, leveraging sensor data, network connectivity, and cloud computing to collect and transmit real-time data from the production site to a centralized system.
- **Edge Computing**: Edge computing is utilized to perform data processing and analysis tasks at the edge of the network, closer to the data source, enabling faster response times and reducing the dependence on cloud infrastructure.
- **Real-Time Monitoring**: The current framework enables real-time monitoring of crucial parameters such as oil flow rate, temperature, pressure, and equipment status. This information is visualized through an IIoT dashboard, providing operators with a comprehensive view of the production process.
- **Data Analytics**: The collected data is analyzed using advanced analytics techniques, including data analytic and machine learning algorithms, to identify patterns, anomalies, and predictive insights. This analysis aids in optimizing production, detecting equipment failures, and enabling predictive maintenance.
- **Decision-Making**: The framework supports data-driven decision-making by providing dashboard operators with actionable insights derived from the real-time data. This empowers them to take proactive measures, optimize production processes, and minimize downtime.
- **Benefits**: The implementation of the above framework offers several benefits, including enhanced operational visibility, improved production efficiency, reduced downtime, optimized maintenance, and cost savings.

The article showcases the significance of leveraging IIoT and Edge Computing technologies in the crude oil production industry. By adopting the I2OT-EC framework, companies can achieve real-time monitoring, data-driven decision-making, and ultimately optimize their crude oil production processes [101].

5.4.2 REVOLUTIONIZING AGRICULTURE: IoT-ENABLED SMART AGRI DASHBOARDS

Kayetha and Pabboju discuss the development of an IoT-based smart device for agricultural purposes [102]. Here are some useful pieces of information related to enhancing operational visibility and data-driven decision-making with IIoT dashboards:

- **Objective**: The principal goal of the proposed work is to produce a connection between farmers and farms by developing an IoT-based system and smart device that collects and stores sensor-based data to repossess water and soil parameters. The device also provides crop recommendations based on the collected/stored data.

- **Methodology**: Internet of Things (IoT) system, sensor networks, big data, data mining, machine learning algorithms. Components such as Raspberry Pi, Sensors like DHT11 (Digital humidity and temperature sensor), soil moisture, LDR (Light Dependent Resistor sensor), ultrasonic sensor, NPK (Nitrogen, Phosphorus, and Potassium sensor), pH sensor, and others are used to collect data related to soil properties and weather conditions.
- **Crop Prediction**: The prediction module contains Gaussian Naive Bayes algorithm to predict suitable/appropriate crops based on parameters such as pH, N, P, K, humidity, temperature, and rainfall. The model for crop prediction is trained using a dataset from the Kaggle database.
- **Comparison with Traditional Methods**: The proposed system is compared to existing outdated methods such as laboratory-based soil testing. The traditional methods involve very lengthy and expensive policies and procedures for soil testing and as well as for crop prediction. In contrast, this proposed IoT-based dashboard system provides faster results at a lesser cost and makes instant digital data obtainable on a cloud-server.
- **Efficiency and Accuracy**: This system demonstrates efficient performance with a 99.3% accuracy rate with comparison to a previous accuracy of 97.18%. The system allows a single device for multiple soil tests, and the other advantage is the instant result viewing feature, eliminating the need for time-consuming lab-based testing.
- **Novelty**: The proposed system differs from existing systems by using Raspberry Pi (small, affordable single board computer) used for soil tests. This also supports high-end sensors and is companionable with the advanced and recent machine-level algorithms. It also uses an NPK sensor to directly measure the nutrient values instead of using a soil electrical conductivity sensor and color sensor, making the process more efficient.
- **Integration with IoT Dashboards**: The data collected from sensors is stored in the ThingSpeak cloud server, which enables monitoring of crop conditions. The data can be visualized and analyzed using IoT dashboards, providing operational visibility and facilitating data-driven decision-making.

Overall, the article highlights the use of IoT dashboards and data-driven approaches in agriculture to enhance operational visibility and enable stakeholders to make informed decisions based on real-time data [102,103].

5.5 CONCLUSION

Transforming Industry 5.0: Real-Time Monitoring and Decision-Making with IIoT dashboards have highlighted the significant impact of real-time monitoring and decision-making process enabled by IIoT in shaping the future of industries. Throughout this chapter, we have explored the various applications, benefits, and challenges associated with implementing IIoT technologies.

Enhancing operational visibility through IIoT dashboards is a powerful strategy for industries to improve understanding, optimize performance, and drive operational excellence. By capturing and visualizing real-time data from connected devices, sensors, and systems, decision-makers can gain insights, monitor KPIs, and assess the overall health of industrial operations. The application of IIoT dashboards in manufacturing plants and the crude oil production industry demonstrates their effectiveness in identifying issues, optimizing processes, and enabling data-driven decision-making. Similarly, in agriculture, IoT-enabled smart agriculture dashboards empower farmers to collect and analyze sensor-based data, predict suitable crop types, and make informed decisions for optimized farming practices. However, along with the opportunities, challenges have also emerged in this new era of Industry 5.0. The complete volume and complexity of raw data produced by IIoT channels/devices pose challenges in terms of data management, storage, and security. Ensuring the privacy and security of sensitive data has become a crucial concern for industries. Additionally, the integration of legacy systems with IIoT technologies and the need for skilled professionals proficient in IIoT implementation present further challenges [104].

Looking into the near future, it is evident that IIoT will endure to play a pivotal role in transforming industries in sustainable way. We can anticipate several interesting future trends that will shape the landscape of Industry 5.0. First, recent advancements in artificial intelligence and edge computing will enable faster and more accurate process monitoring, real-time decision-making, empowering industries to respond swiftly to changing conditions. Second, the convergence of IIoT with other emerging technologies such as block chain, robotics, and 5G will unlock new possibilities, creating intelligent and interconnected ecosystems. Moreover, addressing the challenges associated with IIoT implementation will be crucial. Industry leaders and stakeholders must invest in robust cybersecurity measures to protect sensitive data and build trust in the ecosystem and to improve the data integrity. Efforts should also focus on upskilling the workforce to bridge the skills gap and enable seamless integration of IIoT technologies into existing systems.

In conclusion, the transformative potential of real-time monitoring and decision-making with IIoT is immense. By embracing these technologies, industries can unlock new levels of efficiency, productivity, and competitiveness with above evidences of several industries such as oil industry and agriculture. However, it is essential to navigate the challenges and proactively adapt to the evolving trends to fully harness the benefits of IIoT and drive the future of Industry 5.0.

REFERENCES

[1] Bali, S., Aggarwal, S., & Sharma, S. (Eds.). (2021). *Industry 4.0 Technologies for Business Excellence: Frameworks, Practices, and Applications* (1st ed.). Boca Raton: CRC Press.

[2] Internet Source: Pew Research Center, "AI, Robotics, and the Future of Jobs" - https://www.pewresearch.org/internet/2020/02/13/ai-robotics-and-the-future-of-jobs/.

[3] Internet Source: IEEE Spectrum, "How Augmented Reality Is Transforming Work" - https://spectrum.ieee.org/augmented-reality-transforming-work.

[4] Internet Source: ScienceDirect, "A Review of Human Motion Capture and Gesture Recognition Techniques" - https://www.sciencedirect.com/science/article/pii/S2352340917305880.

[5] Internet Source: Nature, "A Brain-Computer Interface Decoded Motor Imagery Signals from the Rat Frontal Cortex" - https://www.nature.com/articles/s41598-021-81192-7.

[6] Internet Source: ACM Transactions on Interactive Intelligent Systems, "Multimodal Emotion Recognition: Advances and Challenges" - https://dl.acm.org/doi/10.1145/3125493.

[7] Internet Source: Forbes, "The Importance Of Edge Computing In Autonomous Cars" - https://www.forbes.com/sites/forbestechcouncil/2021/08/19/the-importance-of-edge-computing-in-autonomous-cars/.

[8] Elangovan, U. (2021). *Industry 5.0: The Future of the Industrial Economy* (1st ed.). Florida, Boca Raton, Florida, USA: CRC Press. ISBN 9781032041278.

[9] Kumari, K. A., Sadasivam, G. S., Dharani, D., & Niranjanamurthy, M. (2021). *Edge Computing: Fundamentals, Advances, and Applications* (1st ed.). CRC Press. ISBN 9781032126081.

[10] Mourtzis, D., Doukas, M., & Bernidaki, A. (2019). 3D printing applications in industry 4.0: A review. *Procedia CIRP*, 81, 656–661.

[11] Yang, Y., Li, H., Zhang, H., Zuo, Y., & Liu, W. (2021). A review of sustainable technologies in industry 4.0 and their application in industry 5.0. *Journal of Cleaner Production*, 318, 128502.

[12] Maddikunta, P. K. R., Pham, Q.-V., Prabadevi, B., Deepa, N., Dev, K., Gadekallu, T. R., Ruby, R., & Liyanage, M. (2022). Industry 5.0: A survey on enabling technologies and potential applications☆. *Journal of Industrial Information Integration*, 26, 100257.

[13] Internet Source: Ford Media Center, "Collaborative Robotics: Humans and Robots Working Side by Side at Ford" - https://media.ford.com/content/fordmedia/fna/us/en/news/2017/02/22/collaborative-robotics-humans-and-robots-working-side-by-side-a.html.

[14] Li, X., Hu, Z., Huang, G. Q., & Ye, Y. (2018). Real-time production monitoring and control in smart manufacturing. *Journal of Manufacturing Systems*, 48, 157–169.

[15] Chalal, R., Boudjlida, N., & Zerhouni, N. (2017). Real-time monitoring for quality control in the industry 4.0 context. *Procedia Manufacturing*, 11, 1394–1402.

[16] Barata, J., Oliveira, A. I., & Pereira, A. I. (2020). Predictive maintenance in industry 4.0: A systematic review. *Computers in Industry*, 122, 103298.

[17] Aftab, H., & Al-Bayatti, A. H. (2017). Real-time monitoring and safety management in industrial environments using IoT-based systems. *Journal of Sensor and Actuator Networks*, 6(4), 21.

[18] Fayaz, H., Awang, M., & Hassan, A. (2018). Real-time monitoring and control systems: A review. *Measurement*, 121, 266–280.

[19] Immerman, G. (2019). *Proving Operational Efficiency with Industrial IoT*. Easthampton, MA: MachineMetrics.

[20] Peñalver, L., & Parra, L. (Eds.). (2021). Industrial IoT Technologies and Applications. *4th EAI International Conference, Industrial IoT 2020, Virtual Event, December 11, 2020, Proceedings. Lecture Notes of the Institute for Computer Sciences, Social Informatics and Telecommunications Engineering*. Cham: Springer. https://doi.org/10.1007/978-3-030-71061-3.

[21] Lloret, J., & Parra, L. (2022). Industrial internet of things. Mobile networks and applications, ISSN 1572-8153. Advance online publication. https://doi.org/10.1007/s11036-022-02014-5.

[22] Internet Source: Industrial IoT Dashboards Improve Effectiveness in Modern Manufacturing Facilities - https://synergycodes.com/our-work/industrial-iot-dashboards/.

[23] Shunmughavel, V. (2021). *Innovations in the Industrial Internet of Things (IIoT) and Smart Factory, Challenges to Industrial Internet of Things (IIoT) Adoption*. https://doi.org/10.4018/978-1-7998-3375-8.ch009.

[24] Sundas, A., & Panda, S. N. (2021). Real-time data communication with iot sensors and thingsspeak cloud. In *Wireless Sensor Networks and the Internet of Things* (1st ed., p. 17). Apple Academic Press. eBook ISBN 9781003131229.

[25] Sharma, Nikhil. (2020). Evolution of IoT to IIoT: Applications & challenges. *SSRN Electronic Journal,* 1–6.

[26] Jaidka, Himanshu, Sharma, Nikhil, & Singh, Rajinder. (2020). Evolution of IoT to IIoT: Applications & challenges. *SSRN Electronic Journal.* https://doi.org/10.2139/ssrn.3603739.

[27] Lu, Y. (2017). Industry 4.0: A survey on technologies, applications and open research issues. *Journal of Industrial Information Integration,* 6, 1–10. https://doi.org/10.1016/j.jii.2017.04.005.

[28] Madakam, S, & Uchiya, T (2019). Industrial internet of things (IIoT): Principles, processes and protocols. *The Internet of Things in the Industrial Sector.* Springer. https://doi.org/10.1007/978-3-030-24892-5_2.

[29] Maqbool, R., Saiba, M.R. & Ashfaq, S. (2023). Emerging industry 4.0 and Internet of Things (IoT) technologies in the Ghanaian construction industry: Sustainability, implementation challenges, and benefits. *Environmental Science and Pollution Research* 30, 37076–37091. https://doi.org/10.1007/s11356-022-24764-1.

[30] The Top 20 Industrial IoT Applications. https://www.iotworldtoday.com/iiot/the-top-20-industrial-iot-applications (accessed on 11 June 2023).

[31] Internet source: How to Create an Industrial IoT Dashboard. A Step-by-Step Guide - https://www.machinechat.io/post/how-to-create-an-industrial-iot-dashboard-a-step-by-step-guide (accessed on 11 June 2023).

[32] Lin, S.W., Miller, B., Durand, J., Bleakley, G., Chigani, A., Martin, R., Murphy, B., Crawford, M. (2017). *The Industrial Internet of Things Volume G1: Reference Architecture.* Needham, MA: Industrial Internet Consortium, pp. 10–46.

[33] Hattinger, Monika, Snis, Ulrika & Islind, Anna. (2021). Real-time analytics through industrial internet of things: Lessons learned from data-driven industry. In *27th Annual Americas Conference on Information Systems (AMCIS), ELECTR NETWORK,* August 9–13, 2021. Montreal, Canada: Association for Information Systems.

[34] IoT in Manufacturing: Predictive Maintenance and Quality Control. https://www.peer-bits.com/blog/iot-in-manufacturing-predictive-maintenance-and-quality-control.html (accessed on 11 June 2023).

[35] Singhal, R., Nunez, D., & Pegg, J. (2022). Achieving operational efficiency in energy, AVEVA Group plc and its subsidiaries, Retrieved from https://discover.aveva.com/paid-search-oee/whitepaper-achieving-operational-efficiency-in-energy (accessed on 11 June 2023).

[36] Verma, S., Kawamoto, Y., Fadlullah, Z. M., Nishiyama, H., & Kato, N. (2017). A survey on network methodologies for real-time analytics of massive IoT data and open research issues. *IEEE Communications Surveys & Tutorials,* 19(3), 1457–1477.

[37] Williams, S., Hardy, C., & Nitschke, P. (2019). Configuring the Internet of things (IoT): a review and implications for big data analytics. Paper presented at the Proceedings of the 52nd Hawaii International Conference on System Sciences, Honolulu, HI.

[38] Canli, T., Khokhar, A. (2009). Data acquisition and dissemination in sensor networks. In: Liu, L., Özsu, M. T. (eds). *Encyclopedia of Database Systems.* Boston, MA: Springer. https://doi.org/10.1007/978-0-387-39940-9_92.

[39] Analytics for IIoT: IIoT data management and analytics for large manufacturers. https://yalantis.com/blog/iiot-data-management-and-analytics/ (accessed on 11 June 2023).

[40] Javaid, M., Haleem, A., Singh, R. P., Rab, S., & Suman, R. (2021). Upgrading the manufacturing sector via applications of industrial internet of things (IIoT). *Sensors International,* 2, 100129.

[41] Using IoT Sensors to Improve Productivity in Manufacturing. https://www.advancedtech. com/blog/common-sensors-used-in-manufacturing/ (accessed on 11 June 2023).

[42] 5 Types of Sensors that can be used on Manufacturing Equipment. https://www.iot-forall.com/using-iot-sensors-to-improve-productivity-in-manufacturing (accessed on 11 June 2023).

[43] Chen, C. (2022). IoT architecture-based mechanism for digital transmission of key aspects of the enterprise. *Computational Intelligence and Neuroscience*, 2022, 3461850. https://doi.org/10.1155/2022/3461850.

[44] Xu, Jiangtao, Tao, Fengbo, Liu, Yang, Hu, Chengbo, Xu, Yang, Keivanimehr, Farhad, Nabipour, Narjes. (2020). Data transmission method for sensor devices in internet of things based on multivariate analysis. *Measurement*, 157, 107536. https://doi.org/10.1016/j.measurement.2020.107536.

[45] Ann, Fernandes & Wagh, Rupali. (2019). Quality assurance in big data analytics: An IoT perspective. *Telfor Journal*, 11, 114–118. https://doi.org/10.5937/telfor1902114A.

[46] Yi Ği Tler, H.N., Badihi, B., & Jäntti, R. (2020). Overview of time synchronization for IoT deployments: Clock discipline algorithms and protocols. *Sensors (Basel)*, 20(20), 5928. https://doi.org/10.3390/s20205928.

[47] Duan, C., Wu, Y., Song, L., & Liu, L. (2021). The new method of sensor data privacy protection for IoT. *Shock and Vibration*, 2021, 3920579. https://doi.org/10.1155/2021/3920579.

[48] A guide to simplifying IoT data management: Sensor integration and ingestion solutions. https://datorios.com/blog/simplifying-iot-data-management/ (accessed on 11 June 2023).

[49] Arellanes, Damian & Lau, Kung-Kiu. (2020). Evaluating IoT service composition mechanisms for the scalability of IoT systems. *Future Generation Computer Systems*, 108. https://doi.org/10.1016/j.future.2020.02.073.

[50] Nunes, P., Santos, J., & Rocha, E. (2023). Challenges in predictive maintenance - A review. *CIRP Journal of Manufacturing Science and Technology*, 40, 53–67. ISSN 1755-5817. https://doi.org/10.1016/j.cirpj.2022.11.004.

[51] Al-Fuqaha, A., Guizani, M., Mohammadi, M., Aledhari, M., & Ayyash, M. (2015). Internet of things: A survey on enabling technologies, protocols, and applications, *IEEE Communications Surveys & Tutorials*, 17(4), 2347–2376.

[52] Izaddoost, A., & Siewierski, M. (2020). Energy efficient data transmission in iot platforms. *Procedia Computer Science*, 175, 387–394. ISSN 1877-0509. https://doi.org/10.1016/j.procs.2020.07.055.

[53] Chakchouk, N. (2015). A survey on opportunistic routing in wireless communication networks" *IEEE Communications Surveys & Tutorials*, 17 (4), 2214–2241.

[54] Debauche, O., Mahmoudi, S., Mahmoudi, S. A., Manneback, P., & Lebeau, F. (2020). A new edge architecture for AI-IoT services deployment. *Procedia Computer Science*, 175, 10–19. ISSN 1877-0509. https://doi.org/10.1016/j.procs.2020.07.006.

[55] Alsuwaidan, Lulwah. (2020). The role of data management in the industrial internet of things. *Concurrency and Computation: Practice and Experience*, 33. https://doi.org/10.1002/cpe.6031.

[56] Alonso, Á., Pozo, A., Cantera, J.M., De la Vega, F., & Hierro, J.J. (2018). Industrial data space architecture implementation using FIWARE. *Sensors*, 18, 2226. https://doi.org/10.3390/s18072226.

[57] 10 Benefits of Cloud Storage. Available online: https://cloudacademy.com/blog/10-benefits-of-using-cloud-storage/ (accessed on 11 June 2023).

[58] Al-Issa, Y., Ottom, M.A., & Tamrawi, A. (2019). eHealth cloud security challenges: A survey. *Journal of Healthcare Engineering*, 2019, 7516035. https://doi.org/10.1155/2019/7516035.

[59] Top Databases in The Market For IoT Applications. Available online: https://www.intuz.com/guide-on-top-iot-databases (accessed on 11 June 2023).

[60] Fadhel, Muntazir, Sekerinski, Emil, & Yao, Shucai. (2019). A comparison of time series databases for storing water quality data. In *Mobile Technologies and Applications for the Internet of Things: Proceedings of the 12th IMCL Conference*, pp. 302–313. https://doi.org/10.1007/978-3-030-11434-3_33.

[61] Trunzer, Emanuel, Kirchen, Iris, Folmer, Jens, Koltun, Gennadiy, & Vogel-Heuser, Birgit. (2017). A flexible architecture for data mining from heterogeneous data sources in automated production systems. In *2017 IEEE International Conference on Industrial Technology (ICIT)*, pp. 1106–1111. https://doi.org/10.1109/ICIT.2017.7915517.

[62] Nambiar, A., & Mundra, D. (2022). An overview of data warehouse and data lake in modern enterprise data management. *Big Data and Cognitive Computing*, 6(4), 132. https://doi.org/10.3390/bdcc6040132.

[63] Dixit, Rashmi, & Kongara, Ravindranath. (2018). Encryption techniques & access control models for data security: A survey. *International Journal of Engineering and Technology (UAE)*, 7, 107–110. https://doi.org/10.14419/ijet.v7i1.5.9130.

[64] de Carvalho Junior, M.A., & Bandiera-Paiva, P. (2018). Health Information System Role-Based Access Control Current Security Trends and Challenges. *Journal of Healthcare Engineering*, 19, 6510249. https://doi.org/10.1155/2018/6510249.

[65] Improving Data Value with Data Lifecycle Management. Available online: https://bigid.com/blog/improving-data-value-with-data-lifecycle-management/ (accessed on 11 June 2023).

[66] Juma, M., Alattar, F., & Touqan, B. (2023). Securing big data integrity for industrial IoT in smart manufacturing based on the trusted consortium blockchain (TCB). *IoT*, 4(1), 27–55. https://doi.org/10.3390/iot4010002.

[67] Bourechak, A., Zedadra, O., Kouahla, M.N., Guerrieri, A., Seridi, H., & Fortino, G. (2023). At the confluence of artificial intelligence and edge computing in IoT-based applications: A review and new perspectives. *Sensors*, 23(3), 1639. https://doi.org/10.3390/s23031639.

[68] Mahdavinejad, M. S., Rezvan, M., Barekatain, M., Adibi, P., Barnaghi, P., & Sheth, A. P. (2018). Machine learning for internet of things data analysis: A survey. *Digital Communications and Networks*, 4(3), 161–175. https://doi.org/10.1016/j.dcan.2017.10.002.

[69] Chatterjee, A., & Ahmed, B. S. (2022). IoT anomaly detection methods and applications: A survey. *Internet of Things*, 19, 100568. https://doi.org/10.1016/j.iot.2022.100568.

[70] Javaid, Mohd, Haleem, Abid, & Suman, Rajiv. (2023). Digital twin applications toward industry 4.0: A review. *Cognitive Robotics*, 3, 71–92. ISSN 2667-2413. https://doi.org/10.1016/j.cogr.2023.04.003.

[71] Mirani, A.A., Velasco-Hernandez, G., Awasthi, A., & Walsh, J. (2022). Key Challenges and Emerging Technologies in Industrial IoT Architectures: A Review. *Sensors*, 22(15), 5836. https://doi.org/10.3390/s22155836.

[72] Isah, Haruna, Abughofa, Tariq, Mahfuz, Sazia, Ajerla, Dharmitha, Zulkernine, Farhana & Khan, Shahzad. (2019). A survey of distributed data stream processing frameworks. *IEEE Access*, 7, 1–1. https://doi.org/10.1109/ACCESS.2019.2946884.

[73] Shree, Rishika, Choudhury, Tanupriya, Gupta, Subhash, & Kumar, Praveen. (2017). KAFKA: The modern platform for data management and analysis in big data domain. In *2017 2nd International Conference on Telecommunication and Networks (TEL-NET)*, pp. 1–5. https://doi.org/10.1109/TEL-NET.2017.8343593.

[74] Kefalakis, N., Roukounaki, A., & Soldatos, J. (2019). Configurable distributed data management for the internet of the things. *Information*, 10(12), 360. https://doi.org/10.3390/info10120360.

[75] Rashid, Mamoon, Singh, Harjeet, Goyal, Vishal, Ahmad, Nazir, & Mongla, Neeraj. (2019). Efficient big data-based storage and processing model in internet of things for improving accuracy fault detection in industrial processes. In *Research Anthology on Big Data Analytics, Architectures, and Applications*, pp. 945–957. https://doi.org/10.4018/978-1-7998-0373-7.ch009.

[76] Calatrava, Carlos, Fontal, Yolanda, & Cucchietti, Fernando. (2022). A holistic scalability strategy for time series databases following cascading polyglot persistence. *Big Data and Cognitive Computing*, 6(3), 86. https://doi.org/10.3390/bdcc6030086.

[77] Venkatramulu, S., Phridviraj, M.S.B., Srinivas, C. & Rao, Vadithala. (2021). Implementation of Grafana as open source visualization and query processing platform for data scientists and researchers. *Materials Today: Proceedings*. https://doi.org/10.1016/j.matpr.2021.03.364.

[78] Ren, Sothearin, Kim, Jae-Sung, Cho, Wan-Sup, Soeng, Saravit, Kong, Sovanreach, & Lee, Kyung-Hee. (2021). *Big Data Platform for Intelligence Industrial IoT Sensor Monitoring System Based on Edge Computing and AI*, 480–482. https://doi.org/10.1109/ICAIIC51459.2021.9415189.

[79] Isah, Haruna, Abughofa, Tariq, Mahfuz, Sazia, Ajerla, Dharmitha, Zulkernine, Farhana, & Khan, Shahzad. (2019). A survey of distributed data stream processing frameworks. *IEEE Access*, 7, 1–1. https://doi.org/10.1109/ACCESS.2019.2946884.

[80] Patel, M., Mehta, A., & Chauhan, N. C. (2021). Design of smart dashboard based on IoT & fog computing for smart cities. *2021 5th International Conference on Trends in Electronics and Informatics (ICOEI)*, pp. 458–462, Tirunelveli, India. https://doi.org/10.1109/ICOEI51242.2021.9452744.

[81] Costa, F.S., Nassar, S.M., Gusmeroli, S., Schultz, R., Conceição, A.G.S., Xavier, M., Hessel, F., Dantas, M.A.R. (2020). FASTEN IIoT: An Open Real-Time Platform for Vertical, Horizontal and End-To-End Integration. *Sensors*, 20(19), 5499. https://doi.org/10.3390/s20195499.

[82] Costa, Felipe, Nassar, Silvia, & Dantas, Mario. (2020). FASTEN IIoT: An open real-time platform for vertical, horizontal and end-to-end integration. *Sensors*, 20. https://doi.org/10.3390/s20195499.

[83] Protopsaltis, Antonis, Sarigiannidis, Panagiotis, Margounakis, Dimitrios & Lytos, Anastasios. (2020). Data visualization in internet of things: tools, methodologies, and challenges. In *Proceedings of the 15th International Conference on Availability, Reliability and Security*, pp. 1–11 https://doi.org/10.1145/3407023.3409228.

[84] Trendowicz, Adam, Groen, Eduard, Henningsen, Jens, Siebert, Julien, Bartels, Nedo, Storck, Sven, & Kuhn, Thomas. (2023). User experience key performance indicators for industrial IoT systems: A multivocal literature review. *Digital Business*, 3, 100057. https://doi.org/10.1016/j.digbus.2023.100057.

[85] Gyamfi, E., & Jurcut, A. (2022). Intrusion detection in internet of things systems: A review on design approaches leveraging multi-access edge computing, machine learning, and datasets. *Sensors*, 22(10), 3744. https://doi.org/10.3390/s22103744.

[86] Widget types in custom dashboards. Available online: https://help.youscan.io/en/articles/4889946-widget-types-in-custom-dashboards (accessed on 11 June 2023).

[87] Praharaj, S., Solis, P., & Wentz, E.A. (2022). Deploying geospatial visualization dashboards to combat the socioeconomic impacts of COVID-19. *Environment and Planning. B, Urban Analytics and City Science*. https://doi.org/10.1177/23998083221142863.

[88] Munawar HS, Qayyum S, Ullah F, Sepasgozar S. (2020). Big data and its applications in smart real estate and the disaster management life cycle: A systematic analysis. *Big Data and Cognitive Computing*, 4(2), 4. https://doi.org/10.3390/bdcc4020004.

[89] Chai, P. R., Zhang, H., Baugh, C. W., Jambaulikar, G. D., McCabe, J. C., Gorman, J. M., Boyer, E. W., & Landman, A. (2018). Internet of things buttons for real-time notifications in hospital operations: proposal for hospital implementation. *Journal of medical Internet Research*, 20(8), e251. https://doi.org/10.2196/jmir.9454.

[90] Mahmoodpour, Mehdi, Lobov, Andrei, Lanz, Minna, Makela, Petteri & Rundas, Niko. (2018). Role-based visualization of industrial IoT-based systems. 1–8. https://doi.org/10.1109/MESA.2018.8449183.

[91] Javaid, Mohd, Haleem, Abid, Singh, Ravi Pratap, Rab, Shanay, & Suman, Rajiv. (2021). Upgrading the manufacturing sector via applications of Industrial Internet of Things (IIoT). *Sensors International*, 2, 100129. https://doi.org/10.1016/j.sintl.2021.100129.

[92] Dhungana, Deepak, Haselböck, Alois, Meixner, Sebastian, Schall, Daniel, Schmid, Johannes, Trabesinger, Stefan, & Wallner, Stefan. (2021). Multi-factory production planning using edge computing and IIoT platforms. *Journal of Systems and Software*, 182, 111083. https://doi.org/10.1016/j.jss.2021.111083.

[93] N. Stefanovic (2014). Proactive supply chain performance management with predictive analytics. *The Scientific World Journal*, 2014, 528917. https://doi.org/10.1155/2014/528917.

[94] Haleem, A., & Javaid, M. (2019). Additive manufacturing applications in industry 4.0: a review. *Journal of Industrial Integration and Management*, 4, 4.

[95] Javaid, M. & Haleem, A. (2020). Critical components of Industry 5.0 towards a successful adoption in the field of manufacturing. *Journal of Industrial Integration and Management*, 5, 327–348.

[96] Kathiriya, H., Pandya, A., Dubay, V., & Bavarva, A. (2020). State of art: energy efficient protocols for self-powered wireless sensor network in IIoT to support industry 4.0. *2020 8th International Conference on Reliability, Infocom Technologies and Optimization (Trends and Future Directions) (ICRITO)*, pp. 1311–1314. Noida, India: IEEE.

[97] Alexopoulos, K., Sipsas, K., Xanthakis, E., Makris, S. & Mourtzis, D. (2018). An industrial Internet of things based platform for context-aware information services in manufacturing. *International Journal of Computer Integrated Manufacturing*, 31(11), 1111–1123.

[98] Rosales, J., Deshpande, S., & Anand, S. (2021). IIoT based augmented reality for factory data collection and visualization. *Procedia Manufacturing*, 53, 618–627.

[99] Truong, Hong-Linh. (2018). Integrated analytics for IIoT predictive maintenance using IoT big data cloud systems, 109–118. https://doi.org/10.1109/ICII.2018.00020.

[100] Hoelscher, J., & Mortimer, (2018). A. Using Tableau to visualize data and drive decision-making. *Journal of Accounting Education*, 44, 49–59. https://doi.org/10.1016/j.jaccedu.2018.05.002.

[101] Ramzey, Hazem, El-Hosseini, Mostafa, & Abdelbaset, Adel. (2023). I2OT-EC: A framework for smart real-time monitoring and controlling crude oil production exploiting IIOT and edge computing. *Energies*, 16. https://doi.org/10.3390/en16042023.

[102] Kayetha, Spandana & Pabboju, Suresh. (2023). IoT enabled smart agriculture using digital dashboard. *Indian Journal Of Science And Technology*, 16, 1–11. https://doi.org/10.17485/IJST/v16i1.1680.

[103] Alonso, Á., Pozo, A., Cantera, J.M., De la Vega, F., & Hierro, J.J. (2018). Industrial data space architecture implementation using FIWARE. *Sensors*, 18, 2226. https://doi.org/10.3390/s18072226.

[104] IDLab Obelisk: A Platform for Building Scalable Applications on IoT Centric Timeseries Data. Available online: https://obelisk.ilabt.imec.be/ (accessed on 11 June 2023).

6 Energy Efficiency and Renewable Energy in Industry 5.0

Aihloor Subramanyam Sreelatha
Aalborg University

Bandi Pallavi
Stanley College of Engineering & Technology for Women

Sheriff Olalekan Ajala
Roban Energy

6.1 INTRODUCTION

6.1.1 OVERVIEW OF THE IMPORTANCE OF ENERGY EFFICIENCY AND RENEWABLE ENERGY IN INDUSTRY 5.0

The industrial field is a key driver of economic and societal transformations, and it must embrace digitalization and sustainability to maintain its role as a catalyst for prosperity. This comprehensive approach goes beyond mere efficiency and productivity, recognizing the industry's broader contributions to society. It prioritizes worker well-being, harnesses emerging technologies for comprehensive success, and ensures environmental sustainability. Building upon the foundation of "Industry 4.0," this approach leverages research and innovation to cultivate a sustainable, people-centered, and resilient industry [1].

Industry 5.0 represents the forthcoming industrial revolution, aiming to combine the creative capabilities of human experts with efficient, sustainable, intelligent [2], and precise machines. Its objective is to achieve manufacturing solutions that are resource-efficient and tailored to user preferences, surpassing the achievements of Industry 4.0. By merging human expertise with advanced technologies, Industry 5.0 strives to optimize productivity while placing sustainability and user preferences at the forefront [3]. This evolution signifies a significant advancement towards more efficient and inclusive industrial practices.

Sustainability involves reducing energy consumption and greenhouse emissions to protect natural resources from depletion and degradation while meeting the present generation's needs without compromising the future's well-being. Advanced technologies like Artificial Intelligence (AI) and additive manufacturing play a crucial

DOI: 10.1201/9781032686363-6

107

role in achieving these objectives. By optimizing resource efficiency and minimizing waste, these technologies contribute to a more sustainable future. Their application empowers us to prioritize environmental conservation and create a better world for future generations [4].

The concept of resilience in industrial production refers to the ability to withstand disruptions and the ability to provide and maintain critical infrastructure during crises. It underscores the need to develop robust safeguards and contingency plans to mitigate risks and maintain uninterrupted operations. By prioritizing resilience, industrial production can effectively navigate challenges and contribute to the stability and continuity of essential services, even in the face of adversity [5].

6.1.2 Definition of Industry 5.0

Industry 5.0 acknowledges that industrial sector holds the capacity to transcend mere job generation and economic advancement, transforming into a resilient fountain of well-being by harmonizing manufacturing with sustainability and giving primacy to a human-centered approach.

European policy has long prioritized sustainable development, anchored in treaties. The EU is fully committed to achieving the 17 Sustainable Development Goals by 2030 [6]. The Green Deal outlines the necessary steps for a sustainable economy, with innovations in green technology, energy efficiency (EE) and digitization embraced by industries. Companies are integrating sustainability into their business models, realizing benefits in reputation and cost savings. However, there has been a slowdown in EE improvements in industries since 2005, particularly in energy-intensive sectors. Sectoral analysis is crucial for targeted research and innovation to enhance EE and shape focused energy policies.

Industry 5.0 has a limited amount of literature that deals with sustainability and EE, with a large amount of emphasis on human-centered concepts and Industry 5.0 in particular. While there is literature available on EE in Industry 4.0 [5], there is a lack of specific research on sustainable energy sources and EE in Industry 5.0.

Therefore, this chapter provides an overview of how EE and renewable energy are contributing to Industry 5.0, which represents the latest phase of the industrial revolution characterized by efficiency, sustainability, and digital integration. The objective of this chapter is to investigate the benefits and obstacles linked to the implementation of EE and renewable energy in the industrial sector, highlighting exemplary instances from diverse industries. Moreover, it emphasizes how EE and renewable energy can be integrated to create a positive impact on the environment.

A discussion of industrial EE and renewable energy policy and regulation is also provided in this chapter. It identifies potential policy changes that can facilitate wider adoption of sustainable practices. By offering a comprehensive analysis, this chapter contributes to the understanding of energy-related aspects in Industry 5.0 and provides insights for policymakers and industry stakeholders.

6.1.3 RENEWABLE ENERGY AND ENERGY EFFICIENCY IN INDUSTRY 5.0: POTENTIAL BENEFITS

Implementing renewable energy and promoting EE can have several advantages for an industry [7,8]. Figure 6.1 visualizes the potential benefits of incorporating EE and renewable energy in the context of Industry 5.0. The following are some ways in which industries can benefit from these practices [9].

6.1.3.1 Boosted Consumer Trust

In today's fiercely competitive business landscape, enterprises often require more than just the satisfaction of contributing to the well-being of our planet. The drive for profitability plays a crucial role in motivating businesses to take action. However, there is good news: environmental concerns have gained widespread acceptance, and consumers now highly appreciate companies that prioritize sustainability. By embracing renewable energy sources (RES), businesses can not only enhance consumer confidence but also attract new customers. This, in turn, leads to increased profitability for all parties involved.

6.1.3.2 Ensuring Energy Resilience: The Strength and Stability of Renewable Sources

While abundant fossil fuel reserves exist worldwide, it is imperative to recognize their finite nature, ultimately leading to depletion. On the other hand, RES possess

FIGURE 6.1 Benefits of adopting sustainable energy sources and energy efficiency programs in Industry 5.0.

an inherent advantage—they are infinite and constantly replenished. As a result, renewables offer unparalleled energy security and stability compared to oil, coal, or gas. Furthermore, the decentralized and modular structure of most renewable energy facilities enhances their resilience, safeguarding against accidents, sabotage, or natural disasters.

6.1.3.3   Staying Ahead in Global Competition: Embracing Eco-Friendly Innovations

Countries worldwide are rapidly embracing eco-friendly technologies, with Nordic nations like Finland, Sweden, and Denmark leading the way in renewable implementation. Germany is also making significant strides in green energy. Surprisingly, even China, the largest carbon polluter globally, has invested more in renewable research and installations than the rest of the world combined in recent years. In this dynamic landscape, industrial users in the UK cannot afford to lag behind their international counterparts. To maintain competitiveness, it is crucial for UK businesses to embrace sustainable practices and stay ahead in the global race towards eco-friendly innovation.

6.1.3.4   Fostering Employment Opportunities: The Renewable Energy Advantage

It's a lesser-known fact that RES typically require a larger workforce compared to fossil fuel power plants. Installing solar farms calls for skilled engineers, while maintaining wind turbines necessitates technicians. In fact, a 2009 report by the Union of Concerned Scientists revealed that increasing the renewable energy share in the U.S. to 25% by 2025 would generate over three times the number of employment opportunities compared to a similar increase in fossil fuels. These figures do not even account for the additional positive impacts on the broader economy. The transition to renewables presents a significant opportunity for job creation, further emphasizing the benefits of sustainable energy initiatives.

6.1.3.5   Cost Saving

Improving EE in businesses leads to cost savings. Energy usage, once considered uncontrollable, is now recognized as controllable and directly impacts financial outcomes. For Instance, UK government data shows potential savings of 39% in non-domestic buildings, equivalent to £3.7 billion. Lighting alone accounted for £1.1 billion in potential savings, consuming 20% of electricity in commercial and industrial buildings. As an ideal place to start implementing EE programs, lighting projects can generate a quick return on investment and require little initial investment. Despite initial costs, reducing energy consumption frees up funds for other business investments.

6.1.3.6   Mitigated Risk: Navigating Volatile Energy Markets

Global energy markets have experienced heightened volatility in recent years, resulting in significant price fluctuations. With the rise of the global population and the subsequent growth in energy demand, the International Energy Agency (IEA) predicts that this trend will continue. For example, in the UK, between 2005 and 2018, gas and electricity costs in the UK more than doubled, which has contributed to the surge in energy costs. Further, energy prices surged by 5.3% during a mere 3-month period in 2018 (February–May), largely due to rising wholesale prices.

6.1.3.7 Enhanced Brand Reputation: Embracing Energy Efficiency

EE not only brings financial benefits but also strengthens your brand's reputation, positively impacting business performance. However, it's crucial to avoid green-washing, as it can harm your reputation. Research shows that Customers, suppliers, and stakeholders benefit from EE strategies. According to a nationwide study by Unilever, 33% of consumers today prefer brands that are socially and environmentally conscious. Many companies, including Sainsbury's, Google, Microsoft, and Coca-Cola, actively pursue energy reduction initiatives. Establishing an EE strategy can benefit your business and seeking guidance can assist in getting started.

6.1.3.8 Enhanced Working Conditions: The Positive Impact of Energy Efficiency

EE not only reduces costs and improves brand reputation but also plays a vital role in creating optimal working conditions for employees. Despite earlier perceptions that EE endangered comfort, recent research has contradicted this belief. According to studies published in Frontiers of Psychology, employees in companies that prioritize EE are more productive. Heating, Ventilation, and Air Conditioning (HVAC) systems that are well installed and provide adequate lighting contribute significantly to employee well-being and productivity.

6.1.3.9 Environmental Benefit

It's essential to address climate change concerns by improving EE. While the focus is often on households, businesses have a significant responsibility as they accounted for 18% of UK carbon dioxide emissions in 2018. Switching to 100% renewable energy suppliers, as demonstrated by Apple and Google, is an effective way to reduce environmental impact. With more competitive prices, businesses can lower their carbon footprint while saving on energy costs, benefiting both the organization and the planet.

6.1.3.10 Compliance and Future-Proofing -The Importance of Energy Efficiency

In order for countries to achieve net-zero emissions of greenhouse gases by 2050, businesses must be actively involved. Approximately 18% of carbon dioxide emissions are emitted by businesses, so improving EE is vital for achieving these targets. Proactive businesses that prioritize EE will be better positioned as stricter regulations approach closer to 2050. Display Energy Certificates (DECs), or operational energy ratings, are being considered as mandatory ratings, with severe financial penalties for non-compliant businesses. Starting early to reduce environmental impact ensures compliance and prepares businesses for upcoming regulations.

6.1.4   DISCUSSION OF THE CHALLENGES AND BARRIERS
TO ADOPTION OF RES AND EE

The previous sections have highlighted the significance of EE and sustainable energy sources in Industry 5.0. Additionally, the potential benefits of embracing sustainable energy resources and EE have been examined. This section will address the challenges and barriers associated with adopting sustainable energy sources and EE. Specifically, we will focus on three commonly utilized use cases in industries: Demand Response (DR) Management, renewable energy adoption in industries, and Industrial Combined Heat and Power (CHP).

The barriers and challenges encompass a wide range of factors, which can be categorized into several key areas: economic and financial barriers, regulatory barriers, technical barriers, market barriers, and social and environmental barriers [10]. Each of these categories presents unique obstacles that need to be addressed when implementing sustainable energy sources and EE measures. Figure 6.2 shows the three use cases and range of factors that act as barriers for adoption RES and EE.

Furthermore, for each of the aforementioned use cases, we will discuss the barriers mentioned above in detail. By examining these barriers, we aim to comprehensively understand the challenges that industries face in adopting sustainable energy sources and EE practices in Industry 5.0 context.

6.1.4.1   Economic and Financial Barriers

6.1.4.1.1   Use Case 1: Industrial Demand Response

The adoption of DR programs in industries can face several challenges. One key hurdle is the restricted customer base using time-based rates. Without access to these rates, there is a restriction on participation in DR programs. Additionally, the

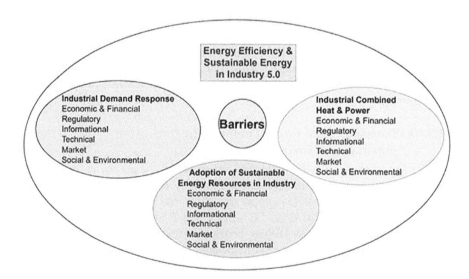

FIGURE 6.2   Barriers for energy efficiency and sustainable energy in Industry 5.0.

absence of sufficient financial incentives can hinder the effectiveness of these programs. When the incentives fail to provide an attractive proposition, customers may be less motivated to participate. Another challenge lies in accurately quantifying and attributing the benefits derived from DR. The complexity involved in valuing these benefits and determining how to properly allocate them can make it difficult to fully recognize and account for the true value of DR initiatives. Overcoming these challenges is crucial to foster wider adoption of DR and realize its full potential in promoting EE and sustainability in industries.

6.1.4.1.2 Use Case 2: Adoption of Sustainable Energy Resources

A high level of industrialization and technological advancement makes importing technologies from such countries more efficient, but they are also more expensive than locally manufactured technologies, which require greater initial investments. Renewable and sustainable energy technologies, in particular, have high initial costs, making them less competitive and potentially discouraging consumer adoption. The initial costs of these technologies are often more important to consumers than the operating costs. Renewable and sustainable energy solutions can be hindered by focusing on affordability at the outset.

Insufficient government incentives and financing impede businesses and industries from adopting renewable and sustainable energy technologies. A significant barrier is the limited availability of credit for purchasing renewable energy technologies. This poses challenges, particularly for small and medium-scale enterprises (SMEs) that often struggle with financial constraints when adopting cleaner technologies [11].

6.1.4.1.3 Use Case 3: Industrial Combined Heat and Power

The implementation of CHP systems in industries faces several challenges. One significant obstacle is the internal competition for capital, where investment decisions are influenced by payback expectations and capital budget constraints. A CHP investment's feasibility is also affected by natural gas availability and long-term prices. A "split-incentive system" between capital improvement and operation and maintenance budgets also complicates accounting practices. Monetary risk poses another barrier, as industrial facilities may struggle to secure low-cost financing due to perceived risks associated with CHP projects. In addition, financing options are limited because favorable tax structures such as Master Limited Partnerships and Real Estate Investment Trusts are not readily available. Additionally, surplus electricity cannot be sold or reasonable sales agreements cannot be established. Addressing these issues is crucial to promote wider adoption of CHP systems and unlock their potential benefits in industrial applications. By overcoming these barriers, industries can enhance their EE and sustainability while reaping the economic advantages offered by CHP technologies.

6.1.4.2 Regulatory Barriers

6.1.4.2.1 Use Case 1: Industrial Demand Response

The adoption of DR programs in industries faces various challenges that hinder its widespread implementation. First, the traditional regulatory model, where utility revenue is linked to building new infrastructure, can discourage DR efforts.

Additionally, the presence of numerous program requirements, varying terms, and aggregation rules that limit smaller industrial facilities can deter potential participants. It is further complicated by the absence of standardized measurement and verification procedures to settle DR contracts, plan operations, and plan long-term resources. Certain electricity market structures prioritize supply side resources, limiting the participation of DR or imposing other barriers. In addition, DR is not incorporated into state EE resource standards (EERS) programs, which can impede its growth and development. Overcoming these challenges is crucial to promote the effective integration of DR in industrial settings, ensuring EE and sustainability goals are met while optimizing economic benefits.

6.1.4.2.2 Use Case 2: Adoption of Sustainable Energy Resources

Subsidies for renewable energy have been implemented in a few states and countries, as either payment rebates or production payments. An installation rebate is a refund of a specific percentage of the total installation costs, for example 30%. Another approach is providing refunds based on the capacity installed per unit of money, ensuring financial support in relation to the energy generation capacity. By providing financial incentives like tax exemptions, low-interest loans, extended credit, subsidies and dedicated funds for grid-connected projects in rural or mountainous areas, businesses can become more financially viable and renewable energy services become more affordable. Developing and implementing renewable energy projects can be facilitated by these measures.

There is a lack of comprehensive policy statements on renewable energy, since most renewable energy technologies are still in development. Policies are issued to encourage the growth of specific renewable energy technologies as and when necessary. There is, however, a discrepancy between these policies and the plans for renewable energy development. In a comprehensive review conducted by [12] an examination of industrial EE policies spanning the years 1980–2005 revealed the implementation of six significant policies during that period. These policies encompassed various measures such as disclosing company-level EE information, providing accelerated depreciation for EE and pollution control equipment, establishing the Energy Management Center, eliminating price and output controls to enhance industrial competitiveness, introducing energy price reforms, and enacting the Energy Conservation Act of 2001 and the Electricity Act of 2003 in India [13].

6.1.4.2.3 Use Case 3: Industrial Combined Heat and Power

The implementation of industrial CHP projects faces several barriers that hinder their adoption and recognition. In some cases, utilities may become disinterested in promoting CHP projects because of the nature of their business model, including cost recovery and revenue lost mechanisms. The implementation of CHP is complicated by environmental permit and regulatory issues, including output-based regulations and New Source Review regulations. Inconsistent interconnection requirements further impede the deployment of CHP systems. Potential emissions reductions from CHP are not recognized because they do not offer environmental benefits or financial benefits. Regulatory evaluations and utility procurement plans often fail to fully recognize the value streams provided by CHP. Standby rates, which do not align charges with the cost of service, create additional obstacles. Furthermore, the exclusion of CHP from clean energy standards programs and limitations in capacity and ancillary services markets restrict the participation of CHP in electricity markets. Addressing these barriers is essential to unlocking the full potential of CHP and promoting its integration into the energy landscape.

6.1.4.3 Informational Barriers

6.1.4.3.1 Use Case 1: Industrial Demand Response

Limited knowledge and resource availability are significant barriers to effective participation in DR programs. It is often the case that low participation rates are caused by an insufficient awareness of federal, state, and utility incentives. Additionally, inadequate in-house technical expertise can hinder organizations from actively engaging in DR initiatives. Without a clear understanding of the available programs and their benefits, businesses may miss out on potential cost savings and other advantages. Furthermore, the absence of sufficient knowledge and expertise can prevent organizations from implementing the necessary strategies and technologies to participate effectively in DR. To overcome these barriers, it is crucial for businesses to invest in education and training programs to enhance their understanding of incentives and develop the technical capabilities required for successful participation in DR programs [10].

6.1.4.3.2 Use Case 2: Adoption of Sustainable Energy Resources

There is an urgent need in rural communities to become more aware and informed about renewable energy technologies and systems. Education and information dissemination initiatives should encompass a wide range of topics, including resource evaluations, providing education on diverse renewable technologies, training, and access to details about government incentives and support information. Technology adoption is hindered by a lack of knowledge about operations and management, as well as a lack of spare parts and maintenance expertise. Overcoming these barriers requires comprehensive educational programs, improved access to information, and enhanced technical support to empower rural communities and enable them to effectively adopt and utilize renewable energy technologies.

6.1.4.3.3 Use Case 3: Industrial Combined Heat and Power

Limited awareness of available incentives and insufficient technical knowledge and resources are significant barriers to the effective execution of CHP projects. Many organizations lack knowledge about the various federal, state, and utility incentives that can support CHP initiatives and are unfamiliar with the eligibility requirements for accessing these incentives. This lack of awareness hinders organizations from taking full advantage of the financial and regulatory benefits that can make CHP projects more viable and attractive. Additionally, the implementation of CHP systems requires specialized technical expertise, which some organizations may lack. Without internal technical expertise knowledge or the capacity to recruit external experts, organizations face challenges in effectively designing, developing, and operating CHP systems. Overcoming these barriers necessitates increasing awareness about available incentives and eligibility criteria, as well as investing in technical training and resources to build the necessary expertise internally or seek external support for successful CHP project implementation.

6.1.4.4 Technical Barriers

6.1.4.4.1 Use Case 1: Industrial Demand Response

The technological aspects of DR and the Smart Grid play a crucial role in determining the barriers to DR implementation. Information and Communication Technology (ICT) is crucial for various DR functionalities such as local metering, transactional communications, and on-premises automation. However, transitioning from niche to normal in delivering DR capability at a larger scale poses a challenge [14]. Standardization is a key factor to overcome technological barriers in sensing, computing, and communication. Sensing involves accurate metering and granular sensing to identify flexibility and measure related factors. Computing deals with managing large volumes of data, handling uncertainty, and ensuring computational capacity meets the requirements. Communication focuses on data exchange, standardization, and addressing security and privacy concerns. However, interoperability issues and the slow process of standardization hinder progress [15]. Additionally, technological skills, including requirement elicitation, design, and technical talent recruitment, are crucial for successful implementation [16]. Overcoming these barriers requires a comprehensive approach that emphasizes standardization, security, privacy, and skilled resources.

6.1.4.4.2 Use Case 2: Adoption of Sustainable Energy Resources

The majority of the renewable energy and sustainable technologies involve technical complexity. Wind energy, for instance, relies on intricate mechanisms that encompass the rotation of the Earth, solar heat energy, ocean's cooling impacts and polar ice sheets, contrasting temperatures of land and sea, and the tangible effects of mountains and other barriers. Bioenergy generation also presents a multi-phase analysis problem, involving location, technology, capacity, and route optimization. As a result of this complexity, the trade-offs between conflicting objectives need to be carefully weighed for a compromise solution. It is crucial to understand the technical intricacies of these renewable energy systems in order to effectively harness their potential and address the challenges associated with their implementation.

The short daylight hours and the uneven distribution of solar resources within the world make solar energy inherently intermittent due to weather conditions and daylight hours [17]. This intermittency necessitates the requirement of backup or storage devices to ensure an uninterrupted and continuous power supply. Addressing the technical complexities of integrating backup storage systems is crucial in overcoming the intermittent nature of solar power. It is essential to develop sustainable and environmentally friendly solutions for energy storage to efficiently store excess solar energy and bridge the gaps in power generation and consumption.

Technology transfer within an industry is hindered by insufficient communication and information flow. The establishment of effective links and the implementation of efficient renewable energy technologies require adequate information support. By leveraging information technology resources, businesses can optimize resource utilization, supporting operations more efficiently and minimizing paper consumption. Technology transfer can also be negatively affected by information technology, which is a major concern. Ensuring robust information flow and effective communication channels are in place is essential for facilitating successful technology transfer and promoting the adoption of renewable energy technologies.

6.1.4.4.3   Use Case 3: Industrial Combined Heat and Power

Subsequent research has revealed a lack of comprehensive analysis of cogeneration possibilities, primarily attributed to difficulties in accessing proprietary data and the wide range of system designs. Cogeneration systems include both bottoming and topping cycle configurations, with diverse options for fuels and system setups depending on the type of "prime mover" technology employed. In recent years, solar resources have emerged as alternative sources of energy, encompassing gas turbines, reciprocating engines, fuel cells, microturbines, and boiler/steam turbines. The varied nature of these factors adds complexity to the assessment of cogeneration opportunities.

6.1.4.5   Market Barriers

6.1.4.5.1   Use Case 1: Industrial Demand Response

Establishing a baseline methodology for DR poses challenges to DR business cases. High-resolution metering data alone cannot determine the baseline consumption/generation profile without DR. Agreeing on a baseline between buyers and sellers is necessary to assess compliance with contractual obligations. However, the baseline definition can be a barrier to DR deployment, hindering proper product valuation. Standardization of energy and capacity products in which DR operates can also present barriers. Restrictive product definitions may exclude certain DR providers or limit the full realization of DR's value, leading to suboptimal system efficiency. Balancing the need for standardization to reduce transaction costs with the desire for flexible definitions to maximize DR value creates tension in the industry.

6.1.4.5.2   Use Case 2: Embracing Sustainable Energy Sources

Projects focused on renewable energy and companies generally operate on a smaller scale, which means they have limited resources compared to larger generation companies or integrated utilities. This lack of resources hampers their ability to directly communicate with a large customer base. Also, it hinders their ability to participate in legislative and regulatory proceedings that establish new regulations for the electricity market, as well as in industry forums that shape those regulations [17]. In many countries, the sustainable electricity market is not sufficiently large. Consequently, private investment in sustainable energy is discouraged by a lack of market size, which is exacerbated by a lack of policies that encourage adequate private investment and provide development assistance [18]. Addressing these challenges is crucial to level the playing field for renewable energy companies, foster private investment, and create a conducive environment for the widespread integration of sustainable energy technologies.

In many countries, the sustainable electricity market is not sufficiently large. This lack of market size discourages private investment [19] and is compounded by a lack of policies that incentivize adequate Non-public investments and provide developmental support to promote the adoption of sustainable energy technologies. Addressing these challenges is crucial to level the playing field for renewable energy companies, foster private investment, and create a conducive environment for the widespread adoption of sustainable energy technologies.

Land use competition poses a significant challenge in many countries, especially those heavily reliant on tourism. The development of renewable energy (RE) projects often faces resistance from landowners who are hesitant to allocate land for such purposes [20].

6.1.4.5.3 Use Case 3: Industrial Combined Heat and Power

CHP faces challenges in terms of energy prices. A significant spark spread can be achieved by CHP with high electricity prices and low gas prices, resulting in a favorable price scenario. Electricity spark spreads are the differences between revenue generated and natural gas cost from electricity generation. Certain regions, such as Georgia, USA, have lower average electricity prices ($0.0962/kWh) than the national average ($0.1048/kWh). According to interviews with developers and supporters of CHP, the unfavorable spark spread is a major barrier to implementing the technology. CHP projects may become economically unviable in states with low electricity rates due to the significant fuel costs involved.

6.1.4.6 Social and Environmental Barriers

6.1.4.6.1 Use Case 1: Industrial Demand Response

Social barriers encompass organizational and behavioral aspects. Organizational barriers, such as power dynamics and cultural norms within structured organizations, can hinder the implementation of DR programs. Limited power of individuals responsible for DR initiatives may impede the adoption of enabling technologies, behavior change, and investment in flexibility. This barrier is closely tied to the broader organizational culture, where energy, environmental, and economic considerations may not be prioritized. Behavioral barriers, on the other hand, arise from individual deviations from fully rational behavior. Factors like convenience, comfort, and personal utility influence decision-making, alongside economic considerations. These behavioral barriers affect both firms aiming for profit maximization and individuals seeking utility maximization [14].

6.1.4.6.2 Use Case 2: Adoption of Sustainable Energy Resources

In order to avoid significant scarcity issues, the world is turning towards alternative sources of energy to avoid the environmental costs associated with fossil fuel, hydroelectric, and nuclear energy consumption. Proper reforestation can solve the environmental and ecological issues associated with these energy sources. Addressing social issues necessitates the implementation of inclusive, democratic, and participatory policies for rehabilitation. Generally, wind power is viewed as having negative impacts on public health and the environment because of its sound and visual effects. On the contrary, solar power carries potential environmental impacts including land use and habitat loss, water consumption, and the utilization of hazardous materials in manufacturing processes.

There is a demand for individuals with technical expertise and individuals possessing robust managerial abilities. The preferred method of training Asians, especially when the local language is used, is through hands-on experiences and group work.

Achieving long-term change in Indian attitudes toward intellectual property requires addressing the issue of training in intellectual property rights. This is a long-term challenge that needs to be addressed. Another issue is deficiency in guidance provision and technical aid for operators, which impedes the effective utilization of resources that are renewable and sustainable.

6.1.4.6.3   Use Case 3: Industrial Combined Heat and Power

The lack of qualification of social benefits makes it less appealing to expand the implementation of CHP industries. When the social benefits of CHP, such as environmental advantages and EE improvements, are not adequately recognized or valued, it diminishes the overall attractiveness of investing in CHP projects. Consequently, the limited consideration given to the broader societal benefits of CHP hampers its widespread adoption and expansion in various industries.

The organization of this book chapter is structured as follows: The upcoming section delves into the importance of EE in Industry 5.0. In the subsequent subsections, we define and explain the concept of EE within the context of Industry 5.0. We also provide a review of various EE technologies and practices, including process optimization, energy management systems, and energy audits. Furthermore, we present case studies highlighting successful EE projects implemented across different industries.

Moving forward, the subsequent section focuses on the adoption of sustainable energy resources in Industry 5.0. This section is divided into three subsections. First, we define and explain sustainable energy resources such as solar, wind, and biomass. Second, we provide a concise outline of the advantages and obstacles linked to the integration of RES in Industry 5.0. Lastly, we discuss the suitability of various sustainable energy resources for different industries and showcase case studies of successful implementations within diverse sectors.

The third section examines the synergies between EE and sustainable energy resources in Industry 5.0. Within this section, we explore the inherent connection between EE and sustainable energy resources. Additionally, we discuss arrangements that combine EE practices with sustainable energy resources, such as onsite generation, demand-side management, power purchase agreements, and energy storage.

Finally, we present case studies that demonstrate successful projects integrating both EE and sustainable energy resources.

In the fourth section, we delve into the framework of policies and regulations pertaining to EE and sustainable energy resources in Industry 5.0. This section comprises three subsections. First, we provide a brief overview of the current practices of policies and regulatory frameworks adopted within industries. Second, we discuss potential challenges and changes needed to achieve a sustainable Industry 5.0 through policy and regulatory means. Finally, we present case studies showcasing successful policies and regulatory frameworks that have been implemented to achieve a sustainable Industry 5.0.

This book chapter concludes with a summary and discussions on the prospects for EE and sustainable energy in the context of Industry 5.0.

6.2   ENERGY EFFICIENCY IN INDUSTRY 5.0

In Industry 5.0, advanced technologies and intelligent systems are integrated to create more robust production processes. The focus on EE has become a top priority for governments and industries. In Industry 5.0, EE is crucial for optimizing industrial processes and minimizing resource consumption. By adopting energy-efficient technologies and practices, businesses can achieve the same level of output while reducing energy inputs. For instance, implementing energy-efficient manufacturing equipment and optimizing production lines can lead to substantial energy savings [21].

Additionally, EE is compatible with Industry 5.0's broader objectives of digitalization, automation, and sustainability. Real-time monitoring control and optimization of energy consumption are made possible in industrial contexts by technologies such as IoT sensors, AI, and data analytics. Businesses can take advantage of this data–driven strategy to identify inefficiencies, optimize energy consumption patterns, and improve EE in general [22].

Moreover, energy-efficient practices can strengthen resilience against volatile energy prices and supply disruptions, ensuring the stability and continuity of industrial operations.

To fully leverage the potential of EE in Industry 5.0, collaboration between governments, industries, and research institutions is vital. This collaboration can drive innovation, knowledge sharing, and the development of energy-efficient technologies tailored to specific industrial processes [3]. Additionally, supportive policies, incentives, and regulations can incentivize businesses to prioritize EE and accelerate its adoption across various sectors.

6.2.1   DEFINITION AND EXPLANATION OF ENERGY EFFICIENCY

EE refers to the ability to accomplish a desired energy service while utilizing less energy. By reducing energy consumption without compromising output, EE involves optimizing devices, systems, and procedures. LED light bulbs provide the same amount of light as incandescent bulbs while consuming less energy [23].

6.2.2   PRINCIPAL FACTORS FOR ENERGY EFFICIENCY IN INDUSTRY

The summarized representation of factors enhancing EE in Industry can be observed in Figure 6.3.

6.2.2.1   Energy as a Service

Implement a service-based energy business model where customers pay a fixed monthly energy service fee, allowing them to save while benefiting from advanced technologies. Focus on offering the best energy solutions rather than selling energy products.

6.2.2.2   Sustainable Lighting with Low Consumption

Replace traditional lighting systems with efficient alternatives, potentially reducing energy consumption in this area by up to 80%. Prioritize LED technology, which

Principal Factors of Energy Efficiency in Industry 5.0

Energy as Service

Implement a service-based energy business model where customers pay a fixed monthly energy service fee, allowing them to save while benefiting from advanced technologies. Focus on offering the best energy solutions rather than selling energy products.

Sustainable Lighting with Low Consumption

Replace traditional lighting systems with efficient alternatives, potentially reducing energy consumption in this area by up to 80%. Prioritize LED technology, which offers significant savings potential. Utilize automatic lighting control systems to schedule routines and minimize energy waste.

Change in Energy Sources

Embrace renewable energy sources, particularly solar energy. Consider investing in photovoltaic systems as a cost-effective and high-energy potential option. Reduce dependence on conventional electricity markets with volatile prices by generating and managing your own renewable energy.

Optimization of Industrial Processes

Focus on optimizing energy-intensive operational and production processes. Enhance machinery efficiency to reduce energy consumption without compromising productivity. Strive for greater energy performance to achieve energy efficiency goals. Implementing these strategies in industry can lead to guaranteed energy savings, support decarbonization efforts, and contribute to a more sustainable future.

FIGURE 6.3 Principal factors of energy efficiency in Industry 5.0.

offers significant savings potential. Utilize automatic lighting control systems to schedule routines and minimize energy waste [24].

6.2.2.3   Change in Energy Sources

Embrace RES, particularly solar energy. Consider investing in photovoltaic systems as a cost-effective and high-energy potential option. Reduce dependence on conventional electricity markets with volatile prices by generating and managing your own renewable energy.

6.2.2.4   Optimization of Industrial Processes

Focus on optimizing energy-intensive operational and production processes. Enhance machinery efficiency to reduce energy consumption without compromising productivity. Strive for greater energy performance to achieve EE goals. Implementing these strategies in industry can lead to guaranteed energy savings, support decarbonization efforts, and contribute to a more sustainable future [25].

6.2.3   REVIEW OF TECHNOLOGIES AND PRACTICES RELATED TO ENERGY EFFICIENCY

Amidst the advent of Industry 5.0, it is crucial for industries to prioritize EE measures that promote sustainable resource utilization, minimize environmental impact, and enhance productivity. By optimizing energy generation, conversion, transmission, and consumption, industries can achieve significant energy savings, cost reduction, and improved operational performance [24]. This section explores key EE measures within the context of Industry 5.0.

6.2.3.1   Supply Side Energy Efficiency Measures

To achieve higher EE in Industry 5.0, it is essential to focus on more efficient generation and conversion of energy. Industries can employ the following strategies to maximize energy utilization and minimize waste:

- Reducing excess heat production and harnessing waste heat to its optimal economic level to minimize energy losses.
- Implementing improved maintenance practices to ensure optimal equipment performance and reduce energy wastage caused by inefficiencies or malfunctions.
- Making use of modern equipment that meets the highest efficiency standards, such as transformers, electric motors, gas and steam turbines, and boilers, to improve overall energy performance.
- Technologically advancing processes, including clean coal technologies, to promote cleaner and more efficient energy generation.
- Implementing cogeneration, especially when combined with biomass fuel or waste heat utilization, to enable simultaneous production of heat and electricity, enhancing overall EE.
- Implementing improved monitoring systems and metering of essential performance indicators to enable real-time monitoring and optimization of energy consumption.

More efficient transmission and distribution systems are vital for EE in Industry 5.0. The following measures are recommended to enhance EE in these systems:

- Enhanced supervision and superior management of current systems, such as optimized equilibrium of phases, voltage regulation, and enhancement of power factor, to reduce energy losses during transmission and distribution.
- Increased use of distributed generation, which involves generating energy closer to the point of consumption, to reduce transmission losses and enhance system efficiency.
- Adoption of higher transmission voltages to enable efficient electricity transfer over long distances, minimizing energy losses.
- Improved monitoring, control, and analysis of energy flows by incorporating state-of-the-art technologies such as low-loss transformers, fiber optic data acquisition, and smart meters [26].

6.2.3.2 Demand Side Energy Efficiency Measures

Industry 5.0 emphasizes the use of energy-efficient equipment and appliances across all sectors. This includes:

- Employing energy-saving motors, boilers, furnaces, pumps, compressors, illumination, household appliances, and cooling systems. Efficient equipment reduces energy consumption and waste [27].
- Implementing improved maintenance practices to ensure optimal performance and EE.
- By monitoring fuel, electricity, and steam flow rates in addition to the performance of critical operations, better energy management, performance evaluation, and improvement opportunities can be identified.
- Control and energy system optimization, through variable speed drives, thermostats, ripple signaling, smart appliances, and enhancement of power quality, further enhance EE by aligning energy usage with actual needs [26].

6.2.3.3 Behavioral Changes

Promoting behavioral changes among industry stakeholders is a critical aspect of achieving EE in Industry 5.0 [28]. These changes include:

- Establishing operational criteria and performance benchmarks for EE in significant energy-consuming industrial processes and machinery.
- Encouraging systematic reporting of detection and notification of leaks and equipment malfunctions to prioritize repairs and replacements, minimizing energy losses and associated costs.
- Adopting new work practices, such as remote work and flextime, to reduce energy consumption related to commuting and office operations.

6.2.4   The Impact of Industrial Systems on Energy Efficiency

Inefficient industrial steam and motor systems exert a substantial ecological footprint, as they consume nearly twice the energy compared to their optimized counterparts. They also contribute to substandard goods, excess material and scrap. Properly operating systems reduce energy input requirements and decrease energy consumption in the tools and equipment they support. Table 6.1 provides a condensed overview of Energy Efficiency Technologies and Practices within the realm of Industry 5.0.

6.2.4.1   Sustaining System Optimization

Energy audits provide recommendations based on current production levels. However, it may be difficult to sustain the recommended improvements if no proper procedures are in place to ensure ongoing system operation. Establishing mechanisms for continued monitoring, maintenance, and optimization of systems beyond the initial audit phase is essential.

6.2.4.2   Linking Energy Audits to Existing Management Systems

Integrating energy audits into existing management systems allows companies to incorporate energy management practices effectively. By leveraging frameworks such as ISO 9000/14000 [24], Total Quality Management, or Six Sigma, energy optimization becomes part of the decision-making process, aligning it with other operational considerations.

6.2.4.3   Energy Management Standards

Energy management standards, such as ANSI/MSE 2000:2005, developed by the Georgia Institute of Technology and compatible with Energy Star Guidelines [24], establish a framework and uniformity for organizations to proactively oversee and regulate their energy assets. Several countries are also developing energy management standards that include strategic planning, cross-divisional management teams, policies and procedures, energy-saving projects, energy manuals, key performance indicators, and periodic reporting.

6.2.4.4   Energy Audit

Energy audits are vital tools in the energy management process. They assess current energy consumption patterns, identify inefficiencies, and provide recommendations for improvement. By thoroughly examining industrial systems and processes, energy audits reveal opportunities for optimizing energy use, reducing waste, and lowering operational costs [29]. Energy audits consider factors such as equipment efficiency, maintenance practices, control systems, and overall energy management practices, analyzing energy consumption patterns over time.

6.2.4.5   Energy Audit

Energy audits are vital tools in the energy management process. They assess current energy consumption patterns, identify inefficiencies, and provide recommendations for improvement. By thoroughly examining industrial systems and processes, energy audits reveal opportunities for optimizing energy use, reducing waste, and lowering

TABLE 6.1
Energy Efficiency Technologies and Practices in Industry 5.0

Supply Side EE Measures	Demand Side EE Measures	Integration with Existing Management Systems	Impact of Industrial System to EE	Sustaining System Optimization	Linking Energy Audits to EMS	Energy Management	Energy Audit	Behavioral Changes
Waste Heat Recovery	Energy Labelled Equipment	Leverage Existing EMS	Inefficient System use 2X more Energy	Ensure Sustainability of procedures	Integration with ISO for Continuous Improvement	ANSI/MSE 2000:2005	Maintenance Practices	Monitoring Energy Consumption
Improved Maintenance Practices	Real Time Data Recording	Optimize Complex Processes	Environmental Impact	Risk of Efficiency Loss	Existing Management Systems	Proactive Energy Management	Energy Consumption Pattern	Monitoring Energy Consumption
Modern Equipment & Technologies	Enhanced Metering & Monitoring	Integrate ISO 9000/140000	Process can Produce off quality Products	Mechanisms for Sustainability	Link ISO Energy Management Standards	Strategic Planning	Recommendations for Improvement	Monitoring Energy Consumption

operational costs [29]. Energy audits consider factors such as equipment efficiency, maintenance practices, control systems, and overall energy management practices, analyzing energy consumption patterns over time.

6.2.5 CASE STUDIES OF SUCCESSFUL ENERGY EFFICIENCY PROJECTS IN DIFFERENT INDUSTRIES

6.2.5.1 Case Study-1

Simplot, a leading privately held company in the US, has experienced significant growth since its establishment in 1929. The company's success skyrocketed after striking a deal with McDonald's to supply frozen French fries.

As part of Simplot's business operations, the company also produces potatoes, agribusiness, ranching, meatpacking, and food processing. Manufacturing more than 3 billion pounds of frozen potato products on a yearly basis is a significant participant in the frozen potato processing industry. Simplot is also prominent in phosphate mining, ranking as the fourth-largest company in North America. With 120 facilities across eight states, Simplot relies on multiple utilities and diesel fuel for its energy needs.

6.2.5.1.1 Simplot's Pursuit of Energy Efficiency –Goals

A substantial amount of EE projects has been implemented by Simplot since 2000. They took important steps in 2005 by designating part-time energy champions at their extensive industrial sites, supported by the Northwest Energy Efficiency Alliance (NEEA). Food processing and agribusiness divisions were selected to lead an EE team formed at the corporate level in 2007.

Simplot additionally collaborated with the EPA in 2008 to attain ENERGY STAR accreditation for two of their facilities. Since 10 years, Simplot is among top 25% industries for ENERGY STAR for EE programs [30].

Simplot's EE team, led by a dedicated corporate energy director, is complemented by energy champions at each site who drive energy conservation initiatives and foster a culture of efficiency. Acknowledgment and engagement in a yearly energy assessment motivate their efforts, proving the value of incentivizing EE work.

6.2.5.1.2 Recognition, Choosing and Deployment of Energy-Efficient Solutions

Simplot heavily relies on its plant-level EE team to achieve its EE goals. The energy champions and on-site energy specialists at the plant level play a crucial role in observing and understanding plant operations to identify energy-saving opportunities. They receive support from business-unit-level energy engineers to vie for financial support. Emphasizing training and providing assistance to the staff at the plant level takes precedence, fostering a culture of EE within Simplot. The use of interns and DOE training further enhances their capabilities. Identified EE projects undergo packaging and compete for capital budget based on Internal Rate of Return (IRR), with a minimum requirement of 15% [31]. New plant construction poses a challenge as EE planning is often overlooked, resulting in potentially energy-inefficient designs.

6.2.5.2 Case Study-2

General Motors (GM) is a well-known automobile manufacturer with a century-long history. With its U.S.-based and global manufacturing facilities, the company has long been a leader in the industry. GM filed for insolvency in 2009 due to declining sales and substantial debt, resulting in a complete reorganization of the company. Since then, GM has made significant progress in regaining its sales growth through the introduction of innovative, fuel-efficient vehicles that reflect shifting consumer preferences. GM recognizes the accelerated evolution of the automotive industry and anticipates more significant changes in the next 5 years than in the previous five decades. With numerous brands and manufacturing facilities across the United States, GM continues to be a major force in the automobile industry.

6.2.5.2.1 General Motors (GM)–Goals

Over the past 15 years, GM has established an impressive EE program. The Energy Savings Project Initiative (ESPI) was created in 2000, providing a dedicated team and resources for EE efforts. Initially allocated with a $5 million annual budget, the ESPI funding has gradually increased to around $20 million. GM's collaboration with utility companies, such as DTE Energy and Consumers Energy, ensures the provision of full-time energy engineers for their plants, fostering a trusted long-term partnership. In 2008, GM joined the Department of Energy's (DOE) Energy Leaders program, committing to a 25% reduction in energy intensity per vehicle by 2018. And GM is aiming for 100% renewable energy by 2035. In addition to the above goals GM is spending about $ 20 million yearly for EE programs [32].

6.2.5.2.2 Recognition, Choosing and Deployment of Energy-Efficient Solutions

GM emphasizes EE through the establishment of targets for plants and facilities, which are prominently displayed and integrated into plant business plans and evaluations. EE projects are initiated by on-site utility managers and energy engineers, who build strong relationships with plant staff to identify and implement projects effectively. The corporate-level EE team approves projects based on various criteria, such as payback period and cash flow positivity. The ESPI funding program supports utility budgets and holds plants accountable for projected energy savings. Achieving EE in new or refurbished facilities requires close cooperation between the EE team and the Global Facilities Engineering Group. This collaboration facilitates the integration of EE factors into plant design. It is generally considered that investments in EE in new production must provide a return on investment within half the assets' lifespan.

6.2.5.3 Case Study-3

General Mills, a prominent grain and cereal processor in North America, has a long history and a portfolio of brands that includes well-known names such as Betty Crocker and Cheerios. The corporation has grown through acquisitions and spin-offs, with the most recent significant acquisition being Pillsbury. To address challenges in the food industry and maintain profitability, General Mills has focused on cost reduction while expanding into emerging segments like Greek yogurt. They have also aimed to enhance the appeal of their cereal line by incorporating whole grains. With a global net sale of over $17.6 billion in 2015, General Mills operates manufacturing facilities across several states in the United States, producing cereals, yogurt, flour, and other food products [31].

6.2.5.3.1 General Mills-Goals

General Mills has made significant strides in implementing EE measures, with a focus on Industry 5.0 principles. The company introduced company-wide EE targets in 2005, and in 2008, they piloted a project in Georgia with an energy engineer, Graham Thorsteinson, over the course of 4 years, the energy spending of the plant dropped from $13 million to $7.5 million. This success prompted General Mills to hire energy engineers in all major factories, ultimately employing 15 engineers, with dedicated engineers for cereal plants and others shared across different locations. Each energy engineer was given a target to save four times their salary in energy.

Graham's role expanded to become the corporate energy manager, developing continuous improvement and energy analytics tools for the entire EE program. General Mills also embraced the concept of "energy as an ingredient," emphasizing the efficient use and avoidance of waste in their products, similar to essential ingredients like flour or sugar.

Although General Mills' initial goal was to reduce energy consumption per tonne of product produced by 20% by 2015, they only achieved a 10% reduction by 2014, predominantly as a result of a shift in product composition towards energy-intensive items. New goals were established in 2015, including a 2% annual reduction in energy consumption through 2025 and a 28% reduction in greenhouse gas emissions throughout the supply chain over the same period. Using these energy improvement programs GM was able to save 12 million kWh and saves about $4.8 million [33]. Remarkably, General Mills has surpassed these goals, achieving energy intensity reductions exceeding 3% per year.

6.2.5.3.2 Recognition, Choosing, and Deployment of Energy-Efficient Solutions

General Mills' dedication to EE measures, Industry 5.0 principles, and the successful integration of energy engineers have contributed to their remarkable progress in reducing energy consumption and greenhouse gas emissions.

General Mills is committed to EE and has embraced the principles of Industry 5.0 by integrating EE measures into its corporate structure and culture. The company has established corporate EE targets that cascade down to various levels within the organization. Each plant has environmental targets, including energy targets, which impact the plant's ratings and management evaluations, fostering a strong drive for EE measures.

General Mills employs full-time EE personnel at each plant to bolster its decentralized framework. Corporate EE provides support to these energy engineers and reports to the plant manager. They promote EE projects, share ideas across plants, and are dedicated to energy-related tasks, including energy procurement, at the large plants.

In terms of project authorization, minor initiatives can be approved by the finance team operating at the plant level, drawing from the plant's allocated capital budget. Larger projects require approval from the corporate finance group but are funded from the financial resources allocated to the plant. The EE team selects projects based on a standardized spreadsheet distributed to each member that surpasses a specified internal rate of return (IRR).

General Mills does not have a dedicated fund pool for EE projects; instead, projects are evaluated and approved on a case-by-case basis and included in the annual budget. This approach poses challenges for ad hoc projects throughout the year, and the availability of funds varies based on capital availability. The plant energy budgets have been adjusted according to projected energy savings, as the EE program is justified as a cost-reduction measure. Non-energy benefits must demonstrate budget reductions in other areas to be included in project returns.

The company has invested significantly in sub-metering, enabling the implementation of energy targets for individual equipment. Sub-metering provides valuable insights into energy usage at the plant, aiding the identification of potential EE projects. Furthermore, it is anticipated to enhance behavioral EE practices by heightening employee consciousness regarding energy consumption associated with individual machines.

Despite the absence of certain elements, General Mills lacks a formalized system for ensuring EE in new production and facilities, funding applications for new projects include a checkbox specifically addressing EE. A collaborative process between engineers and energy specialists ensures energy-conscious design and execution of projects through the integration of EE.

6.2.5.4   Case Study-4

Intel, founded in 1968, is the world's largest semiconductor manufacturer. It has witnessed rapid growth, driven by personal computer proliferation, and operates data centers. In 2014, its revenues reached almost $56 billion with manufacturing facilities in various U.S. states.

6.2.5.4.1   Intel Goals

Intel, a sustainability leader, prioritizes greenhouse gas emissions and EE. Since 1996, they publicly report energy use and commit to reducing emissions. Their objective is to achieve an annual reduction in energy intensity of $4\%/cm^2$ of silicon annually, aggregating specific EE measures for a corporate energy savings metric. Intel has a 2020 EE goal divided by region and site. By 2015, they achieved over 1.6 billion kWh in energy reductions since 2012 [34], aligning with the principles of Industry 5.0.

6.2.5.4.2   Recognition, Choosing and Deployment of Energy-Efficient Solutions

Intel's EE program aligns with Industry 5.0 through its centralized organization and dedicated energy champions at each manufacturing site. The EE team of 16 members' fosters collaboration and standardization across sites. Identified projects are optimized by the central team and seek funding through the annual budget.

The company prioritizes projects based on NPV and prefers internal capital over energy performance contracting. Pursuing EE projects helps Intel reduce its carbon footprint, support sustainability, and mitigate costs. While EE measures mainly focus on facility services, they are also considered in production line upgrades and new building designs to ensure EE is prioritized.

6.3   RENEWABLE ENERGY IN INDUSTRY 5.0

A renewable energy source is solar, wind, biomass, and geothermal energy. They can meet energy needs while emitting zero or negligible greenhouse gases. Through the advancement of renewable energy systems, it becomes feasible to address considerable challenges such as the increase of energy reliability, the advocacy for enhanced fuel efficiency, the strengthening of indigenous energy sources and water supplies, and the facilitation of sustainable development in remote locations [35]. It is possible to mitigate the possibility of rural-to-urban migration by deploying renewable energy projects in rural regions. Rural and small-scale applications can achieve reliable, cost-effective, and environmentally responsible energy solutions by harvesting renewable energy decentralized. These advancements align with the principles of Industry 5.0 [36].

6.3.1   DEFINITION AND EXPLANATION OF RENEWABLE ENERGY SOURCES

The term "bioenergy" refers to a renewable source of energy produced from biological sources. Bioenergy finds application across a diverse array of uses, including transportation, electric generation, cooking, and heating. It encompasses diverse sources like wood residues, agricultural residues, and animal husk. One advantage is that bioenergy often utilizes by-products or waste, avoiding competition with food production [10].

6.3.1.1   Wind Energy Systems

Wind energy, harnessed through wind turbines, has been utilized for centuries for milling wheat and water pumping. The latest wind turbines generate electricity with increased efficiency and reduced costs. Offshore wind farms, taking advantage of stronger coastal winds, are being constructed worldwide [37]. Wind power has the advantage of continuous electricity generation, day and night, unlike solar photovoltaic systems. Small wind systems may require backup batteries, but generally, wind power offers great potential for renewable energy generation in Industry 5.0. The concept of wind dams presents a promising strategy for utilizing wind resources effectively [10].

6.3.1.2   Solar Energy Systems

Solar energy, encompassing a multitude of solar-powered technologies like solar heating, residential solar heating, solar drying, and solar devices, assumes a pivotal role in the integration of sustainable energy sources. Solar panels and photovoltaic systems are extensively used, and the market for these technologies is rapidly expanding. Solar energy systems, operated by families or local communities, provide electricity, water pumping, and irrigation. These advancements align with the integration of renewable energy in Industry 5.0.

6.3.1.3 Geothermal Energy

Geothermal energy refers to the thermal energy extracted from the Earth's subsurface via natural mechanisms. It originates from the planet's internal structure and physical processes. The heat is unevenly distributed and often at depths that are challenging to access. A geothermal reservoir supplies fluids that can be used for generating electricity and heat energy. Hydrothermal reservoirs are a type of geothermal reservoir, whereas enhanced geothermal systems are the others. A variety of applications can be achieved through geothermal energy, which is obtained through drilling wells and removing fluid [10].

6.3.1.4 Hydro Power

Hydroelectricity can be generated by transporting water from high to low elevations in order to generate electricity. As part of this program, dams, run-of-river systems, and in-stream projects will be implemented. Hydropower projects provide multiple benefits like flood control, irrigation, and navigation [35]. In a hydro power plant, water potential and kinetic energy are converted into electricity through turbines. Energy storage, environmental friendliness, and adaptability make hydropower a valuable resource. It offers a reliable and sustainable energy solution with minimal pollution.

6.3.1.5 Ocean Energy

Tidal, wave, current, and temperature differences are all sources of ocean energy. Oceans contain enormous amounts of energy, and wind passing over them creates waves. Commercial ocean energy devices, like SeaGen and Pelamis, have been installed to harness this energy. The four primary methods of obtaining energy from the ocean are wind, tides, waves, and thermal differences. Ocean energy has significant potential to meet global power demands sustainably.

6.3.1.6 Fuel Cell

A fuel cell is an electrochemical device that converts chemical energy from a conventional fuel directly into direct current (DC). Hydrogen, an abundant chemical element in the universe, serves as a clean energy carrier. It constitutes a significant portion of normal matter, comprising 75% of its mass and over 90% of its atoms [38]. Through electrochemical oxidation in fuel cell systems, hydrogen gas can generate pure water as a by-product without emitting carbon dioxide. In addition to being used as a feedstock for ammonia, methanol, and oil refining, hydrogen is also becoming an increasingly popular form of energy generation. It finds expanding applications in various sectors, including transportation, power generation, and military equipment. This is due to its notable advantages of high efficiency and low emissions.

6.3.2 OVERVIEW OF THE BENEFITS OF SUSTAINABLE ENERGY RESOURCES IN INDUSTRY 5.0

The benefits of Sustainable energy resources are discussed and presented in Figure 6.4.

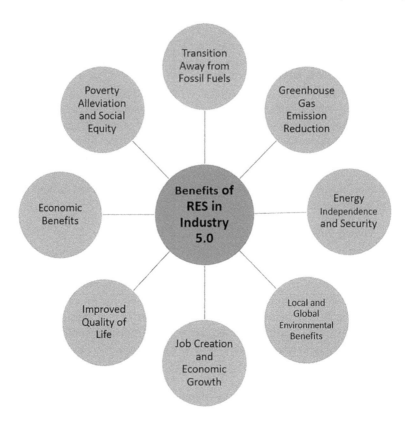

FIGURE 6.4   Benefits of sustainable energy resources in Industry 5.0.

6.3.2.1   Greenhouse Gas Emission Reduction

Through the replacement of fossil fuels with hydrogen in domains like power generation, heating, and transportation, the utilization of hydrogen and renewable energy
resources aids in the mitigation of greenhouse gas emissions. By reducing air pollution and combating climate change, local and global environmental conditions are
improved.

6.3.2.2   Energy Independence and Security

By expanding energy sources and diminishing dependence on fossil fuels, hydrogen
and renewables enhance energy independence and national energy security. They
minimize the risk of power failures, ensure a stable energy supply, and reduce vulnerability to geopolitical tensions.

6.3.2.3   Job Creation and Economic Growth

SMEs regularly contribute significantly to the economic growth in local and regional
areas, which is driven by the renewable energy sector, which includes hydrogen
technologies.

6.3.2.4 Improved Quality of Life

Hydrogen, for instance, can be used to enhance rural and disadvantageous regions' quality of life by using renewable energy technologies. As a result, respiratory illnesses are reduced and productive endeavors are made possible by providing access to pure energy services such as cooking, lighting, and heating.

6.3.2.5 Poverty Alleviation and Social Equity

By generating additional income for rural communities and creating employment opportunities, renewable energy projects help alleviate poverty and promote social equity. Local authorities often support these initiatives enthusiastically, recognizing their positive impact on communities. Indigenous renewable resources empower regions, enhance national energy security, and reduce the economic burden of fossil fuel imports.

6.3.2.6 Economic Benefits

Renewable energy, including hydrogen, is expected to generate significant economic benefits. Global GDP could increase significantly if the proportion of renewable energy in the global energy balance experienced a twofold increase by 2030 [39]. There is a potential for economic growth if renewable energy investments attract substantial capital. The economic benefits of renewable energy systems can be realized over a long period of time once they are installed and installed well.

6.3.2.7 Transition from Fossil Fuels to Renewable Energy Sources

Through the transition from non-renewable fossil fuels to sustainable energy sources, we are reducing the use of limited resources, mitigating climate change, and avoiding financial losses. Many nations are implementing policies and strategies to reshape their energy balance in order to transition to healthier energy sources.

6.3.2.8 Local and Global Environmental Benefits

In addition to mitigating air pollution, water quality enhancement, and desertification, renewable energy has environmental advantages on a local and global scale. Conventional energy sources have an adverse effect on the environment and contribute to the safeguarding of ecological resources, biodiversity, and the protection of the environment.

As well as the advantages mentioned above, the emergence of Industry 5.0, which is characterized by the integration of advanced technologies and sustainable practices, underscores the importance of hydrogen and renewable energy for driving innovation, efficiency, and environmental sustainability across a broad range of industries.

6.3.3 Challenges Faced by Renewable Energy in Industry 5.0

Adopting sustainable energy resources in Industry 5.0 presents several challenges. The visual representation of challenges is shown in Figure 6.5. Some of the challenges are presented below.

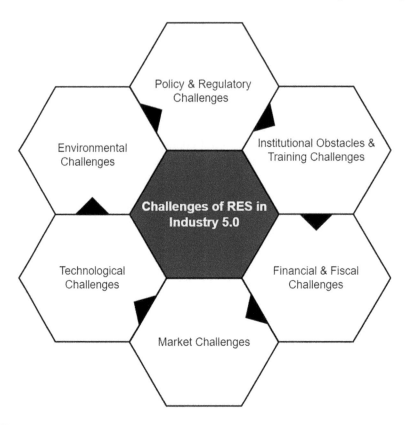

FIGURE 6.5 Challenges of renewable energy sources in Industry 5.0.

Adopting sustainable energy resources in India's renewable sector faces challenges due to the absence of a comprehensive regulatory framework. Policies often do not align with renewable energy development plans, and state-level variations in regulations create investment risks. The biomass sector lacks an established framework, and the maintenance of wind projects is not adequately addressed. The lack of clarity in renewable purchase obligations (RPOs) and penalty mechanisms further complicates compliance [40]. Transparency in tariff determination and restrictions on third-party sales limit profitability for renewable generators.

In the context of Industry 5.0, poor inter-institutional coordination, delays in policy implementation, and an inadequate workforce hinder the progress of renewable energy development. The single-window project approval system is unreliable, pre-feasibility reports have deficiencies, and there is a lack of research centers and customer care support. Insufficient institutions and laboratories hamper the establishment of standards and quality control for renewable technologies.

The renewable sector in Industry 5.0 faces significant challenges due to budgetary constraints and delayed fund allocation. Developers struggle with high initial capital costs, uncertainties in resource assessment, and perceived risks, which hinder their financial progress. Transparency concerns surrounding subsidies and declining tariffs also discourage investor participation. Additionally, limited developer engagement, a lack of institutional track record, and insufficient financial support further impede project development. Moreover, the limited understanding of renewable energy projects by financial institutions and delayed payments exacerbates the debt burden on small developers.

Subsidies favoring conventional fossil fuels create an unfair structure that prioritizes them over renewables in Industry 5.0. India's renewable markets—government, government-driven, loan, and cash—are not adequately promoted. The biomass market faces supply gaps, unreliable pricing, and variations in biomass types across states. Cost-plus methods for calculating renewable power overlook environmental costs. Inadequate evacuation infrastructure and grid integration hinder renewable projects, forcing costly power purchases from neighboring states. Transmission limitations, distribution plans, and licenses further impede renewable power. Despite increased capacity, capital costs remain high due to machinery exports, limited capacity, and equipment supplier cartelization. Insufficient land availability stifles capacity expansion in multiple states [39].

In the realm of Industry 5.0, the renewable energy sector encounters intricate threat challenges arising from environmental fluctuations, calamities, logistical complexities, device malfunctions, and anticipated profit reduction. Despite the issuance of a standardization policy by MNRE in December 2017, it still lags behind international practices [38]. Establishing a robust quality infrastructure is crucial to ensuring the Component Dependability, imported equipment, and subsystems. Testing laboratories, referral institutes, review mechanisms, inspections, and monitoring guidelines are lacking in the sector. Furthermore, the inadequate presence of R&D centers, insufficient efforts in order to prioritize research and innovation, there is a need to reduce subsidies and invest in research, reliance on international suppliers for technology and equipment, and scarcity of locally manufactured spare parts impede progress in the renewable industry within the context of Industry 5.0.

In Industry 5.0, the renewable energy sector faces challenges related to a shortage of skilled workers and insufficient maintenance support. There is a lack of knowledge and awareness among the public, hindering land acquisition for renewable projects. People's perception of high costs and limited understanding of environmental benefits also impact the adoption of renewables. Additionally, varying climates and low per capita income contribute to the less popular appeal of renewable technologies.

In Industry 5.0, the expansion of wind and solar energy systems presents various environmental challenges. The clustering of wind turbines and the size of off-shore installations occupy significant land and affect ocean activities and marine wildlife. Collisions with birds and bats, as well as sound and visual impacts, raise concerns. The environmental impact of shadow flicker and the life cycle of wind turbines require more attention. Large-scale solar plants contribute to land degradation, and the manufacturing process of photovoltaic cells poses risks from hazardous chemicals and improper waste disposal [40]. Hydroelectric power turbines also harm aquatic ecosystems and fail to control algae and aquatic weeds effectively.

6.3.4   DISCUSSION OF THE DIFFERENT TYPES OF RENEWABLE ENERGY TECHNOLOGIES AND THEIR SUITABILITY FOR DIFFERENT COUNTRIES

6.3.4.1   Denmark

The Danish government traditionally relied on massive coal-fired power plants to generate electricity. While the government has implemented policies to encourage the development of offshore wind power, onshore wind power, combined heat and Solar PV power, it has also implemented policies to encourage the development of solar power on land. The wind energy supply accounted for 40.7% of the total supply in 2018, followed by solar PV at 2.8%, fossil fuels at 23.5%, biomass and waste combustion at 17.5%, and imports at 15.5%. Denmark adopts a market-based approach, with an emphasis on flexible production and the day-ahead market. Integration efforts include strong transmission grids, international electricity markets, flexible generation systems, specialized forecasting tools, and established rules and business models. In 2030, Denmark will achieve 100% renewable electricity, and in 2050, 100% renewable energy [41].

6.3.4.2   Kauai, United States

Kauai Island Utility Cooperative (KIUC) holds the sole responsibility for supplying electricity to Kauai Island in Hawaii. 96 MW of solar power was installed to meet the demand of 55–65 MW in 2018, a great improvement over the 92% supply of oil in 2010. To address the increasing photovoltaic (PV) levels, flexibility was introduced in thermal oil-based production, gradually reducing the minimum operational load to 10%. However, this proved insufficient, leading to an expansion of energy storage. In 2018, Tesla commissioned a new 30 MW/100 MWh battery storage facility along with 13 MW of PV [41].

6.3.4.3   South Australia

During 2018, wind generation in South Australia exceeded demand 5% of the time, with 30% of households having photovoltaic systems. Adapting to inverter-based wind systems will require the grid system to move away from synchronous generators. Thorough system analyses provide recommend keeping synchronous machines online, curtailing wind output during peak generation, and relying on interconnections for balance. South Australia aims to meet 50% of its demand with distributed energy resources (DERs), which may reach 100% by 2027, requiring control, communication, and ride-through capabilities [41].

6.3.4.4   India

Several days in 2029–2030 may require a cutback in generation of renewable energy, according to CEA and IEA modeling. Solar and wind energy can be fully absorbed with reduced minimum load and increased gas-based capacity, but coal plants operate at 55% of minimum load. Gas-based generation can increase, and solar and wind system inverters can contribute to grid functions.

Based on the IEA's model, the Gujarat state could produce 40% of its energy from renewable sources by 2030, with 44 GW of solar and wind energy generated there and 20 GW imported. Steps include demand side response, flexible coal plant operation, and provision of 4,000 MW battery storage, enabling up to 100% renewable energy on certain days [41].

6.3.5 Case Studies of Successful Renewable Energy Projects

6.3.5.1 Kasai Village, MP, India

Kasai is a tribal village in Madhya Pradesh, India with no grid connection but abundant biomass resources. Since 2005, a government-funded 10 KW biomass plant has been managed by the local community. Villagers contribute to operating costs, and a committee oversees the project. The plant provides lighting, entertainment, water pumping, and more. It has reduced migration, increased agricultural production, and opened opportunities for dairy and flour milling. The project also promotes health by considering a gas supply for cooking, reducing indoor pollution from traditional biomass burning [41].

6.3.5.2 Gram Vikas Projects in Odisha

Gram Vikas, in partnership with Christian Aid, operates in 732 villages in Orissa, providing piped water supply and lighting using stand-alone renewable pumping systems. Solar power, biodiesel, and gravity flow are used to pump water from wells or springs to households. Each household receives a toilet, washroom, and piped water to the kitchen and yard. Biodiesel and solar are both more economical than gravity flow. Gram Vikas ensures community participation and sets up maintenance funds. Scaling up these projects will require more investment. UNFCCC finance could support their expansion and transform energy supply in whole districts.

6.3.5.3 Solar Applications World's Largest Solar Steam
Cooking System at Tirumala, Andhra Pradesh

In Andhra Pradesh, the Tirumala Tirupathi Devasthanam (TTD) has installed the world's largest solar steam cooking system. Using automatic tracking solar dish concentrators, the system is capable of cooking food for 15,000 people per day. It operates in conjunction with an existing diesel boiler, ensuring reliability in all weather conditions. A central steam pipeline leads from 106 parabolic concentrators to the kitchen of this modular system. The annual saving is expected to be 118,000 L of petroleum worth Rs. 2.3 million. The project was implemented by M/s Gadhia Solar Energy Systems, with support from MNES and TTD trust. This technology is particularly beneficial in rice-centric regions with large-scale cooking needs [38].

6.3.5.4 Agro-Waste and Industrial Waste Utilizing Gasifier, Hyderabad

A Biomass Power Project with an 8 MW capacity has been established in Patancheru, Andhra Pradesh. It utilizes agricultural and industrial waste materials, including sugar cane trash, coffee shells, and poultry manure, to generate power. Plant Load Factor (PLF) was 90% in the year of operation for the project, which began operations in February 2002. AP Forest Development Corporation Limited has partnered with the company to cultivate eucalyptus plantations for fuel production using indigenous technology. Over 110 jobs have been created as a result of the initiative, contributing to the economic development of the region [38].

6.4   INTEGRATION OF ENERGY EFFICIENCY AND RENEWABLE ENERGY IN INDUSTRY 5.0

6.4.1   EXPLANATION OF THE SYNERGIES BETWEEN ENERGY EFFICIENCY AND RENEWABLE ENERGY ADOPTION

The transition towards Industry 5.0 hinges upon the utilization of sustainable energy sources and the optimization of energy usage. Efforts could be made to merge these two components in order to create a future with minimum carbon emissions and sustainable practices. The synergy between renewable energy systems and EE is depicted in Figure 6.6.

Buildings exhibit synergies between EE and renewable energy. By employing EE measures and using RES, nearly zero energy buildings (NZEBs) in an industry reduce energy consumption greatly. For a building to achieve a net zero-energy balance, less renewable energy is required the more efficient its systems. This not only

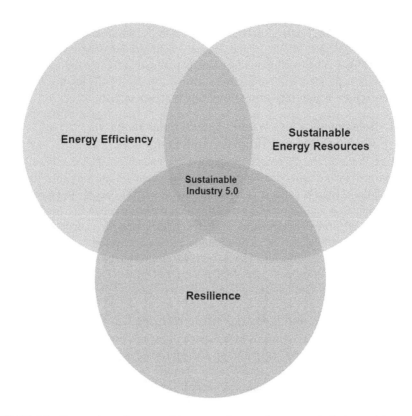

FIGURE 6.6   Integration of energy efficiency and renewable energy in Industry 5.0.

reduces the environmental impact but also increases the cost-effectiveness of NZEBs by reducing the size and capacity of renewable energy systems needed.

Advanced insulation, airtightness, efficient lighting, and appliances are examples of EE measures in NZEBs [41]. A NZEB can generate renewable energy both on site through building-integrated solar systems and off site through solar power plants or wind farms.

The transportation sector is another area in which renewable energy and EE can complement each other. For electric vehicles (EVs), electricity provides the main source of energy, and it improves transportation efficiency and reduces emissions, especially when it is generated from renewable sources like hydropower and wind power. The market for EVs is growing rapidly, and the decreasing cost of batteries is making them more competitive. EVs can maximize their environmental benefits by improving efficiency and decarbonizing electricity supplies.

A district energy system has the potential to be a synergistic system that can both meet renewable energy goals and be energy efficient. Utilizing locally accessible RES and leveraging waste heat can improve EE and improve the proportion of renewable energy in the energy mix. Energy from renewable sources is used to provide heating, cooling, and electricity to a network of buildings. Buildings requiring less heating and cooling are best served by district energy systems. In a district energy system, waste heat is recycled and local RES are used to increase renewable energy production and improve EE [42].

Significant amount of investment is necessary to promote EE and the adoption of sustainable energy sources. There will be about USD 2.8 trillion invested in renewable energy and EE at the global level in 2023. Investing in EE programs and sustainable energy resources is expected to increase by 24% in 2023 [43]. In addition to increasing EE and renewable energy use, these investments contribute to their development and deployment.

The interdependence of renewable energy and EE is apparent across diverse sectors. We can achieve greater energy savings, reduce greenhouse gas emissions, and accelerate the transition to a sustainable, low-carbon future by combining these two elements. For Industry 5.0 to succeed and for global sustainability goals to be achieved, renewable energy and EE measures are essential.

6.4.1.1 Technical Synergies

Each stage of delivering energy services generates potential losses, including extraction, transformation, transportation, transmission, and consumption. EE can also be enhanced during these stages and overall system performance can be optimized. This phenomenon of improving EE applies regardless of the primary energy source.

Moreover, there are synergies that can be aligned with the principles of Industry 5.0 between RES and EE.

A more sustainable and efficient industrial ecosystem is achieved through the integration of advanced technologies, automation, and human collaboration. Embracing Industry 5.0 principles can help energy companies streamline operations and achieve greater sustainability by utilizing renewable energy and EE.

Energy delivery systems that are more efficient can significantly increase the use of RES as primary energy sources. A decline in renewable energy services occurs as the proportion of primary energy increases. A system-wide collaboration between renewables and EE minimizes environmental and economic costs [44].

Wind, solar, and hydropower are all renewable sources of energy that reduce energy losses because they eliminate the need for thermal conversion. Moreover, the combination of distributed renewable energy and EE improvements can minimize transmission losses, reduce peak electricity demand, and relieve system bottlenecks.

Incorporating Industry 5.0 principles in the energy sector will improve EE and maximize renewable energy deployment by embracing advanced technologies and automation. By collaborating, new energy applications can be developed that were not previously possible, resulting in outcomes that are more effective than the sum of their parts.

In addition to reducing the end-use energy demand, grid congestion, losses, and fuel transportation costs, efficient buildings can also help reduce the reliance on fossil fuels.

Renewable energy investments can reduce costs for end-user services when combined with EE measures. In addition to financing further efficiency improvements, the cost savings can also be reinvested to implement renewable energy technologies in more locations. There are several industries that can benefit from Industry 5.0, such as buildings, electrical services, transportation, and industry.

A recent working paper, co-authored by IRENA and the Copenhagen Center for Energy Efficiency (C2E2), presents an examination of the technical interconnections between renewable energies and EE. Through the use of renewable energy and EE measures, some countries can reduce their energy intensity by 5%–10% by 2030. Combining these possibilities could reduce global energy requirements by 25%– by 2030 [27]. The ability to electrify and employ more efficient cookstoves is one way to reduce emissions. Another way is to accelerate the transition to renewable energy, which is more efficient than thermally based technologies [41]. Additionally, efficiency measures are crucial for off-grid hybrid systems and distributed renewable energy in many developing countries.

6.4.1.2 Policy Synergies

The section emphasizes that EE and renewable energy mutually benefit policy development, and collaboration is essential for achieving sustainability goals. Many countries have established targets and policies for both renewables and EE. Although there has been limited systematic linking of the two, efforts are being made to align them locally and nationally.

Three main policy approaches have emerged to link renewables and EE: encouraging them in parallel, integrating them through portfolio standards, and requiring joint implementation [3]. There are several levels of government adopting these approaches, including the European Union (EU), focusing on the building sector. In addition to the importance of combining renewable energy and EE, organizations dedicated to sustainable development acknowledge the importance of combining both.

Policies and targets aimed at promoting renewable energy can drive investments in EE. The more ambitious the renewable energy targets, the more crucial EE becomes.

Pursuing both in parallel can lower overall costs and contribute to greenhouse gas emissions reduction. In scenarios outlined by the IEA, EE significantly limits global temperature increase, while renewables contribute to emission reductions. To accelerate progress towards clean energy, the text suggests adopting long-term and stable policy frameworks, strengthening support mechanisms, and considering heating, cooling, transport, and holistic energy system perspectives. Achieving distributed renewable energy and EE in developing countries requires better information, awareness, and access to finance.

In order to achieve sustainable energy for all, renewable energy and EE need to be recognized and leveraged. Sustainable energy can be produced by aligning renewable energy and EE with Industry 5.0 principles, which emphasize sustainability.

6.4.2 Discussion of the Different Approaches to Integrating Energy Efficiency and Renewable Energy, such as Onsite generation, Power Purchase Agreements, and Energy Storage

There are several technologies not only contribute to reducing primary energy demand but also enhance the proportion of renewable energy within the total final energy consumption (TFEC).

6.4.2.1 Efficient Cook Stoves

Currently, traditional biomass utilization contributes around 9% of the global TFEC and is considered an inefficient energy source. Increasing the proportion of modern renewable energy, increasing cooking energy efficiency, and making access to modern energy easier can be achieved by replacing traditional biomass with modern and efficient cooking and heating methods. It is crucial to consider that when calculating the share of renewable energy, encompassing both contemporary and traditional forms of renewables, the replacement of inefficient cook stoves with efficient ones could potentially result in a reduction of the overall renewable energy percentage [41].

6.4.2.2 Heat Pumps

Heating constitutes approximately 25% of the global TFEC. Geothermal heat pumps exceed the efficiency of air-to-air heat pumps by three times. Air-to-air heat pumps are about three times more energy efficient than conventional boilers. Heat pumps rely primarily on electricity as an energy source. By utilizing renewable sources to power heat pumps, they become a crucial enabling technology for transitioning to renewable electricity.

6.4.2.3 Variable Renewable Energy Technologies

In comparison to fossil fuels and nuclear power, renewable energy technologies usually provide higher efficiency gains than wind and solar PV with 100% efficiency, where nuclear power, for example, achieves about 33% efficiency.

6.4.2.4 Local District Thermal Networks

Heating and cooling are more cost-effective and efficient with local district thermal networks than with individual units.

6.4.2.5   Decentralized Energy Systems (Mini-Grids)

Decentralized energy systems consist of small-scale energy generation units that supply power to local customers. These systems can operate independently or be interconnected with neighboring units to share resources, forming locally decentralized energy networks. They offer promising prospects for expanding clean energy access to remote communities using local RES. By locating energy production closer to consumption, decentralized systems optimize the utilization of renewable energy and CHP, leading to reduced fossil fuel consumption and increased eco-efficiency. Modern renewable energy systems play an important role in promoting EE and the adoption of modern renewable energy [14, 45].

Decentralized energy systems could be defined as characterized by small-scale energy generation units (structures) that deliver energy to local customers. These production units could be stand-alone or could be connected to nearby others through a network to share resources, i.e. to share the energy surplus. In the latter case, they become locally decentralized energy networks, which may, in turn, be connected with nearby similar networks

6.4.2.6   Demand-Response Management

Demand-Response Management (DRM) strategies offer significant value in terms of data related to renewable energy and EE. DRM involves actively managing and modifying electricity demand based on supply conditions, grid limitations, or pricing signals. By analyzing the data generated through DRM, valuable insights can be obtained regarding the integration of renewable energy and EE. DRM provides data in various areas, including demand-side flexibility, load profiles and peak demand analysis, grid balancing and stability, energy conservation and efficiency, as well as customer engagement and awareness. This data aids in enhancing the adoption of modern RES and improving overall EE.

Some of the widely used strategies for demand side management are Peak Clipping, Valley lifting, load shifting. Peak clipping involves mitigating high demand during peak periods by implementing scheduled outages. Valley lifting involves the establishment of additional off-peak loads. When the incremental cost of electricity in the long run is lower than the electricity average price, this is particularly beneficial. It is often the case that such conditions are created when low-cost fuel is underutilized and underutilized capacity is available. Energy consumption rises without corresponding increases in peak demand, resulting in a rise in total energy consumption. This strategy is typically employed by introducing new off-peak electric loads that were earlier reliant on non-electric fuels, such as overnight charging of electric cars and thermal energy storage. Load shifting involves strategically reducing electricity supply in specific zones during a designated period to effectively manage demand and prevent blackouts [46].

6.4.2.7   Smart-Grid

A smart grid is an advanced electricity network that utilizes digital technologies to monitor and control the transmission of electricity from different sources to meet the dynamic demands of end users. By integrating the requirements and capabilities of generators, grid operators, consumers, and market participants, smart grids aim to optimize the efficiency of the entire system, reducing costs and environmental effects while maximizing reliability, resilience, flexibility, and stability. Through its intelligent infrastructure, a smart grid enables a more efficient, sustainable, and robust electricity distribution system [14,46].

6.4.2.8 Intermediate Energy Storage Systems

Intermediate energy storage in the decentralized renewable energy system will help in improving EE and reducing energy production variability.

6.4.3 Methods for Renewable Energy Integration

Reaching beyond the threshold of 15%, proper measures for integration become imperative within the realm of renewable energy generation. The rationale behind this lies in the notable shifts that can occur in both solar and wind power production as a result of phenomena like cloud cover and various weather-related events. With extensive monitoring conducted across ground based stations and satellites. Our ability to forecast daily variations in solar energy has significantly improved [41].

Additionally, wind forecasting has shown tremendous progress in recent years. The government of India has established Renewable Energy Management Centres in all of the states that have abundant sources of renewable energy. These centers make use of the most recent technologies, including AI, in order to produce precise forecasts for solar and wind energy [41].

6.4.3.1 Flexible Sources of Power Generation

As the proportion of primary energy rises, there is a decline in the magnitude of energy services delivered by renewables. Nevertheless, the contribution of hydro-electric and natural gas power generation systems to India's energy supply is diminishing. It is now being upgraded to be able to operate with a flexible load schedule for coal-based power stations. In addition to operating at 60% load, they are being designed to operate even at 40% load. Flexible operation has yet to be proven in terms of reliability and long-term life expectancy. Lights across India were turned off at 9 pm on 5 April 2020 during lockdown due to the COVID pandemic. The Indian grid handled a swing of 32 GW, mainly because of hydro flexibility (2.74 GW/min) [41,47].

6.4.3.2 Energy Storage System

Integration of renewable energy systems on a large scale requires efficient energy storage technologies. The storage capacity of pump hydroelectric systems still exceeds 95%. As a result, batteries and other storage systems are rapidly developing [41].

6.4.3.3 Integration with Larger Systems

A large area of renewable energy provides a better average availability of renewable energy. Moreover, larger electricity grids create prospects for both import and export activities. Green energy corridor is an ambitious project undertaken by the Government of India. An estimated Rs 10,000 crores will be spent on the construction of 9,400 km of transmission lines and 19,000 MVA of transformers under this project. The majority of this project has been finalized. The construction of interstate and intrastate transmission lines has been completed. The evacuation of solar and wind power will amount to about 20,000 MW [27].

6.4.3.4   Renewable Energy Technology for grid support

It is now possible to have both power generation and reactive power support with inverter-based solar and wind systems. Numerous newly developed inverters have the capability to offer reactive support while functioning at reduced output levels. There has been a lot of discussion recently about RES taking steps to support the grid on their own.

6.4.3.5   Demand Management

The generation and demand of energy can be balanced by curtailing some loads. System balance can also be achieved by reducing voltage in some cases. Allocating resources towards EE in new production generally necessitates a return on investment within half the lifespan of the newly acquired assets.

6.4.3.6   Pump Hydro Energy Storage

Storage technology based on pump hydro continues to dominate. A higher level of water is kept in the reservoirs during off-peak periods. Energy is generated during periods of high demand, similar to conventional hydroelectric generation. Physical locations and substantial expenditures are required for the establishment of these systems. It is estimated that by 2030, 5,000 MW of electricity will be stored in pump hydro storage systems in India [41]. A variable-speed drive can also optimize the operation of pump storage plants.

6.4.3.7   Battery Storage

The lithium-ion battery is one of the technologies that has experienced rapid advancement in recent years. Nevertheless, affordability continues to be a significant obstacle. Other solutions include sodium, sulfur, metal, redox flow, and hydro batteries. Flywheels and supercapacitors serve as alternative sources of energy. Indians are already using thermal storage as a form of storage [41].

6.4.4   Case Studies of Successful Integrated Projects in different Industries

The section below presents real-time case studies that demonstrate different use cases for implementing the combined benefits of EE and renewable energy systems in Industry 5.0 [41]. Figure 6.7 illustrates the harmonious relationship between EE and the utilization of renewable energy in Industry 5.0.

6.4.4.1   Buildings

An NZEB is characterized by a significant reduction in energy demand resulting from EE improvement, with any remaining energy needs being met by RES [10]. Consequently, the amount of renewable energy required to meet a building's

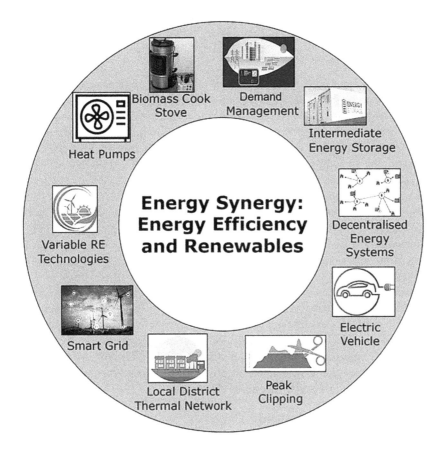

FIGURE 6.7   Synergies of energy efficiency and renewables.

energy demand depends on its EE. Increasing the efficiency of a system reduces the amount of renewable energy needed in order to achieve net zero energy balance. Thus, NZEBs become more cost-effective because they require fewer renewable energy systems to meet their energy needs, which reduces their size and capacity.

Energy-efficient measures commonly implemented in Nearly Zero Energy Buildings (NZEBs) comprise enhanced insulation, minimized thermal bridging, air sealing, utilization of thermal inertia, daylight utilization, strategic ventilation approaches, as well as the use of energy-saving lighting and appliances. A NZEB can generate renewable energy both on- and off-site. In the case of on-site generation, the incorporation of thermal collectors and photovoltaic panels is integrated directly into a building or structure, whereas off-site generation involves the importation of solar power plants or wind farms for energy production.

NZEB targets are being established within specific timeframes within the EU, which is a positive trend. For instance, the Netherlands set a target to build 60,000 new NZEBs by the year 2015. In Malta, there is an anticipation that at least 5% of newly constructed buildings owned and occupied by public authorities will adhere to the NZEB criteria [41].

6.4.4.2 Transport

EE and reduced emissions are among the advantages of using electricity as the primary fuel for transportation. The adoption of electric and hybrid vehicles is swiftly increasing in developed nations. The sales of these vehicles experienced a remarkable surge of 229% in the United States from 2012 to 2013 [48]. As a result of decreasing battery costs, EVs are becoming more competitive. From 2008 to 2012, the price of batteries in the United States witnessed a decline from USD 1,000 to USD 485 per kWh [41].

EVs exemplify the potential synergies between EE and renewable energy, despite their market presence remains relatively modest. Notably, Norway achieved a penetration rate of 6.6% in 2013, followed by the Netherlands at 5.6%, California at 4%, and the United States as a whole at 1.3% in the same year [41]. Hydro, wind, and solar power are all RES that can charge these vehicles and provide these benefits.

University of Minnesota research found that EVs powered by renewable sources of electricity such as wind, water, and solar produce the least environmental pollution. Comparatively, conventional gasoline cars have a greater impact on air quality than cars powered by corn ethanol or electricity from the average grid. According to the study, it is important to improve fuel efficiency and reduce the carbon footprint of electricity generation [49]. While EVs offer sustainability advantages, their competitiveness may be affected by declining oil prices.

6.4.4.3 District Energy Systems

Utilizing RES, district energy systems can provide heating, cooling, and electricity to an entire network of buildings. It is best to use these systems when heating and cooling energy-efficient buildings. EE is enhanced by integrating RES and waste heat into modern district energy systems, which can integrate thermal energy and power supply.

Cities across Europe, the United States, and Canada have been implementing district energy systems for many years. Approximately half of urban energy consumption is derived from heating and cooling [50].

District heating systems play an important role in heating cities such as Helsinki, Finland, and Copenhagen, Denmark. By utilizing these systems, multiple benefits can be obtained, such as an elevated proportion of renewable energy in the energy composition, diminished expenditures, heightened reliability, enhanced atmospheric conditions, and a decrease in emissions. Indeed, district heating systems presently contribute approximately 13% to the existing heat market in residential and service sectors across Europe [51].

District energy systems serve as a sustainable solution, aligning with the goal of reducing greenhouse gas emissions and transitioning to cleaner energy sources. They facilitate the efficient utilization of renewable energy and contribute to the overall sustainability of urban environments [52].

6.5 POLICY AND REGULATORY FRAMEWORK FOR ENERGY EFFICIENCY AND RENEWABLE ENERGY IN INDUSTRY 5.0

An overview of the current policy and regulatory landscape for EE and renewable energy in industry is provided in this section. Policy and regulatory frameworks in various countries and regions are discussed so that EE and renewable energy can be adopted more widely.

6.5.1 REVIEW OF THE CURRENT POLICY AND REGULATORY LANDSCAPE IN THE INDUSTRY - ENERGY EFFICIENCY AND RENEWABLE ENERGY

Many countries have evolved their energy policy over the years, depending on a variety of factors. Prior to the 1973 oil crisis, energy policy primarily centered on ensuring energy supply to meet the growing demand. In order to increase energy security of supply, energy diversification and EE measures were emphasized as a result of the oil crisis.

Energy policy began to focus more heavily on environmental concerns during the 1980s and 1990s. Energy programs in various countries highlighted the importance of coupling energy consumption with environmental impact. From 1995, many countries set three key objectives for their energy policies: environmental protection, improvement of competitiveness, and increased security of supply [53].

Alongside environmental considerations, the liberalization and privatization of energy markets also influenced energy policy in many countries. Efforts were made to create internal markets for gas and electricity, leading to the adoption of important directives for the internal market in electricity and natural gas.

The ideal model for solar energy is seen as a decentralized system, taking into account local needs and resources. Passive solar energy and bioclimatic architecture are considered essential elements. This model, combined with hydrogen obtained from RES and energy storage technologies, could address supply instability issues. Massive production of energy from RES offers benefits such as reducing energy imports, mitigating oil and gas price fluctuations, reducing greenhouse gas emissions, and creating local jobs. However, it also presents new environmental challenges related to manufacturing RES units and land use for RES installations and biofuel production.

The widespread use of RES must be complemented by a transformation of the economic development model, focusing on EE. This involves adopting measures proposed by energy directives and implementing structural changes, including fiscal measures like carbon taxes, altering building patterns, and reducing motorized mobility. The goal is to decouple energy and resource consumption from economic growth.

Eliminating current barriers in the energy market and addressing energy price distortions are crucial for RES to become a viable alternative to conventional energy sources. In 1997, many countries adopted strategies to promote renewable energy, setting targets for the share of RES in their gross domestic energy consumption. However, achieving these targets has proven challenging [54].

6.5.2 DISCUSSION OF THE POTENTIAL POLICY AND REGULATORY CHANGES NEEDED TO SUPPORT GREATER ADOPTION OF ENERGY EFFICIENCY AND RENEWABLE ENERGY IN INDUSTRY

Increasing industrial building EE is difficult due to lack of funding. The global financial crisis has constrained investment capital, impeding the realization of cost-efficient energy savings. Businesses and consumers can reduce their cost frameworks by modifying their fiscal policies and establishing financing initiatives, making EE upgrades appear like operations rather than capital investments. Mayors and the National Governors Association recognize financing as a significant barrier to EE deployment and have sought funding to achieve full implementation. Various countries, such as the United States and Germany, offer financial incentives like tax rebates and low-interest loans to incentivize EE improvements [55]. Additionally, innovative financing programs like PACE, performance contracts, and on-bill financing leverage limited public investment for greater private involvement [54]. Figure 6.8 shows the Policies in RES and EE in the world used for Industry 5.0.

PACE (Property Assessed Clean Energy) projects provide property owners with a means to finance energy upgrades by incorporating assessments into their tax bills. This allows for repayment over an extended period through property taxes. These projects primarily focus on the commercial and industrial sectors, as objections from the mortgage industry have limited their application in other areas.

Another approach to EE and renewable energy integration is through ESPC (Energy Savings Performance Contracting) agreements. Within an ESPC arrangement, an

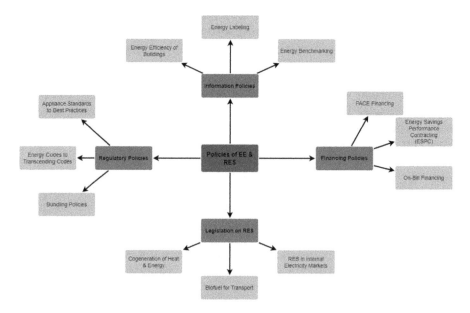

FIGURE 6.8 Current policies of energy efficiency (EE) and renewable energy sources (RES) for sustainability in Industry 5.0.

Energy Service Company (ESCO) assumes financial obligations and retrofitting duties for a building, shouldering a substantial portion of the project risks.

A portion of the energy savings generated by the ESCO will be returned to the ESCO, while the building owner will also benefit from the reduced energy costs. ESPCs have shown success in Europe and the US, particularly in the municipal, university, school, and hospital (MUSH) market. Developing countries have also established "Super ESCOs" to facilitate projects in public facilities and support private ESCOs. Countries like Croatia, the Philippines, South Korea, Hebei Province, and India have implemented ESPC initiatives, currently operational within their respective borders. China, in particular, has shown support for scaling up EE improvements through this approach, with positive evaluations demonstrating economic benefits and the potential for clean energy financing models [54].

On-bill financing is another financial product gaining traction, whereby utility companies handle the servicing and collection of repayment for EE upgrades through customers' monthly bills. This approach, expanding in several states and the UK, allows for the long-term savings to outweigh the upfront costs. The UK's Green Deal program, for instance, enables consumers to recoup payments for building improvements through installments on their electricity bills, with the debt tied to the energy meter. However, concerns remain regarding its effectiveness compared to previous programs and its suitability for building owners with tenants.

Product-specific energy labeling initiatives, such as the EU Energy Label and Energy Star label in the United States, play a vital role in encouraging consumers to choose more energy-efficient products. These labels provide standardized information on energy consumption, empowering consumers to make informed decisions. The EU Energy Label rates EE from A to G, while Energy Star is widely recognized in the US and has expanded to other countries. Such labeling frameworks cover various products, including white goods, light bulbs, and office equipment.

Benchmarking energy consumption in residential and commercial buildings can effectively reduce information asymmetry, decrease consumer discount rates, and drive investments in EE. Mandated disclosure and benchmarking programs, like the Portfolio Manager in the US, offer data for comparisons and improve energy performance assessments. Studies have demonstrated that benchmarking and labeling can increase market demand for high-efficiency buildings and influence consumer choices positively.

To eliminate inefficient models, many countries have enforced Minimum Energy Performance Standards (MEPS) as part of their regulatory measures. Notably, Japan's Top Runner Program sets energy standards based on the most efficient available appliances, proving to be effective and adaptable. The program covers various appliances and is expected to deliver significant benefits [54].

Stringent industrial building energy codes can also play a crucial role in reducing energy consumption and saving costs for building owners and occupants. It is essential to focus on innovations in building codes, enforcement mechanisms, and compliance, along with the establishment of liability structures. Promoting performance beyond code requirements can be achieved through complementary policies and partnerships with utilities.

In the EU, Directive 2001/77/EC was adopted to promote electricity generation from RES within the internal electricity market. The directive sets national targets for RES electricity and an overall target for the EU. However, achieving these targets necessitates the implementation of effective energy consumption control policies. By encouraging the use of biofuels and other renewable fuels, Directive 2003/30/EC contributes to the development of renewable energy integration within the transport sector [53].

6.5.3   CASE STUDIES OF POLICY AND REGULATORY FRAMEWORKS IN DIFFERENT REGIONS AND COUNTRIES

Renewable energy projects have been boosted by policy and legal factors, which justifies continued state involvement in the energy sector. With the increase in wind power capacity over the past few decades, jobs have been created, power grids have become more resilient, energy access has been expanded, and energy costs have decreased. As a result, renewable energy costs could rise without government support, potentially increasing carbon dioxide emissions from fossil fuel-based technologies.

A number of technological advances have made it possible to harness energy from tides, waves, and sunshine through the use of wind turbines and solar photovoltaics. While there may be opposition to wind turbines, falling prices and their solid contribution to the energy mix demonstrate the value of this resource. Many U.S. states and cities have set renewable energy standards, with some committing to reaching 100% renewable energy [55]. The COVID-19 pandemic and economic recession prompted further decarbonization plans from states, cities, utilities, and businesses, with incentives and stimulus measures supporting the development of green infrastructure.

Policy initiatives have been introduced to encourage the installation and purchase of renewable energy systems. Programs aimed at training graduates in solar panel installation and operations have been implemented in certain countries. International collaborations like the International Solar Alliance (ISA) headquarters in India have been established to advance solar energy. Uniform environmental standards, research and development initiatives, and streamlined permitting processes ensure responsible and rapid development of renewable energy projects, promoting economic growth and community involvement.

Ghana and China have adopted energy policy documents outlining their renewable energy targets. Ghana aims to develop an efficient energy market to support the country's economic development, while China's National Energy Plan sets guidelines and challenges for the energy sector [56]. Renewable energy certificates (RECs) provide tradable certificates representing the ecological attributes of electricity generated from renewable sources. Various settings, such as government buildings and biomass cogeneration systems, are generating renewable energy on-site through green pricing programs.

A green pricing program allows consumers to purchase renewable energy, which contributes to the production of renewable energy on-site at various locations, including government buildings and biomass cogeneration plants. Many case studies have illustrated the use of market-based policies to reduce greenhouse gas emissions and promote EE. Emissions trading systems that price carbon have been successful in reducing emissions and putting a price on it. A cap-and-trade mechanism has also been adopted by regional initiatives such as the Regional Greenhouse Gas Initiative (RGGI) in the United States [55,57].

Countries such as Northern Europe, Canada, Australia, and the United Kingdom have implemented carbon taxes. These taxes provide a direct means of pricing carbon emissions and incentivize reductions. Local-level carbon taxes have been introduced in areas like the San Francisco Bay Area and municipalities such as Babylon, New York, and Boulder, Colorado [55].

Market-based strategies have also extended to the creation of tradable EE certificates, known as white certificates. These certificates have been implemented in countries like the United Kingdom, France, Italy, and Australia to certify energy savings obligations [29].

To further promote EE, the EU adopted Directive 2012/27/EU, which mandates annual improvements in EE and sets national targets [54]. Within the United States, EE certificates are being employed in multiple states to meet the requirements of EERS.

India has implemented an EE trading scheme, resembling the cap-and-trade system, aimed at diminishing energy intensity in SMEs [15]. Although market-based instruments are acknowledged for their economic efficiency, supplementary policies are imperative to tackle market constraints and consumer perceptions regarding EE.

6.6 CONCLUSION

With its emphasis on productivity, sustainability, and digital integration, Industry 5.0 offers significant opportunities for EE and renewable energy adoption. Integrating sophisticated technologies and intelligent systems enables businesses to maintain the same output level while consuming less energy, resulting in cost savings, improved operational efficiency, and a strengthened market reputation. EE measures, such as optimizing supply- and demand-side EE, implementing modern process technologies, and adopting improved control systems, are essential to attaining energy performance objectives.

RES, such as solar, wind, biomass, and geothermal energy, provide alternatives to traditional fossil fuels that are pure and sustainable. Adoption of these resources can reduce greenhouse gas emissions, increase energy resilience, generate job opportunities, and enhance brand reputation. However, obstacles must be overcome, such as the absence of a comprehensive regulatory framework, insufficient coordination, high initial capital costs, and a shortage of skilled employees.

Collaboration between governments, industries, and research institutions is essential for Industry 5.0 to completely leverage the benefits of EE and renewable energy. With supportive policies, incentives, and regulations, businesses can be incentivized to prioritize EE and embrace renewable energy. In addition, increasing public awareness and addressing concerns regarding transparency can foster a favorable environment for sustainable energy practices.

Despite the obstacles encountered, a multitude of triumphant case studies exemplify the feasibility and advantages of integrating EE and renewable energy endeavors across diverse industries. By overcoming obstacles and adopting sustainable energy practices, businesses can contribute to a more sustainable and environmentally friendly future while reaping the benefits of increased consumer confidence, energy resilience, cost savings, enhanced brand reputation, and adherence to international laws.

The transition to Industry 5.0 necessitates a concerted effort from all stakeholders in order to surmount obstacles and seize opportunities presented by EE and renewable energy. By adopting these practices, industries can foster innovation, enhance their competitiveness, and contribute to a more sustainable and resilient industrial sector for the benefit of future generations.

REFERENCES

[1] P. K. R. Maddikunta et al., "Industry 5.0: A survey on enabling technologies and potential applications," *J. Ind. Inf. Integr.*, vol. 26, p. 100257, 2022. doi: 10.1016/j. jii.2021.100257.

[2] P. R. Anisha, C. K. K. Reddy, N. G. Nguyen, M. Bhushan, A. Kumar, and M. Mohd Hanafiah, *Intelligent Systems and Machine Learning for Industry*. CRC Press, 2022. doi: 10.1201/9781003286745.

[3] M. Ghobakhloo, M. Iranmanesh, M. F. Mubarak, M. Mubarik, A. Rejeb, and M. Nilashi, "Identifying industry 5.0 contributions to sustainable development: A strategy roadmap for delivering sustainability values," *Sustain. Prod. Consum.*, vol. 33, pp. 716–737, 2022, doi: 10.1016/j.spc.2022.08.003.

[4] J. Barata and I. Kayser, "Industry 5.0 - Past, present, and near future," *Procedia. Comput. Sci.*, vol. 219, pp. 778–788, 2023, doi: 10.1016/j.procs.2023.01.351.

[5] A. Adel, "Future of industry 5.0 in society: Human-centric solutions, challenges and prospective research areas," *J. Cloud Comput.*, vol. 11, no. 1, pp. 1–15, 2022, doi: 10.1186/S13677-022-00314-5.

[6] M. Ghobakhloo, M. Iranmanesh, M. F. Mubarak, M. Mubarik, A. Rejeb, and M. Nilashi, "Identifying industry 5.0 contributions to sustainable development: A strategy roadmap for delivering sustainability values," *Sustain. Prod. Consum.*, vol. 33, pp. 716–737, 2022, doi: 10.1016/J.SPC.2022.08.003.

[7] P. Solutions, "What are the benefits of renewable energy for industrial users? Pollution solutions online," *Pollut. Solut.*, 2021. https://www.pollutionsolutions-online.com/ news/green-energy/42/breaking-news/what-are-the-benefits-of-renewable-energy-for-industrial-users/55392 (accessed Jun. 23, 2023).

[8] Surple, "6 top energy efficiency benefits for businesses in 2021," *Energy Manag.* 2021. https://surple.co.uk/energy-efficiency-benefits/ (accessed Jun. 23, 2023).

[9] U.S. EPA, "Part one - The multiple benefits of energy efficiency and renewable energy," 2018. [Online]. Available: https://www.epa.gov/statelocalenergy/quantifying-multiple-benefits-energy-efficiency-and-renewable-energy-guide-state.

[10] S. Luthra, S. Kumar, D. Garg, and A. Haleem, "Barriers to renewable/sustainable energy technologies adoption: Indian perspective," *Renew. Sustain. Energy Rev.*, vol. 41, pp. 762–776, 2015, doi: 10.1016/j.rser.2014.08.077.

[11] Seetharaman, K. Moorthy, N. Patwa, Saravanan, and Y. Gupta, "Breaking barriers in deployment of renewable energy," *Heliyon*, vol. 5, no. 1, p. e01166, 2019, doi: 10.1016/j. heliyon.2019.e01166.

[12] M. Yang, "Energy efficiency policy impact in India: case study of investment in industrial energy efficiency," *Energy Policy*, vol. 34, no. 17, pp. 3104–3114, 2006, doi: 10.1016/j.enpol.2005.05.014.

[13] S. Sen and S. Ganguly, "Opportunities, barriers and issues with renewable energy development - A discussion," *Renew. Sustain. Energy Rev.*, vol. 69, pp. 1170–1181, 2017, doi: 10.1016/J.RSER.2016.09.137.

[14] N. Good, K. A. Ellis, and P. Mancarella, "Review and classification of barriers and enablers of demand response in the smart grid," *Renew. Sustain. Energy Rev.*, vol. 72, pp. 57–72, 2017, doi: 10.1016/j.rser.2017.01.043.

[15] M. Kennedy and B. Basu, "Overcoming barriers to low carbon technology transfer and deployment: An exploration of the impact of projects in developing and emerging economies," *Renew. Sustain. Energy Rev.*, vol. 26, pp. 685–693, 2013, doi: 10.1016/j.rser.2013.05.071.

[16] V. S. K. V. Harish and A. Kumar, "Demand side management in India: Action plan, policies and regulations," *Renew. Sustain. Energy Rev.*, vol. 33, pp. 613–624, 2014, doi: 10.1016/j.rser.2014.02.021.

[17] E. K. Stigka, J. A. Paravantis, and G. K. Mihalakakou, "Social acceptance of renewable energy sources: A review of contingent valuation applications," *Renew. Sustain. Energy Rev.*, vol. 32, pp. 100–106, 2014, doi: 10.1016/j.rser.2013.12.026.

[18] N. H. Ravindranath and P. Balachandra, "Sustainable bioenergy for India: Technical, economic and policy analysis," *Energy*, vol. 34, no. 8, pp. 1003–1013, 2009, doi: 10.1016/j.energy.2008.12.012.

[19] P. Blechinger, C. Cader, P. Bertheau, H. Huyskens, R. Seguin, and C. Breyer, "Global analysis of the techno-economic potential of renewable energy hybrid systems on small islands," *Energy Policy*, vol. 98, pp. 674–687, 2016, doi: 10.1016/j.enpol.2016.03.043.

[20] A. Adel, "Future of industry 5.0 in society: human-centric solutions, challenges and prospective research areas," *J. Cloud Comput.*, vol. 11, no. 1, 2022, doi: 10.1186/s13677-022-00314-5.

[21] M. Maciaszczyk, Z. Makieła, and R. Miśkiewicz, "Industry 5.0," In *Innovation in the Digital Economy*, London: Routledge, pp. 51–61, 2023. doi: 10.4324/9781003384311-5.

[22] M. G. Patterson, "What is energy efficiency? Concepts, indicators and methodological issues," *Energy Policy*, vol. 24, no. 5, pp. 377–390, 1996, doi: 10.1016/0301-4215(96)00017-1.

[23] S. Gennitsaris et al., "Energy efficiency management in small and medium-sized enterprises: Current situation, case studies and best practices," *Sustain.*, vol. 15, no. 4, pp. 1–26, 2023, doi: 10.3390/su15043727.

[24] SERPA, "Industrial energy efficiency and systems optimization sustainable energy regulation and policymaking for africa," pp. 1–86, 2009, [Online]. Available: https://www.unido.org/sites/default/files/2009-02/Module17_0.pdf.

[25] Renewable Energy & Energy Efficiency Partnership, "Energy efficiency technologies and benefits," *Int. Energy Agency*, no. April, pp. 1–29, 2012, [Online]. Available: https://africa-toolkit.reeep.org/modules/Module12.pdf.

[26] D. Maheswaran, V. Rangaraj, K. K. J. Kailas, and W. A. Kumar, "Energy efficiency in electrical systems," *PEDES 2012- IEEE Int. Conf. Power Electron. Drives Energy Syst.*, 2012, doi: 10.1109/PEDES.2012.6484460.

[27] K. Cleary and K. P. June, "Energy efficiency 101," Resources for the Future, 2020. https://media.rff.org/documents/Energy_Efficiency_101.pdf (accessed Jun. 23, 2023).

[28] J. Malinauskaite, H. Jouhara, L. Ahmad, M. Milani, L. Montorsi, and M. Venturelli, "Energy efficiency in industry: EU and national policies in Italy and the UK," *Energy*, vol. 172, no. 2019, pp. 255–269, 2019, doi: 10.1016/j.energy.2019.01.130.

[29] M. I. Staff, *J.R. Simplot company - Manitoba Inc.* Manitoba Inc., 2021. https://manitoba-inc.ca/j-r-simplot-company/ (accessed Jul. 04, 2023).

[30] Local Energy Efficiency Action Network, "Saving energy in industrial companies: Case studies of energy efficiency programs in large U.S. Industrial corporations and the role of ratepayer-funded support," 2017. www.seeaction.energy.gov.

[31] General Motors, "Our renewable energy journey," *GM Sustainability*, 2021. https://www.gm.com/stories/renewable-energy-sustainable-strategy (accessed Jul. 04, 2023).

[32] General Mills, "General mills focuses on energy efficiency, hopes to save $25M a year," *Environment plus Energy Leader*, 2022. https://www.environmentalleader.com/2022/04/general-mills-focuses-on-energy-efficiency-to-create-energy-savings/ (accessed Jul. 04, 2023).

[33] Intel, "Renewable energy technology powered by Intel," *Intel*, 2023. https://www.intel.in/content/www/in/en/energy/renewable-energy.html (accessed Jul. 04, 2023).

[34] C. Philibert, *Materials and Fuels*, Paris, 2017, International Energy Agency (IEA) Publications.

[35] K. A. Demir and H. Cicibaş, "The next industrial revolution: Industry 5.0 and discussions on industry 4.0," *Ind. 4.0 from MIS Perspect.*, no. February, pp. 247–260, 2019.

[36] B. Liu, J. R. Lund, S. Liao, X. Jin, L. Liu, and C. Cheng, "Optimal power peak shaving using hydropower to complement wind and solar power uncertainty," *Energy Convers. Manag.*, vol. 209, no. January, p. 112628, 2020, doi: 10.1016/j.enconman.2020.112628.

[37] P. Chaturvedi, "Renewable energy in india programmes and case studies," *ISECO Sci. Technol. Vis.*, vol. 1, no. May, pp. 61–64, 2005.

[38] W. Strielkowski, E. Tarkhanova, M. Tvaronavi˘, and Y. Petrenko, *"Renewable energy in the sustainable development of electrical,"* pp. 1–24, 2021.

[39] C. R. K. J and M. A. Majid, "Renewable energy for sustainable development in India: current status, future prospects, challenges, employment, and investment opportunities. *Energy, Sustain. Soc.*, vol. 10, no. 2, pp. 1–36, 2020, [Online]. Available: https://sci-hub.se/https://doi.org/10.1186/s13705-019-0232-1.

[40] B. G. Desai, "Case studies for integration of renewable energy sources in power grid - lessons for India," *Curr. Sci.*, vol. 120, no. 12, pp. 1827–1832, 2021, doi: 10.18520/cs/v120/i12/1827-1832.

[41] M. Yuan, J. Z. Thellufsen, P. Sorknæs, H. Lund, and Y. Liang, "District heating in 100% renewable energy systems: Combining industrial excess heat and heat pumps," *Energy Convers. Manag.*, vol. 244, p. 114527, 2021, doi: 10.1016/j.enconman.2021.114527.

[42] IEA, *"Overview and key findings - World energy investment 2022 - Analysis -,"* *International Energy Agency*, 2022. https://www.iea.org/reports/world-energy-investment-2023/overview-and-key-findings (accessed Jul. 03, 2023).

[43] P. A. Owusu and S. Asumadu-Sarkodie, "A review of renewable energy sources, sustainability issues and climate change mitigation," *Cogent. Eng.*, vol. 3, no. 1, 2016, doi: 10.1080/23311916.2016.1167990.

[44] U.N. ESCAP, "Low carbon green growth roadmap for Asia and the Pacific: Decentralized energy system," *Low Carbon Green Growth Roadmap Asia Pacific*, no. December, pp. 57–61, 2012.

[45] N. Good, K. A. Ellis, and P. Mancarella, "Review and classification of barriers and enablers of demand response in the smart grid," *Renew. Sustain. Energy Rev.*, vol. 72, pp. 57–72, 2017, doi: 10.1016/j.rser.2017.01.043.

[46] D. Verma, A. Shukla, and P. Jain, "COVID19: Impact on Indian power sector," *2020 5th IEEE Int. Conf. Recent Adv. Innov. Eng. ICRAIE 2020- Proceeding*, vol. 2020, pp. 24–29, 2020, doi: 10.1109/ICRAIE51050.2020.9358342.

[47] Z. Shahan, "Electric car sales increased 228.88% in 2013 (US EV & Hybrid Sales Update)," *evobsession.com*, 2014. https://evobsession.com/electric-car-sales-increased-228-88-2013/ (accessed Jun. 23, 2023).

[48] C. W. Tessum, J. D. Hill, and J. D. Marshall, "Life cycle air quality impacts of conventional and alternative light-duty transportation in the United States," *Proc. Natl. Acad. Sci. U. S. A.*, vol. 111, no. 52, pp. 18490–18495, 2014, doi: 10.1073/pnas.1406853111.

[49] ICC, "IPCC Updates for A Level Geography," 2014. https://www.metlink.org/resource/ipcc-updates-for-a-level-geography/.

[50] Connolly, D., Mathiesen, B. V., Østergaard, P. A., Möller, B., Nielsen, S., Lund, H., Persson, U., Werner, S., Grözinger, J., Boermans, T., Bosquet, M., & Trier, D, "Aalborg Universitet heat roadmap Europe 2 second pre-study for the EU27." https://vbn.aau.dk/en/publications/ (accessed Jun. 23, 2023).

[51] M. Yuan, J. Z. Thellufsen, P. Sorknæs, H. Lund, and Y. Liang, "District heating in 100% renewable energy systems: Combining industrial excess heat and heat pumps," *Energy Convers. Manag.*, vol. 244, p. 114527, 2021, doi: 10.1016/j.enconman.2021.114527.

[52] I. M. de Alegría Mancisidor, P. Díaz de Basurto Uraga, I. Martínez de Alegría Mancisidor, and P. Ruiz de Arbulo López, "European Union's renewable energy sources and energy efficiency policy review: The Spanish perspective," *Renew. Sustain. Energy Rev.*, vol. 13, no. 1, pp. 100–114, 2009, doi: 10.1016/j.rser.2007.07.003.

[53] M. Brown, "Innovative energy-efficiency policies: An international review," *Wiley Interdiscip. Rev. Energy Environ.*, vol. 4, no. 1, pp. 1–25, Jan. 2015, doi: 10.1002/WENE.125.

[54] S. Carley and T. R. Browne, "Innovative US energy policy: A review of states' policy experiences," *Wiley Interdiscip. Rev. Energy Environ.*, vol. 2, no. 5, pp. 488–506, 2013, doi: 10.1002/WENE.58.

[55] S. V. Valentine, "The socio-political economy of electricity generation in China," *Renew. Sustain. Energy Rev.*, vol. 32, pp. 416–429, 2014, doi: 10.1016/j.rser.2014.01.017.

[56] M. A. Brown and S. Zhou, "Smart-grid policies: An international review," *Wiley Interdiscip. Rev. Energy Environ.*, vol. 2, no. 2, pp. 121–139, Mar. 2013, doi: 10.1002/WENE.53.

[57] R. Bardhan, R. Debnath, and A. Jana, "Evolution of sustainable energy policies in India since 1947: A review," *Wiley Interdiscip. Rev. Energy Environ.*, vol. 8, no. 5, 2019, doi: 10.1002/WENE.340.

7 A Study of Cloud of Things Enabled Machine Learning-Based Smart Health Monitoring System

Ayontika Das and Riya Paul
Adamas University

Anindya Nag and Biva Das
Khulna University

7.1 INTRODUCTION

Patients needing medical care in rural areas can benefit from a remote health monitoring system that enables communication with doctors in cities. This system utilizes a platform that enhances the speed and efficiency of communication between patients and doctors, allowing for the monitoring of vital signs such as heart rate, ECG, blood pressure, and body temperature. By collecting this information from patients, the system transmits it to an Internet Protocol-based application for analysis [1]. To ensure quick response in emergencies, cloud machine learning is employed to identify appropriate doctors and provide them with real-time updates on a patient's medical condition. IoT is critical in facilitating the seamless sharing of vital information among various network nodes, enabling fast and accurate decision-making. Its integration into the healthcare industry has created an efficient environment for medical care, aiding in preventing life-threatening conditions like cancer and heart disease [2]. Smart healthcare monitoring systems rely on the combined utilization of IoT and Wireless sensor networks (WSNs), significantly improving the transfer and analysis of patient data for medical professionals and healthcare facilities. Regarding accuracy, (Support Vector Machine) SVM outperformed decision trees (DT), random forests (RF), and multilayer perceptrons [3]. The convergence of smart sensing devices and IoT addresses challenges faced by networks, businesses, and governments worldwide. As an innovative internet form, IoT leverages sensors, (Radio-Frequency Identification) RFID, Global Positioning System (GPS), and infrared sensors to gather data on targeted objects' physical and chemical properties [4]. WSNs have witnessed remarkable applications, interfaces, scaling, interoperability, and data processing growth. Technological advancements such as RFID and breakthroughs in wireless and cellular networks have further strengthened the IoT.

DOI: 10.1201/9781032686363-7

WSNs provide real-time monitoring of physical and environmental conditions, encompassing temperature, pressure, vibration, pollution, sound, and motion [5]. This monitoring can be conveniently conducted from a centralized location without additional infrastructure, facilitating data collection and interpretation. By connecting multiple low-power and cost-effective sensor nodes through wireless links over short distances, WSNs enable the efficient transmission of data [6]. Utilizing machine learning (ML) models, it becomes possible to predict the near-term health status of patients, assessing whether their condition is likely to deteriorate, improve, or require immediate assistance. Automating decision-making processes through modern technologies, particularly ML models and cloud computing has been proposed to monitor and control devices based on patients' health and test results [7,8]. The architecture of the IoT offers practical solutions that leverage sensors, network connections, Artificial intelligence (AI), and big data, highlighting the importance of control and performance in these systems and solutions. Conversely, cloud computing facilitates the provision of various computer services and utilities, such as servers, storage, databases, networking, software, and analytics, over the Internet. This enables the remote delivery of various services tailored to the specific requirements of end customers [9].

7.1.1 INTERNET OF THINGS (IoT)

IoT is poised to become the next major transformative trend in the realm of the Internet. It envisions a world where various objects can sense their environment, establish connections, and exchange information via a Private Internet Protocol. By interconnecting these smart devices and enabling them to collect and analyze data regularly, an intelligent network emerges capable of evaluation, planning, and decision-making. Technology is vital in delivering medical care through sensing devices and recording, displaying, and communicating critical information in the healthcare landscape. To address this need, the IoT has been introduced as an innovative solution for healthcare communication, finding applications in numerous healthcare scenarios as a catalyst for transformation [10,11].

7.1.2 CLOUD COMPUTING

Cloud computing is a web-based service that offers a diverse array of Information Technology (IT) capabilities, encompassing Platforms, Software, and Infrastructure, with a payment structure based on usage. The concept of an alternative to dedicated IT infrastructure has gained significant attention in the field of research [12]. Clients have the ability to access a network of nodes that can be scaled up or down through the utilization of cloud computing. This allows them to obtain software, platforms, and infrastructure as services. This model enables clients to utilize cloud infrastructures for data storage and application hustings, such as web servers and databases, and pay only for the resources they consume, eliminating the need for investing in physical infrastructure [13]. Virtual servers or virtual private servers allow the creation of logical servers in the cloud, which can be distributed over the internet. Major cloud services providers like AWS, Google Cloud, and Microsoft Azure offer cloud computing services, providing flexibility in choosing operating systems for cloud servers [14]. Cloud computing is a computing model that involves the distribution of resources, such as servers, storage devices, networks, and software development platforms, in a virtualized environment, allowing users to access them. Extensive research has been conducted on the utilization of this technology in educational environments. Users can leverage cloud computing, relying on service providers instead of maintaining their physical infrastructure [15]. Cloud networks handle a substantial service load, reducing the burden on local PCs during application operations. Shifting the computing workload to the cloud can help reduce hardware and software requirements. Accessing cloud computing only requires a computer and a web browser, making it highly accessible [16].

7.1.3 SMART HEALTH MONITORING SYSTEM

IoT refers to the network of interconnected physical devices, such as smartphones, tablets, and laptops, that are able to communicate and exchange data via the Internet. The technology has the potential to bring about significant changes in multiple domains of society, including but not limited to healthcare, environments, cities, transportation, and retail [17]. IoT in healthcare can significantly enhance communication and patient care, reducing costs and improving treatment outcomes, disease management, error reduction, and medication management. The monitoring system enables remote observation of multiple patient parameters simultaneously, allowing doctors to adjust medication dosages as necessary [18]. Figure 7.1 depicts a real-time IoT-based health monitoring system capable of diagnosing multiple parameters simultaneously.

Figure 7.1 depicts a block diagram of a health monitoring system that integrates various components, including Oxygen Saturation measurement, temperature monitoring, and pulse rate measurement. The system utilizes a MQTT broker hosted on an Amazon Elastic Compute Cloud-based server [19]. The Arduino board establishes a connection with a wireless router to interface with a device that is capable of detecting and recording the body temperature of a patient. The recorded data is then transmitted over Wi-Fi using the MQTT protocol [20]. Medical monitoring systems can significantly benefit hypertensive patients. Various authors have explored innovative methods, including volume oscillometers and sensor networks for continuous blood pressure and temperature measurement. Additionally, pulse wave velocity approaches offer non-invasive continuous blood pressure monitoring without calibration requirements. The average daily census method samples and quantifies the amplified signal for blood pressure estimation [21]. Changes in physiological functioning and vital signs, such as blood pressure, often indicate illnesses. Hospital doctors conduct tests to evaluate deviations from typical physiological rates, aiding in diagnosing disorders. Table 7.1 provides a description of vital signs that can be effectively monitored through the utilization of smart health monitoring systems.

Various ML algorithms can be employed to effectively identify different devices in a smart healthcare system, as outlined in Table 7.2.

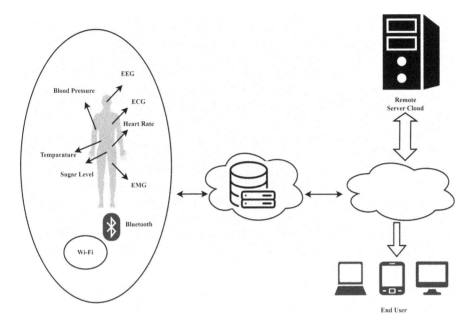

FIGURE 7.1   A health monitoring system based on IoT [18].

TABLE 7.1

Smart Health Monitoring Devices can Monitor Vital Signs [22]

Vital Sign	Description
Heart rate	The number of times your heart beats per minute.
Blood pressure	The force of blood pushing against the walls of your arteries.
Body temperature	Body's internal temperature.
Blood glucose level	The amount of sugar in your blood.
Oxygen saturation	The percentage of oxygen in your blood.
Respiratory rate	The number of times you breathe per minute.

TABLE 7.2

Applications of ML in Smart Health Monitoring Systems [23]

Application	Description
Disease diagnosis	Machine learning algorithms can be used to identify diseases by analyzing medical data.
Risk prediction	Machine learning algorithms can be used to predict the risk of developing a disease.
Treatment planning	Machine learning algorithms can be used to plan treatment for patients with chronic diseases.
Personalized medicine	Machine learning algorithms can be used to develop personalized treatment plans for patients.

7.1.3.1 IoT Integration with a Health Monitoring System

The progress made in the field of IoT and WSN has enabled the remote accessibility of medical data, thereby obviating the necessity for in-person hospital visits. The advent of cloud computing has brought about a significant transformation in the realm of processing and storage within health monitoring systems based on the IoT [24]. This paradigm shift has resulted in the establishment of robust mechanisms for the secure handling and storage of patient data in cloud-based environments. This study introduces a robust and punctual approach for the storage of sensitive health records in cloud-based systems. The utilization of IoT biosensors facilitates the surveillance of an individual's heart rate and oxygen saturation levels within their bloodstream [25]. The field of structural health monitoring (SHM) employs in situ measurements and analysis techniques to evaluate the structural integrity of civil engineering structures, thereby improving safety and minimizing maintenance expenses. The utilization of WSN as a means of data processing for SHM has superseded conventional cable systems shown in Figure 7.2 [26,27]. Sensors for are utilized to observe and

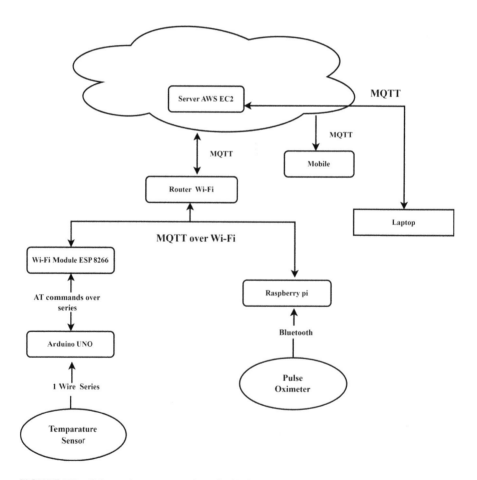

FIGURE 7.2 Schematic representation of a health monitoring system [29].

record pertinent structural information, as well as environmental variables such as humidity and temperature [28]. Figure 7.2 depicts a schematic representation of a health monitoring system, emphasizing the process of health monitoring.

The provision of sufficient healthcare is a widely acknowledged challenge that nations across the globe currently confront. Despite the substantial financial resources allocated to IT in the healthcare sector, the anticipated enhancements in patient safety and workforce efficiency have not been fully achieved [30,31]. Surprisingly, many organizations still rely on manual medical paperwork and handwritten notes for information gathering and decision-making. Digital data remains fragmented across different departments and applications, hindering the effective sharing of patient data among physicians, departments, and patients [32]. To overcome these limitations, adopting cloud computing and IoT technology in healthcare can streamline processes, allowing medical professionals to focus on delivering clinically valuable services and improving patient outcomes [33]. This integration enables timely and convenient healthcare monitoring, diagnostic tests, and treatment while reducing costs. Using technologies like RFID tags, sensors, and intelligent devices, the IoT has the potential to revolutionize healthcare in numerous ways. The system offers various advantages, including but not limited to, facilitating online patient interactions, enabling the monitoring and identification of patient and doctor locations, tracking medical reports and equipment, managing the medical supply chain, providing logistic support, facilitating drug management, and aiding in counterfeit drug detection [34–36].

IoT offers a powerful means of connecting individuals, machines, digital devices, and dynamic systems, thereby enhancing the effectiveness of healthcare and monitoring systems, medical asset monitoring, and medical waste management systems [37]. For instance, wearable bands on a patient's wrist can continuously monitor vital signs such as pulse, heart rate, red blood cell counts, glucose levels, and total cholesterol. These vital sign reports can be seamlessly transmitted to medical professionals' smartphones or tablets for real-time monitoring and analysis. Additionally, wearable bands can send reminders to patients' smartphones, prompting them to take medication, engage in physical activity, and more [38,39]. IoT can revolutionize healthcare by addressing critical aspects such as investment, privacy, security, reliability, and return on investment (ROI). However, for the healthcare industry to fully embrace IoT, several challenging research areas need to be addressed, particularly in the monitoring and analysis of patients and other healthcare actors. These challenges include [40]:

- Cases where diagnoses are missed or delayed
- Inadequate ordering of necessary tests and lack of follow-up
- Limited accessibility to patients' medical records
- Prescribing incorrect pharmaceutical medications
- Uncertainty regarding a patient's allergies to specific medications

IoT devices gather information regarding a patient's health, as seen in Figure 7.3. ML algorithms then examine this data to find patterns and trends. These trends and patterns can help in disease detection, treatment, and prevention. IoT and ML are combined in smart health monitoring systems to offer patients ongoing treatment and monitoring.

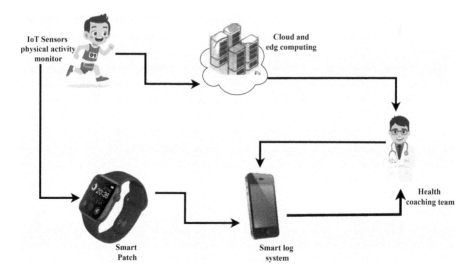

FIGURE 7.3   The intelligent health monitoring system's architecture [41].

7.1.3.2   Integration Cloud Computing Infrastructure with an Health Monitoring System

Cloud computing offers a potentially viable solution for tackling the various challenges faced by the healthcare industry [42]. Figure 7.4 illustrates the manner in which the IoT and cloud computing facilitate the accessibility of shared medical data and infrastructure by users. Cloud computing facilitates expedited deployment, enhanced resource adaptability, and decreased expenses through the utilization of internet-based mechanisms for delivering diverse computer services encompassing server deployments, database administration, networking, software applications, and data analytics [43–45]. Decentralized cloud computing has garnered significant attention due to its ability to securely and cost-effectively process data. Fog computing, a paradigm that leverages edge devices for the purpose of conducting real-time analytics, serves to augment the capabilities of cloud computing [46]. The convergence of portable devices, AI, and cloud computing has established a robust groundwork for the profound influence of the IoT within the healthcare sector. Figure 7.4 illustrates the importance of cloud-based health monitoring systems in enhancing the provision of healthcare [47].

Figure 7.4 illustrates the utilization of cloud computing in the healthcare system, wherein cloud technology is employed for the storage, management, and retrieval of healthcare data and services. Cloud computing presents a multitude of benefits in relation to scalability, flexibility, cost-efficiency, and data protection, rendering it an attractive choice for the healthcare sector.

This paper consists of four sections. Section 7.2 examines the approach used by multiple authors, including their literature reviews and the presentation of findings based on the compiled research. Section 7.3 provides a comparative analysis of the models employed by various authors in the preceding section. Finally, Section 7.4 concludes the paper.

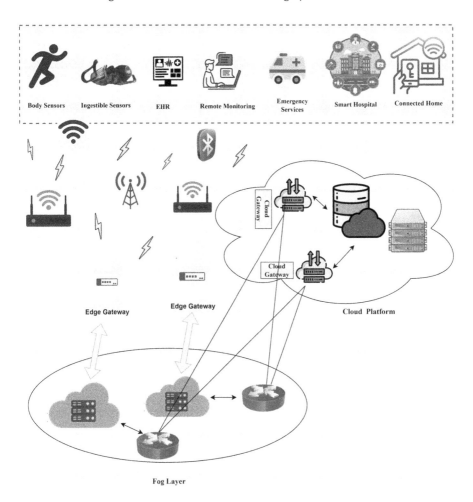

FIGURE 7.4 Cloud based healthcare system framework [48].

7.2 LITERATURE REVIEW

The subsequent part of this paper comprises of literature review. This literature review explores the existing body of literature on the subject of CoT-enabled ML-based Smart Health Monitoring Systems.

Nayak et al. [49] emphasized the importance of health as a fundamental human right that should be accessible to all. The authors emphasized the advantages of utilizing real-time cloud computing and business applications in terms of their reliability and cost-effectiveness for corporate utilization. Cloud computing provides a robust infrastructure and cost-effective pricing, rendering it a feasible choice for enterprises seeking to optimize cost and efficiency. Recent advancements in sensor communication, sensing technology, and microelectronics have mainly focused on managing chronic diseases and potential emergencies. Health monitoring can address the cost of critical challenges or the care provided to individuals. As a result, healthcare professionals can conduct electronic visits, eliminating the need for travel while maintaining seamless communication between doctors and patients. By virtually seeing each other, specialists can visually assess wounds and provide appropriate care. The authors specifically examined the utilization of IoT and cloud-based healthcare monitoring systems for home hospitalization.

Yu et al. [50] highlighted the significant influence of the IoT on enhancing health management in intelligent sports players through the integration and optimized deployment of intelligent sports resources. Utilizing cloud-based computing brought forth key advantages such as virtualization and distributed storage. The cloud also offered essential features like broadband Internet and autonomous administration; by leveraging IoT and cloud computing, a pioneering intelligent sports health monitoring system was developed, employing cutting-edge IT to support smart sports health management.

El-Aziz et al. [51] examined the importance of electronic medical records in monitoring and treating patients in emergencies. They highlighted the potential of leveraging cloud computing and data science approaches to enhance IoT-enabled healthcare monitoring systems. Accurate healthcare data collected by various IoT sensors was the Healthcare Monitoring-Data Science Technique foundation, which incorporated advanced data science techniques and technology. To improve prediction rates, the researchers introduced the Improved Pigeon Optimization method for data aggregation in the cloud. Human healthcare information was classified using the Backtracking Search-Based Deep Neural Network with an accuracy of 93.48%. The proposed system underwent final testing and was compared to other smart healthcare monitoring systems using real-time healthcare datasets.

Sahu et al. [52] focused on the analysis of cardiovascular diseases using ECG, a widely recognized and reliable tool. They explored the utilization of the IoT in developing a real-time remote ECG monitoring system deployed in the cloud. The research presented a cloud-based approach, where AWS facilitated the transmission of ECG data from the subjects to an S3 bucket for remote monitoring of cardiovascular conditions through a mobile gateway. The AWS Cloud leveraged HTTP and MQTT servers to enable data visualization, ensure quick response times and establish long-lived connections between users and devices. The proposed system incorporated filtering algorithms to eliminate distractions, external noise, and motion artifacts.

Lakshmi et al. [53] highlighted the increasing significance of healthcare monitoring systems, which have witnessed remarkable technological advancements in the past decade. Not adequate medical attention has contributed to various health issues, including unforeseen fatalities. An IoT-based solution has been developed to address this challenge. This solution facilitates the uninterrupted wireless monitoring of patients by means of a mobile application that is integrated with a GSM system. Wireless healthcare monitoring systems have the capability to transmit real-time internet data pertaining to a patient's health status. Medical professionals have the capability to consistently observe and assess the patient's essential physiological parameters, including blood pressure, temperature, oxygen saturation levels, ECG readings, and heart rate, by means of a mobile application.

Ru et al. [54] explored the practical applications of the Internet and smart sensing devices in various sectors, including public, commercial, and government organizations worldwide. Their research aimed to enhance the personalization and efficiency of health monitoring by enabling connectivity among devices. The objective of the project was to create wearable health monitoring devices with the capability to assess multiple vital indicators concurrently, including heart rate, temperature, blood pressure and pulse. A wireless sensor was utilized to gather data for the health monitoring system. Through IoT technology, real-time monitoring became possible as the data was processed, connected, and computed. The study's findings indicate that IoT-based health monitoring systems have the potential to empower individuals to manage their daily health and enhance the quality and accessibility of healthcare services.

Reddy et al. [55] explored the utilization of IoT in advancing healthcare technology to address the challenges patients face due to their busy schedules and daily responsibilities. Regular monitoring of patients' conditions, especially the elderly, becomes essential. To simplify this process, a novel system was introduced. Leveraging IoT, vital signs such as blood oxygen levels, body temperature, humidity and heart rate could be continuously monitored. The study employed sensors connected to a microcontroller to demonstrate the implementation and functionality of the patient-monitoring device. These sensors detected and captured the patient's vital signs, enabling effective monitoring and care.

Siam et al. [56] directed their attention toward healthcare professionals and patients, emphasizing the significance of smart health surveillance technology in the early detection of critical abnormalities without requiring direct patient involvement. The advent of IoT introduced the concept of multivocal signal monitoring, allowing for simultaneous monitoring of vital signs such as blood oxygen saturation, body temperature and heart rate. Before transmission to the cloud, the physiological signals underwent encryption and processing using the Advanced Encryption Standard approach. The planned system's measurement was compared to several existing medical devices available.

Tamilselvi et al. [57] focused on health monitoring for coma patients, leveraging the capabilities of IoT. The researchers aimed to improve the accessibility of monitoring for patients in a comatose state through IoT technology. Instead of relying on traditional methods, they found that GSM and IoT were better suited for assessing the patient's condition. Sophisticated sensors were employed to monitor vital signs such as temperature, pulse, eye movement, and blood oxygen saturation. Specifically, a sensor was utilized to measure parameters including peripheral capillary temperature, pulse rate, blink rate, and oxygen saturation. By leveraging a cloud server, the patient's vital statistics could be transmitted to authorized individuals' mobile phones and laptops through cellular data networks. This data could then be stored, processed, and made available for future evaluation and decision-making purposes.

Valsalan et al. [58] addressed the need for a medical surveillance IoT-based solution, particularly in epidemic situations. The healthcare sector is witnessing a surge of IoT studies driven by the Internet's transformative power. The popularity of wearable sensors and smartphones has significantly enhanced remote healthcare monitoring. IoT health monitoring has emerged as a valuable tool, enabling accurate diagnoses even when the attending physician is physically distant. The researchers described a portable monitoring device that enables real-time tracking of crucial physiological indicators, including heart rate, room temperature, and more. They proposed utilizing IoT technology to develop a remote health monitoring system granting authorized individuals' remote access to data stored on an IoT platform. This access would facilitate the diagnosis of patients' ailments using the collected data, thereby improving overall healthcare outcomes.

Paul et al. [59] assessed the use of WSNs in the field of health informatics. WSNs are frequently utilized for the purpose of monitoring individuals who are at a heightened risk of developing chronic diseases. By utilizing wireless and wearable sensors, these patients can be continuously monitored, ensuring compliance with treatment programs and providing immediate assistance in emergencies. The study proposed the adoption of fog computing to collect and process the data generated by these sensors, particularly for monitoring patients with chronic conditions. However, one of the primary challenges identified is the efficient organization and management of patients' health data during the sorting process.

Kumar et al. [60] conducted an analysis focusing on the communication between a temperature controller and a pulse oximeter sensor, which are vital areas of study. A microcontroller was utilized to collect sensor data and transmit it to an online database. This enabled real-time tracking of vital signs and other health indicators by doctors, ensuring continuous access to the data. To address security concerns, the system incorporated measures to ensure authorized access and secure transmission of collected data. Data transmission was performed over the Network and encrypted using the Msg91 standard. Access to the information was restricted to authorized users and physicians, who could log in to an HTML page. In critical situations, the controller's connected GSM module sends an alert message to the attending physician. The system proved efficient, utilizing low power, and demonstrated prompt and accurate response, making it suitable for temporary treatment.

Tyagi et al. [61] elucidated that the IoT envisions a future where objects, individuals, and services are interconnected through advanced electronic and wireless communication. This interconnectedness holds the potential for significant advancements in home automation, smart devices, healthcare IT, inventory management, and supply chain management. This article explores various implementations of the IoT and highlights their standard features and characteristics. Specifically, it delves into the applications of IoT in healthcare delivery, conducting thorough research on its role and the technical aspects that contribute to its realization. A cloud-based conceptual framework has been proposed to support the healthcare industry in implementing IoT-based healthcare solutions.

Ma et al. [62] highlighted several emerging global health challenges, including the unequal distribution of medical resources, the rise in chronic diseases, and escalating healthcare costs. To address these issues, recent advancements in IT offer potential solutions in the medical field. By integrating cutting-edge IT into healthcare systems, the complexity of these problems can be significantly reduced. This paper focuses on the comprehensive health applications system of the IoT and big data in healthcare. It provides a detailed overview of the primary health system's application landscape, system architecture, and critical technologies.

Sundhara Kumar et al. [63] proposed that the rapid development of the IoT field, coupled with advancements in sensor technology and automation, has the potential to bring about significant transformations in the medical industry. Specifically, in the context of autism spectrum disorder, which involves persistent difficulties in social communication and interaction, our framework aims to provide automated monitoring using sensor-based technology. By capturing and analyzing brain signals through sensors, our device enables continuous monitoring and tracking of individuals with autism. The collected data is subjected to analytics, and caregivers are kept informed about the status of the individuals based on the insights derived from the analysis.

Cao et al. [64] concluded that applying the fog computing model in health monitoring, particularly in persistent accident detection for stroke reduction, is highly effective. The risk of death or severe damage increases significantly for stroke patients if they experience a fall. Hence, applying fall detection systems that promptly alert medical professionals is critical in mitigating stroke risk. This study aimed to explore and develop novel fall detection algorithms and construct a real-time fall detection system using fog cloud computing, which leverages distributed analytics and edge intelligence. The proposed system involved collaboration between a server and edge devices, such as a user's smartphone, to facilitate fall detection. With the objective of building and implementing a real-time fall detection system within the fog computing paradigm, the researchers conducted research. They devised innovative fall detection algorithms utilizing cloud servers and other components.

Griebel et al. [65] examined the emerging field of healthcare cloud computing. This technology is relatively new but rapidly expanding, offering numerous possibilities for service creation, delivery, and consumption through pay-per-use models and on-demand access to abundant resources. Despite the increasing interest in cloud computing, there have been limited instances of successful healthcare cloud computing implementations. Cloud computing has often been used interchangeably with terms like virtual machines or web-based services and has yet to explore its unique benefits fully. This study aimed to explore the current state of healthcare cloud computing research and highlight the emerging trends and topics that extend beyond traditional healthcare practices.

Vongsingthong et al. [66] highlighted the transformative potential of the IoT in revolutionizing people's daily lives, similar to how the Internet brought about a paradigm shift in the 1990s. The IoT represents a system enabling new communication between people, objects, and interconnected devices. This research provides an overview of the current state of the IoT, examining its fundamental technology and delving into various domains such as logistics, transportation, healthcare, the environment, and emergency preparedness. The article explores both the benefits and drawbacks of IoT applications. Lastly, the study emphasizes the unresolved challenges of the IoT, urging further interdisciplinary research in this field.

The literature review presented in Table 7.3 summarizes various authors' works, including an overview of their methods and the results they obtained.

TABLE 7.3

An Overview of the Literature Review

Author	Technique	Outcome
Nayak et al., (2022) [49]	Real-time cloud computing	It offered increased reliability and cost-effectiveness for corporate usage, delivering a sturdy, reasonably priced infrastructure.
Yu et al., (2022) [50]	IoT & Cloud computing	A smart sports health monitoring system was being developed using it.
El-Aziz et al., (2022) [51]	Improve pigeon optimization	Its development aimed to aggregate data in the cloud for improved prediction rates.
Sahu et al., (2021) [52]	Real-time remote ECG monitoring	A demonstrated cloud-based remote cardiovascular disease monitoring solution was implemented.
Lakshmi K et al., (2021) [53]	GSM	Wireless healthcare monitoring systems take advantage of this technology, allowing patients' health conditions to be accessed in real time over the Internet.
Ru et al., (2021) [54]	Real-time monitoring	It facilitates the availability of a wireless sensor once data is processed.
Reddy et al., (2021) [55]	IoT	This technology enabled the monitoring essential indicators, including temperature, heart rate, and oxygen saturation.
Siam et al., (2021) [56]	IoT	It establishes a system for monitoring signals that are secure, portable, and capable of handling multiple voices.
Tamilselvi V et al., (2020) [57]	IoT	It is utilized to assess the condition of patients, with a sophisticated sensor tracking all their activities.
Valsalan et al., (2020) [58]	IoT	The growing popularity of wearable sensors has led to the creation of a remote health monitoring system.
Paul et al., (2018) [59]	Wireless sensor network & fog computing	It was employed for monitoring patients with chronic illnesses, where fog computing collected and processed their data.
Kumar et al., (2016) [60]	IoT	The findings of this study showed that the system can deliver timely medical interventions effectively and efficiently.
Tyagi et al., (2016) [61]	IoT & Cloud computing	The authors propose a conceptual framework based on cloud computing that can assist the healthcare sector in developing IoT-based healthcare solutions.
Ma et al., (2016) [62]	IoT & Big Data	This study highlights the comprehensive health application system that leverages IoT and big data in healthcare.

(Continued)

TABLE 7.3 (*Continued*)
An Overview of the Literature Review

Author	Technique	Outcome
Sundhara Kumar et al., (2016) [63]	IoT	Individuals diagnosed with autism will benefit from the proposed autonomous monitoring framework, incorporating sensor technology for continuous monitoring.
Cao et al., (2015) [64]	Fog computing	To demonstrate the effectiveness and efficiency of the fog computing model in health monitoring, this study employed a practical and widespread application for continuous health monitoring.
Griebel et al., (2015) [65]	Cloud computing	The aim was to explore the current status of healthcare research in cloud computing and identify emerging trends.
Vongsingthong et al., (2014) [66]	IoT	This study presented the recent advancements in the IoT, enabling novel interaction between individuals, objects, and interconnected entities.

TABLE 7.4
ML Algorithms Used in Smart Health Monitoring Systems [8,67,68]

Algorithm	Description	Advantages	Disadvantages
Decision trees (DT)	A tree-based algorithm that uses a series of decisions to classify or predict an outcome.	Easy to understand and interpret.	Can be sensitive to overfitting.
Random forests (RF)	An ensemble of decision trees that uses bagging to reduce overfitting.	More accurate than individual decision trees.	Can be computationally expensive.
Support vector machines (SVMs)	A linear classifier that finds the optimal hyperplane to separate two classes.	Good for classification and regression tasks.	Can be computationally expensive.
Neural networks	A type of ML algorithm that learns to approximate a function by adjusting its weights and biases.	Can learn complex relationships between input and output variables.	Can be computationally expensive and difficult to train.

7.3 COMPARATIVE ANALYSIS

In this section, the authors present a comparative analysis of various ML algorithms utilized in the context of smart health monitoring. Table 7.4 presents an overview of the ML algorithms employed in smart health monitoring systems, along with their respective advantages and disadvantages.

The authors conducted a comparative analysis of various models that utilize different ML algorithms and IoT devices, as employed by different authors in this particular section. Various models were developed and tested in the existing literature using classification methods such as DT, SVMs, RF, and Multi-Layer Perceptron (MLP). DT exhibited the highest accuracy of 99.1%, outperforming SVMs, RF, and MLP with 92.4%, 95.1%, and 93%, respectively. In the realm of IoT, sensors are utilized to establish a new type of Internet with an accuracy ranging from 65% to 95%, incorporating technologies such as RFID and GPS. The DT algorithm yielded the highest accuracy, with RF being the second most effective classifier for addressing this problem. Table 7.5 presents the comparative studies of various models, as shown below.

The accuracy comparison graph for the models examined in the study is depicted in Figure 7.5.

TABLE 7.5

The Comparison of Various ML Algorithms

Author	Technology	Accuracy %
M Abd El-Aziz et al., (2022) [47]	BS-DNN	93.48%
Ru et al., (2021) [50]	RFID	65%
	GPS	95%
Souri et al., (2020) [8]	MLP	93%
	SVMs	92.4%
	RF	95.1%
	DT	99.1%

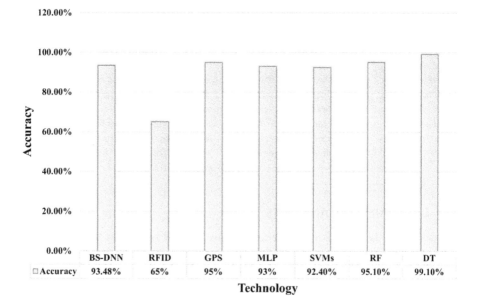

FIGURE 7.5 Accuracy plots for several ML algorithms.

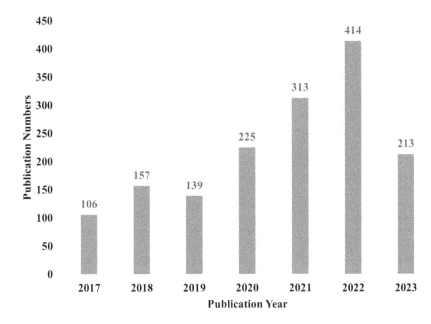

FIGURE 7.6   PubMed results for the query "smart health monitoring system".

Figure 7.6 depicts the PubMed reports pertaining to the search query "Smart health monitoring system" during the period from 2017 to 2023 (June). The data indicates an increase in research activity within the domain of "Smart health monitoring system."

7.4 CONCLUSION AND FUTURE SCOPE

This research study primarily focused on ML-based health monitoring systems that utilize the IoT. Users' vital sign data included heart rate, blood pressure, pulse, and temperature. These health monitoring systems play a crucial role in the early identification of potential health issues, thereby preventing them from escalating into severe conditions. By implementing these methods, there is a potential to reduce medical expenses and minimize the frequency of hospital and doctor visits. A comparative analysis of different models used in health monitoring systems demonstrated that DT achieved the highest accuracy of 99.1%, indicating promising outcomes in line with our objectives. The study proposed developing a secure, cost-effective, and reliable health monitoring system that leverages IoT technology and cloud computing to enable real-time monitoring of biological markers within a secure environment. Furthermore, it recommended future research to focus on long-term data collection and explore the potential of risk prediction to enhance the utilization of IoT-based human health monitoring systems. Ultimately, the goal is to prevent and manage chronic high-risk illnesses in the future effectively.

REFERENCES

[1] Jiwani, N., Gupta, K., & Whig, P. (2022). Machine learning approaches for analysis in Smart Healthcare Informatics. *Machine Learning and Artificial Intelligence in Healthcare Systems*, 129–154. https://doi.org/10.1201/9781003265436-6.

[2] Mincholé, A., Camps, J., Lyon, A., & Rodríguez, B. (2019). Machine learning in the electrocardiogram. *Journal of Electrocardiology*, 57. https://doi.org/10.1016/j.jelectrocard.2019.08.008.

[3] Gatsis, K., & Pappas, G. J. (2017). Wireless control for the IOT. *Proceedings of the Second International Conference on Internet-of-Things Design and Implementation*. https://doi.org/10.1145/3054977.3057313.

[4] Henze, M., Hermerschmidt, L., Kerpen, D., Häußling, R., Rumpe, B., & Wehrle, K. (2016). A comprehensive approach to privacy in the cloud-based internet of things. *Future Generation Computer Systems*, 56, 701–718. https://doi.org/10.1016/j.future.2015.09.016.

[5] Gnana Sheela, K., & Rose Varghese, A. (2020). Machine learning based health monitoring system. *Materials Today: Proceedings*, 24, 1788–1794. https://doi.org/10.1016/j.matpr.2020.03.603.

[6] Lv, Z., Yu, Z., Xie, S., & Alamri, A. (2022). Deep learning-based smart predictive evaluation for interactive multimedia-enabled smart healthcare. *ACM Transactions on Multimedia Computing, Communications, and Applications*, 18(1s), 1–20. https://doi.org/10.1145/3468506.

[7] Bhardwaj, V., Joshi, R., & Gaur, A. M. (2022). IOT-based smart health monitoring system for covid-19. *SN Computer Science*, 3(2). https://doi.org/10.1007/s42979-022-01015-1.

[8] Souri, A., Ghafour, M. Y., Ahmed, A. M., Safara, F., Yamini, A., & Hoseyninezhad, M. (2020). A new machine learning-based healthcare monitoring model for student's condition diagnosis in internet of things environment. *Soft Computing*, 24(22), 17111–17121. https://doi.org/10.1007/s00500-020-05003-6.

[9] Pundir, M., &; Sandhu, J. K. (2021). A systematic review of quality of service in wireless sensor networks using machine learning: Recent trend and future vision. *Journal of Network and Computer Applications*, 188, 103084. https://doi.org/10.1016/j.jnca.2021.103084.

[10] Sabbir, Md., Tushar, A. B., Iqbal, F. R., Ananda, S. G., Hassan, N., & Ahona, S. R. (2021). Web-based health monitoring system and textual mining. *International Journal of Advanced Trends in Computer Science and Engineering*, 10(5), 2991–3003. https://doi.org/10.30534/ijatcse/2021/101052021.

[11] Herasevich, V., Pickering, B. W., Clemmer, T. P., & Mark, R. G. (2021). Patient monitoring systems. *Biomedical Informatics*, 693–732. https://doi.org/10.1007/978-3-030-58721-5_21.

[12] Gia, T. N., Jiang, M., Rahmani, A.-M., Westerlund, T., Liljeberg, P., & Tenhunen, H. (2015). Fog computing in healthcare internet of things: A case study on ECG feature extraction. *2015 IEEE International Conference on Computer and Information Technology; Ubiquitous Computing and Communications; Dependable, Autonomic and Secure Computing; Pervasive Intelligence and Computing*. https://doi.org/10.1109/cit/iucc/dasc/picom.2015.51.

[13] Sujith, A. V. L. N., Sajja, G. S., Mahalakshmi, V., Nuhmani, S., & Prasanalakshmi, B. (2022). Systematic review of smart health monitoring using deep learning and artificial intelligence. *Neuroscience Informatics*, 2(3), 100028. https://doi.org/10.1016/j.neuri.2021.100028.

[14] Neloy, A. A., Alam, S., Bindu, R. A., & Moni, N. J. (2019). Machine learning based health prediction system using IBM cloud as paas. *2019 3rd International Conference on Trends in Electronics and Informatics (ICOEI)*. https://doi.org/10.1109/icoei.2019.8862754.

[15] Alnaim, A. K., & Alwakeel, A. M. (2023). Machine-learning-based IOT-edge computing healthcare solutions. *Electronics*, 12(4), 1027. https://doi.org/10.3390/electronics12041027.

[16] Zhang, H., Guo, F., Ji, H., & Zhu, C. (2017). Combinational auction-based service provider selection in mobile edge computing networks. *IEEE Access*, 5, 13455–13464. https://doi.org/10.1109/access.2017.2721957.

[17] Canedo, J., & Skjellum, A. (2016). Using machine learning to secure IOT Systems. *2016 14th Annual Conference on Privacy, Security and Trust (PST)*. https://doi.org/10.1109/pst.2016.7906930.

[18] Vaccari, I., Chiola, G., Aiello, M., Mongelli, M., & Cambiaso, E. (2020a). MQTTset, a new dataset for machine learning techniques on Mqtt. *Sensors*, 20(22), 6578. https://doi.org/10.3390/s20226578.

[19] Nishitha, K. R., & Vittal Bhat, M. (2021). IOT-based patient health monitoring system using STM32F103C8T6. *Advances in Renewable Energy and Electric Vehicles*, 247–260. https://doi.org/10.1007/978-981-16-1642-6_20.

[20] Nancy, A. A., Ravindran, D., Raj Vincent, P. M., Srinivasan, K., & Gutierrez Reina, D. (2022). IOT-cloud-based smart healthcare monitoring system for heart disease prediction via deep learning. *Electronics*, 11(15), 2292. https://doi.org/10.3390/electronics11152292.

[21] Moye, R. A., Mason, K., Flatt, A., Faircloth, B., Livermore, J., Brown, B., Furr, A., Starnes, C., Yates, J. R., & Hurt, R. (2021). Emergency preparation and mitigation for COVID-19 response in an integrated pharmacy practice model. *American Journal of Health-System Pharmacy*, 78(8), 705–711. https://doi.org/10.1093/ajhp/zxab015.

[22] Talal, M., Zaidan, A. A., Zaidan, B. B., Albahri, A. S., Alamoodi, A. H., Albahri, O. S., Alsalem, M. A., Lim, C. K., Tan, K. L., Shir, W. L., & Mohammed, K. I. (2019). Smart home-based IOT for real-time and secure remote health monitoring of triage and priority system using body sensors: Multi-driven Systematic Review. *Journal of Medical Systems*, 43(3). https://doi.org/10.1007/s10916-019-1158-z.

[23] Gondalia, A., Dixit, D., Parashar, S., Raghava, V., Sengupta, A., & Sarobin, V. R. (2018). IOT-based healthcare monitoring system for war soldiers using machine learning. *Procedia Computer Science*, 133, 1005–1013. https://doi.org/10.1016/j.procs.2018.07.075.

[24] Siam, A. I., Abou Elazm, A., El-Bahnasawy, N. A., El Banby, G., & Fathi E. Abd El-Samie, F. E. (2019). Smart health monitoring system based on IOT and cloud computing. *Menoufia Journal of Electronic Engineering Research*, 28(1), 37–42. https://doi.org/10.21608/mjeer.2019.76711.

[25] Nag, A., Das, A., Sil, R., Kar, A., Mandal, D., & Das, B. (2023). Application of artificial intelligence in mental health. *Intelligent Systems Design and Applications*, 128–141. https://doi.org/10.1007/978-3-031-27440-4_13.

[26] Avci, O., Abdeljaber, O., Kiranyaz, S., Hussein, M., &; Inman, D. J. (2018). Wireless and real-time structural damage detection: A novel decentralized method for wireless sensor networks. *Journal of Sound and Vibration*, 424, 158–172. https://doi.org/10.1016/j.jsv.2018.03.008.

[27] Abdulkarem, M., Samsudin, K., Rokhani, F. Z., &; A Rasid, M. F. (2019). Wireless sensor network for structural health monitoring: A contemporary review of technologies, challenges, and future direction. *Structural Health Monitoring*, 19(3), 693–735. https://doi.org/10.1177/1475921719854528.

[28] Mostafa, B. S., Miry, A. H., & Salman, T. M. (2022). Smart health monitoring and self-analysis system based on internet of things with fuzzy controller. *3rd International Scientific Conference of Alkafeel University (ISCKU 2021)*. https://doi.org/10.1063/5.0067991.

[29] Das, A., Nayeem, Z., Faysal, A. S., Himu, F. H., & Siam, T. R. (2021). Health Monitoring IOT device with risk prediction using cloud computing and machine learning. *2021 National Computing Colleges Conference (NCCC)*. https://doi.org/10.1109/nccc49330.2021.9428798.

[30] Anisha, P. R., Reddy, C. K., Nguyen, N. G., Bhushan, M., Kumar, A., & Mohd Hanafiah, M. (2022). Intelligent Systems and Machine Learning for Industry. https://doi.org/10.1201/9781003286745.

[31] Mala, D. J. (2022). Machine learning-based intelligent assistant for smart healthcare. *Machine Learning and Artificial Intelligence in Healthcare Systems*, 265–286. https://doi.org/10.1201/9781003265436-12.

[32] Desai, F., Chowdhury, D., Kaur, R., Peeters, M., Arya, R. C., Wander, G. S., Gill, S. S., & Buyya, R. (2022). HealthCloud: A system for monitoring health status of heart patients using machine learning and cloud computing. *Internet of Things*, 17, 100485. https://doi.org/10.1016/j.iot.2021.100485.

[33] Anand, L. V., Kotha, M. K., Kannan, N. S., Kumar, S., Meera, M. R., Shawl, R. Q., & Ray, A. P. (2020). Withdrawn: Design and development of IOT based health monitoring system for military applications. *Materials Today: Proceedings*. https://doi.org/10.1016/j.matpr.2020.10.767.

[34] Krishna, C. S., & Sampath, N. (2017). Healthcare monitoring system based on IOT. *2017 2nd International Conference on Computational Systems and Information Technology for Sustainable Solution (CSITSS)*. https://doi.org/10.1109/csitss.2017.8447861.

[35] González-Martínez, J. A., Bote-Lorenzo, M. L., Gómez-Sánchez, E., & Cano-Parra, R. (2015). Cloud computing and education: A state-of-the-art survey. *Computers & Education*, 80, 132–151. https://doi.org/10.1016/j.compedu.2014.08.017.

[36] B. de Matos, F., Rego, P., & Trinta, F. (2021). An empirical study about the adoption of multi-language technique in computation offloading in a mobile cloud computing scenario. *Proceedings of the 11th International Conference on Cloud Computing and Services Science*. https://doi.org/10.5220/0010437802070214.

[37] Chauhan, S., Pahwa, K., & Ahmed, S. (2022). Telemedical and remote healthcare monitoring using IOT and machine learning. *Computational Intelligence in Healthcare*, 47–66. https://doi.org/10.1201/9781003305347-3.

[38] Srivastava, P., & Khan, R. (2018). A review paper on cloud computing. *International Journal of Advanced Research in Computer Science and Software Engineering*, 8(6), 17. https://doi.org/10.23956/ijarcsse.v8i6.711.

[39] Jayswal, R., Gupta, R., & Gupta, K. K. (2017). Patient health monitoring system based on internet of things. *2017 Fourth International Conference on Image Information Processing (ICIIP)*. https://doi.org/10.1109/iciip.2017.8313762.

[40] Xu, B., Xu, L., Cai, H., Jiang, L., Luo, Y., & Gu, Y. (2015). The design of an M-health monitoring system based on a cloud computing platform. *Enterprise Information Systems*, 11(1), 17–36. https://doi.org/10.1080/17517575.2015.1053416.

[41] Tahir, A., Chen, F., Khan, H. U., Ming, Z., Ahmad, A., Nazir, S., & Shafiq, M. (2020). A systematic review on cloud storage mechanisms concerning e-healthcare systems. *Sensors*, 20(18), 5392. https://doi.org/10.3390/s20185392.

[42] Mohammed, J., Lung, C.-H., Ocneanu, A., Thakral, A., Jones, C., & Adler, A. (2014). Internet of things: Remote patient monitoring using web services and cloud computing. *2014 IEEE International Conference on Internet of Things(iThings), and IEEE Green Computing and Communications (GreenCom) and IEEE Cyber, Physical and Social Computing (CPSCom)*. https://doi.org/10.1109/ithings.2014.45.

[43] Krishnan, S., Lokesh, S., & Ramya Devi, M. (2019). An efficient Elman neural network classifier with cloud supported internet of things structure for health monitoring system. *Computer Networks*, 151, 201–210. https://doi.org/10.1016/j.comnet.2019.01.034.

[44] Stone, D., Michalkova, L., & Machova, V. (2022). Machine and deep learning techniques, body sensor networks, and internet of things-based smart healthcare systems in COVID-19 remote patient monitoring. *American Journal of Medical Research*, 9(1), 97. https://doi.org/10.22381/ajmr9120227.

[45] Wan, J., A. A. H. Al-awlaqi, M., Li, M., O'Grady, M., Gu, X., Wang, J., & Cao, N. (2018). Wearable IOT enabled real-time health monitoring system. *EURASIP Journal on Wireless Communications and Networking*, 2018(1). https://doi.org/10.1186/s13638-018-1308-x.

[46] Nashif, S., Raihan, Md. R., Islam, Md. R., & Imam, M. H. (2018). Heart disease detection by using machine learning algorithms and a real-time cardiovascular health monitoring system. *World Journal of Engineering and Technology*, 6(04), 854–873. https://doi.org/10.4236/wjet.2018.64057.

[47] Dang, L. M., Piran, Md. J., Han, D., Min, K., & Moon, H. (2019). A survey on internet of things and cloud computing for healthcare. *Electronics*, 8(7), 768. https://doi.org/10.3390/electronics8070768.

[48] Yu, H., Cai, Z., Xie, W., Xiao, H., Zhang, S., & Wang, F. (2022). Research on the construction of intelligent sports health management system based on internet of things and cloud computing technology. *Wireless Communications and Mobile Computing*, 2022, 1–12. https://doi.org/10.1155/2022/7133810.

[49] Nayak, M., & Barman, A. (2022). A real-time cloud-based healthcare monitoring system. *Advances in Medical Technologies and Clinical Practice*, 229–247. https://doi.org/10.4018/978-1-7998-9831-3.ch011.

[50] Yu, H., Cai, Z., Xie, W., Xiao, H., Zhang, S., & Wang, F. (2022). Research on the construction of intelligent sports health management system based on internet of things and cloud computing technology. *Wireless Communications and Mobile Computing*, 2022, 1–12. https://doi.org/10.1155/2022/7133810.

[51] Abd El-Aziz, R., Alanazi, R., R Shahin, O., Elhadad, A., Abozeid, A., I Taloba, A., & Alshalabi, R. (2022). An effective data science technique for IOT-Assisted Healthcare Monitoring System with a rapid adoption of cloud computing. *Computational Intelligence and Neuroscience*, 2022, 1–9. https://doi.org/10.1155/2022/7425846.

[52] Sahu, M. L., Atulkar, M., Ahirwal, M. K., & Ahamad, A. (2021). IOT-enabled cloud-based real-time remote ECG monitoring system. *Journal of Medical Engineering & Technology*, 45(6), 473–485. https://doi.org/10.1080/03091902.2021.1921870.

[53] Sangeethalakshmi, K., Preethi, U., & Pavithra, S. (2023). Patient health monitoring system using IOT. *Materials Today: Proceedings*, 80, 2228–2231. https://doi.org/10.1016/j.matpr.2021.06.188.

[54] Ru, L., Zhang, B., Duan, J., Ru, G., Sharma, A., Dhiman, G., Gaba, G. S., Jaha, E. S., & Masud, M. (2021). A detailed research on human health monitoring system based on internet of things. *Wireless Communications and Mobile Computing*, 2021, 1–9. https://doi.org/10.1155/2021/5592454.

[55] Reddy, D. L., Naik, M. R., & Srikar, D. (2021). Health Monitoring System based on IOT. *2021 5th International Conference on Trends in Electronics and Informatics (ICOEI)*. https://doi.org/10.1109/icoei51242.2021.9452850.

[56] Siam, A. I., Almaiah, M. A., Al-Zahrani, A., Elazm, A. A., El Banby, G. M., El-Shafai, W., El-Samie, F. E., & El-Bahnasawy, N. A. (2021). Secure health monitoring communication systems based on IOT and cloud computing for medical emergency applications. *Computational Intelligence and Neuroscience*, 2021, 1–23. https://doi.org/10.1155/2021/8016525.

[57] Islam, Md. M., Mahmud, S., Muhammad, L. J., Islam, Md. R., Nooruddin, S., & Ayon, S. I. (2020). Wearable technology to assist the patients infected with novel coronavirus (COVID-19). *SN Computer Science*, 1(6). https://doi.org/10.1007/s42979-020-00335-4.

[58] Valsalan, P., Baomar, T.A.B., & Baabood, A.H.O. (2020). IOT based health monitoring system. *Journal of Critical Reviews*, 7(4). https://doi.org/10.31838/jcr.07.04.137.

[59] Paul, A., Pinjari, H., Hong, W.-H., Seo, H. C., & Rho, S. (2018). Fog computing-based IOT for Health Monitoring System. *Journal of Sensors*, 2018, 1–7. https://doi.org/10.1155/2018/1386470.

[60] A, D., Keerthana, K., Kiruthikanjali, N., Nandhini, G., & Yuvaraj, G. (2017). Secured smart healthcare monitoring system based on IOT. *SSRN Electronic Journal*. https://doi.org/10.2139/ssrn.2941100.

[61] Tyagi, S., Agarwal, A., & Maheshwari, P. (2016). A conceptual framework for IOT-based healthcare system using cloud computing. *2016 6th International Conference–Cloud System and Big Data Engineering (Confluence)*. https://doi.org/10.1109/confluence.2016.7508172.

[62] Ma, Y., Wang, Y., Yang, J., Miao, Y., & Li, W. (2017). Big health application system based on health internet of things and big data. *IEEE Access*, 5, 7885–7897. https://doi.org/10.1109/access.2016.2638449.

[63] Sundhara Kumar, K. B., & Bairavi, K. (2016). IOT based health monitoring system for autistic patients. *Proceedings of the 3rd International Symposium on Big Data and Cloud Computing Challenges (ISBCC – 16')*, 371–376. https://doi.org/10.1007/978-3-319-30348-2_32.

[64] Cao, Y., Hou, P., Brown, D., Wang, J., & Chen, S. (2015). Distributed analytics and edge intelligence. *Proceedings of the 2015 Workshop on Mobile Big Data*. https://doi.org/10.1145/2757384.2757398.

[65] Griebel, L., Prokosch, H.-U., Köpcke, F., Toddenroth, D., Christoph, J., Leb, I., Engel, I., & Sedlmayr, M. (2015). A scoping review of cloud computing in healthcare. *BMC Medical Informatics and Decision Making*, 15(1). https://doi.org/10.1186/s12911-015-0145-7.

[66] Minoli, D., & Occhiogrosso, B. (2018). Internet of things applications for smart cities. *Internet of Things A to Z*, 319–358. https://doi.org/10.1002/9781119456735.ch12.

[67] Chakraborty, A., Adhikary, S., Ghosh, A., & Paul, P. S. (2022). Application of machine intelligence in IOT-enabled healthcare monitoring systems: A case study-based approach. *Smart and Secure Internet of Healthcare Things*, 49–70. https://doi.org/10.1201/9781003239895-4.

[68] Raja, G. B. (2022). Deep learning algorithms for real-time healthcare monitoring systems. *Convergence of Deep Learning and Artificial Intelligence in Internet of Things*, 1–18. https://doi.org/10.1201/9781003355960-1.

8 Lung Cancer Classification Using CNN
Addressing Class Imbalance and Model Performance Analysis

Dr L K Suresh Kumar and Dr Humera Shaziya
Osmania University

Ms Raniah Zaheer
University of Najran

8.1 INTRODUCTION

Lung cancer detection and classification performed automatically on the CT images facilitate its early detection. The selected lung cancer dataset namely, Iraq-Oncology Teaching Hospital/National Center for Cancer Diseases (IQ-OTH/NCCD) [1] has three classes benign, malignant and normal. The proposed work, Lung Cancer Classification (LCC) model has been developed to process IQ-OTH dataset to address three-class classification. The LCC model is based on deep learning and convolutional neural network. The dataset is imbalanced, therefore it is processed with SMOTE [2], a technique for oversampling the minority class by generating synthetic images of the minority class to equalize the count of all of the classes in the dataset. Weighted class score technique is also used to address the class imbalance problem, wherein minority class would be assigned a higher weight compared to majority class thus giving more weightage to the minority class. Data augmentation [3] has also been applied to the dataset for addressing the class imbalance issue prior to providing it as input to the LCC model.

This chapter also aims to compare the developed model with the pretrained models as transfer learning has been implemented by several research publications to leverage the pretrained models. Pretrained models are the huge models that have been rigorously designed, developed and trained to recognize millions of non-medical images. The present work intends to harness the pretrained models available to perform the detection and classification of lung cancer on medical images. The most popular ones have been selected and the same dataset has been leveraged on the chosen pretrained models. The models investigated are MobileNetV2 [4], InceptionV3

DOI: 10.1201/9781032686363-8

[5], Xception [6], ensemble of the previous three models, VGG16 [7], ResNet50V2 [8], VGG19 [7] and ensemble of VGG16 and ResNet50V2. The LCC model performed better than all the chosen pretrained models.

The focus of this work is to address multiclass classification problem to categorize lung CT images into benign, malignant and normal types. Given a lung CT image, the accuracy, sensitivity and specificity with which the CT image is classified into benign, malignant and normal types is to be maximized. The contributions made in this chapter are the development of Convolutional Neural Networks (CNN) model, tuning of the pre-trained model for the purpose of LCC, hyperparameter tuning through manual and automatic methods, experimenting various train test splits ratio.

This chapter presents the proposed work LCC, the CNN based model for classifying CT images into one of the three classes, benign, malignant and normal. Section 8.2 presents the related work. Section 8.3 introduces the LCC model that has been developed to perform multiclass classification. It discusses about the model architecture, hyperparameter tuning, parameter computations and examines the techniques for handling class imbalanced dataset. It further describes pretrained models and the uses of transfer learning. Results are presented and discussed in Section 8.4. Along with the results, dataset and its split are described followed by the explanation of the results obtained. The automatic methods experimented are random, hyperband and Bayesian. Also callbacks were explored to determine the automatic stopping of training when there was no improvement in the results. The number of epochs, convolutional layers, number of filters has been manual tuned and results are observed. Various train-test splits also have been investigated. Finally, conclusion is presented in Section 8.6.

8.2   RELATED WORK

The work [9] discusses how Principal Component Analysis (PCA) is combined with Synthetic Minority Oversampling Technique (SMOTE) to obtain better prediction for the lung cancer. The first step is to apply dimensionality reduction technique PCA on the dataset to eliminate irrelevant features followed by sampling of minority class instances to bring the balance among the class distributions. Finally, the third step applies naive Bayes method to classify the data into lung cancer or non-cancer. The precision is measured by retaining all the features and its value is 65% but when PCA was applied to remove non-essential features, the precision obtained was 50%. Subsequent application of SMOTE technique resulted in an increase of the precision to 73%.

In another work [10], the authors have investigated the combination of Support Vector Machine (SVM) with Random Undersampling (RU) and SMOTE to handle class imbalance problem. The combination of two samplings has shown improvement over the usage of single sampling method. The output is subsequently classified through SVM and had achieved an accuracy of 92.94% for the detection of lung nodules.

A fusion technique presented in [11] examined the integration of feature selection and oversampling along with corresponding scores. Lung cancer dataset of 94 images was considered for simulation with 74 negative and 20 positive patients indicates the imbalanced dataset. To accomplish the task of balancing the classes, SMOTE method applied followed by the application of best first feature selection technique and finally a fusion of 35 Quantitative Image (QI) features and Clinical and Biological markings (CB) were integrated to predict the lung cancer. Area Under Receiver Operating Characteristics Curve (AUROC) was measured for the purpose of prediction. Through K-fold cross validation method, AUROC score observed as 71.6% and improved to 85.9%. The accuracy achieved through this fusion approach is 89.4%. The authors concluded that the SMOTE sampling technique combined with fusion feature selection of QI and CB resulted in better performance.

Deep learning approach for the detection of lung cancer is introduced in [12]. The study focused on extracting the features of lung images through ResNet pretrained model integrated with UNet model. The feature set has been obtained from the images by combining both UNet and ResNet models. The obtained features are provided as input to two classifiers XGBoost (Extreme Gradient Boosting) and Random Forest. Further, the output of these models is ensembled to generate the prediction of whether an image is cancerous or non-cancerous with 84% accuracy.

In [13] authors have experimented only on the AlexNet pretrained model. There are three variants, AlexNet combined with each SVM, deepkNN, and softmax that have been demonstrated. The accuracy for AlexNet with SVM is 98.62%, AlexNet with deepkNN is 97.75% and AlexNet with softmax is 99.52%. Furthermore, the recall or sensitivity is 86.45%, 84.12%, and 88.26%, respectively, for AlexNet+SVM, AlexNet+deepkNN, AlexNet+softmax.

The work presented in [14] has elaborately described about the issue of class imbalanced dataset and the strategies to deal with it. The paper implemented seven class balancing techniques—SMOTE, SVM-SMOTE, SMOTEEN, SMOTETOMEK, ADASYN, Undersampling, Random oversampling. Six machine learning techniques have been chosen—Artificial Neural Networks, SVM, k-Nearest Neighbor, Decision Tree, and Logistic Regression for the prediction of disease over five different clinical datasets namely BCD, ILPD, CKD, CHD and Pima Indians Diabetes. The results obtained indicate that SMOTEEN with KNN showed an improvement in the accuracy by 3% for BCD dataset when compared to classification on original dataset without any class balancing technique.

This chapter [16] discusses about cancer data pre-processing. It emphasizes on the data preprocessing to reduce the impact of data artifacts, validate statistical assumptions, transforms the data to match these assumptions and standardize the location of disease regions across different subjects. It further talks about different cancer types, and concludes by emphasizing the significance of data quality in cancer research.

Authors in chapter [17] appreciate the advantages of deep learning in the direct generation of high level feature representations from raw images; however the black box nature of deep learning raises the concerns about the explainability. The most crucial characteristics are trust and confidence in the clinical implementations. The results of deep learning are compared with the findings of the clinicians and the outcome is promising that highlights the potential of deep learning in aiding medical practitioners.

In [18], a multi-modal image fusion technique for lung cancer diagnosis by combining CT and PET images is presented. The approach decomposes the images into their constituent parts followed by merging the low and high frequency bands executed on Inception V3 architecture. It creates a weight map that integrates pixel data from the images. The fusion images are obtained through the inverse dual tree complex wavelet transform (DTCWT) of the fused coefficient. Deep EfficientNet is employed to extract features from the fused image. The proposed classifier achieves an AUC of 92.34%.

This book [19] explores the concepts and challenges associated with utilizing the Internet of Things (IoT), intelligent systems, machine intelligence systems, and data analytics in various industrial sectors.

8.3 INTRODUCTION TO LCC MODEL

The LCC model has been developed to classify the CT images into three classes namely Benign, Malignant and Normal. The model has been trained with the original dataset and also with the modified versions of the same dataset to deal with class imbalance issue. The strategies applied are SMOTE, weighted class and data augmentation to handle the class imbalance. The dataset [1] selected for the study of the LCC model is having three classes with different number of samples in each class, therefore SMOTE sampling method and data augmentation technique have been applied on the original dataset to balance the data samples. The steps for the proposed work are shown in the flow chart below in Figure 8.1

There are four scenarios that have been implemented in LCC model. The numbers (1, 2, 3, and 4) indicated in the flowchart are mapped to the following list items

1. **LCC with Original Data:** LCC model validated with original data without any class balancing techniques
2. **LCC with SMOTED Data:** LCC model validated after the applications of SMOTE class balancing technique on the dataset
3. **LCC with Class Weights:** LCC model validated by assigning class weights to accomplish class balancing approach
4. **LCC with data Augmentation:** LCC model validated with the dataset has been augmented

The process in the flowchart begins by processing the original dataset. In order to balance the number of instances in each class, SMOTE and DA is applied on the dataset. Further, the LCC model is created, hyperparameters are tuned and the dataset is divided into training and testing sets. Subsequently the LCC model has been trained and validated with original imbalanced dataset followed by training with smoted and augmented datasets and eventually by specifying the class weights. Additionally, pretrained models are trained again by freezing all the preceding layers and adding the last layer with the details of lung cancer CT image dataset. The performance the developed model and pretrained models are compared by measuring the accuracy, sensitivity, and specificity metrics. The results are compared with the existing literature. In addition to the development of LCC model, evaluation of the pretrained models on medical data, the investigation has been made on several significant hyperparameters and techniques of convolutional

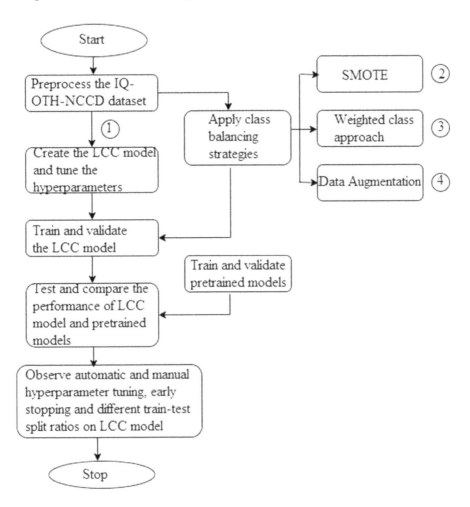

FIGURE 8.1   Flow chart for the LCC model.

neural network model. The following are the tasks that have been taken up to observe the variations in the results.

- **Automatic Hyperparameter Tuning:** Three methods, (a) Random Search (b) Hyperband and (c) Bayesian have been experimented on the lung cancer original imbalanced dataset.
- **Manual Hyperparameter Tuning:** Twelve various configurations of convolutional layers, number of filters and epochs are specified and evaluated with the same dataset as above.
- **Early Stopping:** The training process can be stopped early when there is no improvement in the prediction accuracy. Callback methods have been leveraged to check for how many epochs the training process stops.
- **Train-Test Splits:** The model is evaluated by specifying varying train test splits to determine its impact on the results.

8.3.1 ARCHITECTURE OF LCC MODEL

The architecture comprises of first convolutional input layer with relu activation and maxpool operation and the second convolutional layer having relu and maxpool operations. Subsequently there is a flatten layer to convert the feature map into a vector to be given as input to the dense (fully connected) layers. There are two dense layers and a softmax function to finally perform the classification task.

Figure 8.2 shows the architecture developed to classify the lung images into benign, malignant and normal.

Figure 8.3 presents the LCC model flow. The process begins by defining the convolutional input layer followed by specifying activation function and pooling operations. Subsequent definition of second convolutional layer along with its activation layer and pooling operation. The output of the convolutional layer is called the activations which have two-dimensional values. These have to be transformed into 1D form to be given as input to dense layers which actually perform the classification task through softmax function. Flatten layer does the task of converting 2D into 1D form.

8.3.2 HYPERPARAMETERS OF LCC MODEL

Hyperparameters are number of convolutional layers, number of dense nodes, stride, padding and number of filters with their respective size. Activation functions are quite significant hyperparameters for any convolutional neural network and indeed there is a huge impact of hyperparameters on the outcome of the model. The chosen hyperparameters for LCC model are two convolutional layers and two dense layers. The number of filters for both convolutional layers is 64 and their size is 3×3. The stride value is 1 and there is a 0 padding selected. The activation function for convolutional layer is relu and dense layer is softmax function. The optimization function specified during the

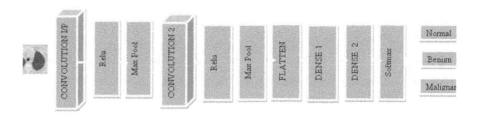

FIGURE 8.2   LCC convolutional neural networks architecture.

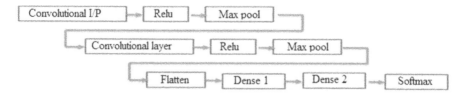

FIGURE 8.3   LCC convolutional neural networks flow.

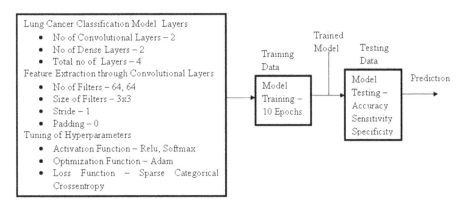

```
Lung Cancer Classification Model  Layers
  •  No of Convolutional Layers – 2
  •  No of Dense Layers – 2
  •  Total no of Layers – 4
Feature Extraction through Convolutional Layers
  •  No of Filters – 64, 64
  •  Size of Filters – 3x3
  •  Stride – 1
  •  Padding – 0
Tuning of Hyperparameters
  •  Activation Function – Relu, Softmax
  •  Optimization Function – Adam
  •  Loss  Function  –  Sparse  Categorical
     Crossentropy
```

FIGURE 8.4   Hyperparameters.

execution of convolutional neural network is adaptive moment estimation (Adam). The loss function is sparse categorical crossentropy as there are three classes and binary crossentropy cannot be used therefore categorical crossentropy has been specified. The chosen hyperparameters for the developed model are shown in Figure 8.4.

Table 8.1 elaborates the architecture description with its hyperparameters and dataset split.

Model parameters are learned by the model during its training process. The images are preprocessed to change the dimensions from 512×512 to 256×256. As there is no padding the input 256×256 is changed to 254×254. The model parameters are presented in Table 8.2.

When 64 filters of dimensions 3×3 are applied to the input, it results in the generation of 640 parameters. The formula used for the computation of parameters is (height of the filter * width of the filter * input feature map * output feature map) + number of filters. For the first convolutional layer, the application of formula is $(3*3*1*64)+64=640$. Activation and pooling layers do not learn any parameters so there are no parameters generated in these two layers. The same formula is used for all the convolutional layers for the generation of the parameters. For the second convolutional layers the generated number of parameters are 36,928 i.e. $(3*3*64*64)+64$. First dense layers parameters are 39,36,272 obtained by multiplying flattened activations of the convolutional layer by the number of nodes at the same dense layer and then adding the number of nodes i.e. $24,6016*16+16$. Three nodes are assigned to the last dense layer. There are 16 nodes in the previous dense nodes so $16*3+3=51$ parameters at the second dense layer. Total parameters generated by the LCC model are 39,73,891 or approximately 3.97 million parameters. The model parameters computations are shown in Table 8.3.

8.3.3   CLASS IMBALANCE TECHNIQUES

Several of the available medical datasets are imbalanced. Data samples belonging to distinct classes are not same in the count. When the data is not balanced, the performance of the model might not be accurate. Therefore, there is a need to equalize

TABLE 8.1
Model Layers

Lung Cancer Classification		Layers	Filters	Size	Activation
Data preprocessing and split		Conv2d	64 filters	3×3	Relu
Target class	One hot encoding	Max Pool2d	-	2×2	-
Train	70%	Conv2d	64 filters	3×3	Relu
Test	30%	Max Pool2d	-	2×2	-
-	-	Flatten	-	-	-
Lung Cancer Classification Architecture					
Architecture	Sequential	Dense	16 nodes	-	Relu
Total layers	4	Dense	3 nodes	-	Softmax
Conv layers	2	Loss	Sparse Categorical Crossentropy	-	-
Dense layers	2	Optimizer	Adam	-	-

TABLE 8.2
Model Parameters

Layer	Layer(Type)	Input Shape	Filter	Output Shape	Parameters
1	Conv2D	(256,256,1)	3×3	(254,254,64)	640
2	Activation	(254,254,64)	2×2	(254,254,64)	0
3	MaxPooling2D	(254,254,64)	NA	(127,127,64)	0
4	Conv2D_1	(127,127,64)	3×3	(125,125,64)	36928
5	MaxPooling2D_1	(125,125,64)	2×2	(62,62,64)	0
6	Flatten	(62,62,64)	NA	246016	0
7	Dense	246016	NA	16	3,936,272
8	Dense_1	16	NA	3	51
Parameter Summary					
Total Parameters				3,973,891	
Trainable Parameters				3,973,891	
Non-Trainable Parameters				0	

the number of data samples of each class. The two ways to balance the samples are oversampling and undersampling. In oversampling, the minority class is increased to match the majority class. Undersampling is to reduce the majority class samples to become equal to minority class.

8.3.3.1 Synthetic Minority Oversampling Technique (SMOTE)

SMOTE [2] is an oversampling method to create synthetic samples of minority class. Synthetic samples are created by choosing five nearest neighbors of a random data point. The differences between the feature vector of random point and its neighbors are obtained which are multiplied by a random number between 0 and 1.

TABLE 8.3
Model Parameters Computations

S.No	Name	Size	Parameters
0	Input	$256 \times 256 \times 1$	0
1	Conv2D_1	$254 \times 254 \times 64$ $((256 - 3 + (2*0))/1)$ $+ 1 = 254$	640 $(3*3*1*64)+64$
2	Activation	$254 \times 254 \times 64$	0
3	MaxPooling2D_1	$127 \times 1274 \times 64$	0
4	Conv2D_2	$125 \times 1254 \times 64$ $((127 - 3 + (2*0))/1)$ $+ 1 = 125$	36,928 $(3*3*64*64) + 64$
5	MaxPooling2D_2	$62 \times 62 \times 64$	0
6	Flatten	246016	0
7	Dense	246016*16	3,936,272
8	Dense_1	16*3	51
Total		$640 + 36,928 + 3,936,272 + 51 = 3,973,891$	
Trainable Parameters			

8.3.3.2 Weighted Class Score

Weights are assigned to each class. Higher weights are assigned to minority class and lower weights to majority class. It is a technique to assign score to the classes in the dataset.

The weights are calculated using the formula wherein the highest score is computed for the minority class and lower scores for the majority class. Therefore, the score of each class corresponds to the number of samples of that class. The formula for the calculation of class weights is shown in equation below

Class Weight (A) = Total Samples/(Total No of Classes * No of Samples of Class A)

An implementation of the equation for the total samples of 767 is shown below. The total numbers of classes are 3, samples of class 0 are 78, samples of class 1 are 390 and samples of class 2 are 299.

- $767/(3 \times 78) = 767/234 = 3.277$
- $767/(3 \times 390) = 767/1170 = 0.655$
- $767/(3 \times 299) = 767/897 = 0.855$

8.3.3.3 Data Augmentation

It is a technique to create new images from the existing images by applying various operations like rotations, shift and flip. The operations applied for the lung cancer dataset in the LCC model is horizontal and vertical flip and has augmented eight images for each one in the dataset.

8.3.4 Transfer Learning and Pretrained Model

The Training of deep learning models require extensive computational resources. It is quite time-consuming process. Imagenet large-scale visual recognition challenge (ILSVRC) was launched in 2012 with the aim to solve image recognition problems on the Imagenet dataset. The first winner, AlexNet was developed using CNN and has achieved better performance than all the other models. Therefore, CNN took the momentum and was widely investigated with a variety of features. Several models were developed and were released as pretrained models in keras library. Transfer learning is to make use of existing pretrained models on one domain and apply on either the same domain or different domains. The pretrained models can be used as it is or can be fine tuned to modify certain layers to suit the requirements of the problem to be solved. In the proposed work to perform the LCC, six pretrained models and two ensemble models are created from pretrained models. A total of eight models have been examined and investigated to figure out the validity and applicability for the medical domain.

8.3.4.1 MobileNetV2

The paper [4] presents MobileNetV2, a mobile architecture to perform operations on images for mobile devices. Apparently, it generates fewer parameters (3.5 Million) relative to other pretrained models. Depth separable convolutions with residuals are the building blocks.

8.3.4.2 InceptionV3

This model is proposed in [5]. The primary concept developed in InceptionV3 is to factorize the 7×7 convolution into three 3×3 convolutions. Label smoothing mechanism has been employed for model regularization. Experiments have been conducted on Imagenet dataset.

8.3.4.3 Xception

Xception [6] is inspired by Inception network. Xception network replaced inception modules with depthwise separable convolutions. The Xception performs slightly better than Inception as it makes the efficient use of parameters of the model.

8.3.4.4 Ensemble of MobileNetV2, InceptionV3, Xception (MIX)

MobileNetV2, InceptionV3, Xception models have been combined to form an ensemble network shown in Figure 8.5. The results obtained from the three models are fed

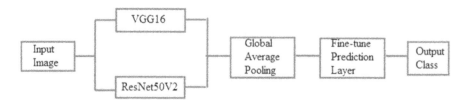

FIGURE 8.5   Ensemble of mobileNetV2, inceptionV3, xception (MIX).

to global average pooling layer, whose output is forwarded to prediction layer. The last layer has been fine tuned in terms of the number of classes. As there are three classes in the chosen dataset, softmax function generates the probabilities for three classes.

8.3.4.5 VGG16

Visual Geometry Group [7] has conducted experiments to explore the impact of the depth of convolutional layers. Developed VGG16 network with 16 layers having 3×3 filters.

8.3.4.6 ResNet50V2

The primary idea of ResNet50V2 [8] was to efficiently train a very deep CNN. Prior to ResNet50 architecture, CNNs models were moderately deep. The novel model comprising of 152 layers was evaluated on Imagenet dataset.

8.3.4.7 VGG19

VGG19 [7], a variant of VGG16 has been developed with 19 layers and 3×3 convolutional filters.

8.3.4.8 Ensemble of VGG16 and ResNet50V2 (VR)

An ensemble network of VGG16 and ResNet50V2 has been developed and is presented in Figure 8.6 to verify whether ensemble model outperforms the individual models or vice-versa. The configuration is to have both the selected model run for the chosen dataset, followed by global average pooling, fine tuning the output layer and produces the output.

8.4 RESULTS COMPARISON WITH EXISTING LITERATURE

8.4.1 Dataset

The dataset [1] with 1097 lung CT images has 120 benign, 561 malignant and 416 normal images. The dataset is imbalanced as the count of the three classes is not same. The split is made in 70% training set and 30% testing set. There are 767 training images comprising of 78, 390 and 299 benign, malignant and normal images, respectively. There are 330 testing images and the count is 42, 171 and 117 for benign, malignant and normal images, respectively. Each image size is 256×256 having single channel. Table 8.4 specifies the data samples for LCC model with imbalanced data, with smoted and augmented data, weighted class and pretrained models.

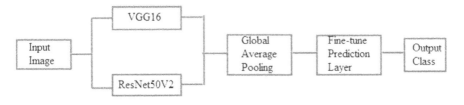

FIGURE 8.6   Ensemble of VGG16 and ResNet50V2 (VR).

TABLE 8.4
Dataset Details and Split

Model	Dataset Samples	Dataset Counter

LCC Model	X Length – 1097
	Train – 767 (767, 256, 256, 1)
	Test – 330 (330, 256, 256, 1)
		Y counts –
		  Counter({1–561,2–416,0–120})
		Train Counter
		  ({1– 390,2– 299,0– 78})
		Test
		  Counter({1– 171,2– 117,0– 42})

LCC with SMOTE	Before SMOTE
	Train Counter
	({1– 390,2– 299,0– 78})
	Test Counter
	({1– 171,2– 117,0– 42})
		After SMOTE
		Train Counter
		  ({1– 390,2– 390,0–390})
		Test
		  Counter({1– 171,2– 117,0– 42})
		767 (767,256,256,1)
		1170 (1170,256,256,1)

LCC with weighted class	X Length – 1097
	Train – 767 (767, 256, 256, 1)
	Test – 330 (330, 256, 256, 1)
		Y counts –
		  Counter({1–561,2–416,0–120})
		Train Counter
		  ({1– 390,2– 299,0– 78})
		Test
		  Counter({1– 171,2– 117,0– 42})
		Class
		  Weights{0–3.27,1–0.65,2–0.85}

LCC with data augmentation	X Length – 1097
	Train – 767 (767, 256, 256, 1)
	Test – 330 (330, 256, 256, 1)
		Y counts –
		  Counter({1–561,2–416,0–120})
		Train Counter
		  ({1– 390,2– 299,0– 78})
		Test
		  Counter({1– 171,2– 117,0– 42})
		Data Augmentation Technique–
		  horizontal_flip, vertical_flip

MobileNetV2 InceptionV3, Xception, Ensemble (MIX)	Train – 767 (767, 256, 256, 1)
	Test – 330 (330, 256, 256, 1)
		Train Counter
		  ({1– 397,2– 282,0– 88})
		Test
		  Counter({1– 164,2– 134,0– 32})

VGG16, ResNet50V2, VGG19 Ensemble (VR)	Train – 767 (767, 256, 256, 1)
	Test – 330 (330, 256, 256, 1)
		Train Counter
		  ({1– 385,2– 303,0– 79})
		Test
		  Counter({1– 176,2– 113,0– 41})

The first row of the table specifies LCC model using the original imbalanced dataset. The second row mentions LCC model with SMOTE technique applied on the dataset. Before SMOTE operation, the number of samples for each of 0, 1, 2 classes has 78, 390, 299 training images and 42, 171, 117 testing images, respectively. After the application of SMOTE, the data sample for each of 0, 1, 2 classes are 390,

390, 390 training and 42, 171, 117 testing samples. Since SMOTE is applied only to training and not to testing samples therefore the training samples would increase from 1,097 to 1,170, while the testing samples count remain the same. The third row is about class weights assigned to class 0 as 3.2777, class 1 as 0.6555 and class 2 as 0.8550 as per the ratio of the samples. The fourth row is LCC model with data augmentation. To augment the images, horizontal and vertical flip operations are applied to each image at the time of training so that the model could learn from more number of images. The fifth row specified the dataset split for MobileNetV2, InceptionV3, Xception and their ensemble, which has 88, 397, 282 images for training and 32, 164, 134 images for testing. The last row provides the dataset split for VGG16, ResNet50V2 and VGG19 and the ensemble of VGG16 and ResNet50V2 that has 79, 385, 303 training and 41, 176, 113 for testing set.

The comparison of sensitivity and specificity is shown in Table 8.5.

LCC model with imbalanced dataset achieved 100%, 97.48%, 98.59% respectively for classes 0, 1, 2. Obtained specificity values are 92.85%, 99.41%, 97.43%. MobileNetV2 achieved sensitivity of 95.97%, 96.98%, 89.28% for classes 0, 1, 2, respectively, and specificity of 31.25%, 99.39%, 88.80%. InceptionV3 obtained sensitivity of 100%, 95.18%, 95.40% for classes 0, 1, 2 respectively with their corresponding specificity values as 56.25%, 100%, 97.76%. Xception obtained sensitivity values for classes 0, 1, 2 as 96.66%, 97.59%, 93.87% and specificity values as 59.37%, 100%, 97.01%. Ensemble model has been created from three models that are MobileNetV2, InceptionV3 and Xception (MIX) has achieved sensitivity for classes 0, 1, 2 are 100%, 99.39%, 90.31% and specificity values are 43.75%, 99.39% and 100%. VGG16 got sensitivity values as 98.61%, 95.45%, 86.17% and specificity values as 26.82%, 99.43%, 91.15.%. ResNet50V2 obtained the specificity value of class 0 as 75.60% which is quite less. It gives 100% sensitivity for class 0 and 100% specificity for class 1. Respective sensitivity values for class 1, 2 are 99.35% and 95.39%. The specificity for class 2 is 99.11%. For VGG19, Class 0 has least specificity of 34.14%. Sensitivity values for classes 0, 1, 2 are 96.88%, 100%, 85.71%, specificity values are 97.72% and 92.03% for class 1 and 2 respectively. Ensemble model (VR) is created from VGG16

TABLE 8.5

Sensitivity and Specificity of LCC Model, Pretrained and Ensemble Models

Model	Sensitivity (%)			Specificity (%)		
	Class 0	Class 1	Class 2	Class 0	Class 1	Class 2
LCC model	100	97.48	98.59	92.85	99.41	97.43
MobileNetV2	95.97	96.98	89.28	31.25	99.39	88.80
InceptionV3	100	95.18	95.40	56.25	100	97.76
Xception	99.66	97.59	93.87	59.37	100	97.01
Ensemble (MIX)	100	99.39	90.31	43.75	99.39	100
VGG16	98.61	95.45	86.17	26.82	99.43	91.15
ResNet50V2	100	99.35	95.39	75.60	100	99.11
VGG19	96.88	100	85.71	34.14	97.72	92.03
Ensemble (VR)	100	99.35	91.24	53.65	100	99.11

and ResNet50V2 sensitivity of 100%, 99.35%, 91.24% and specificity of 53.65%, 100%, 99.11% for classes 0, 1, 2, respectively.

The comparison of the LCC model with that of pretrained and ensemble models is presented in Table 8.6 for validation, testing accuracy, number of parameters generated, the depth of each model and the total execution time in seconds.

LCC model achieved 98.78% validation accuracy and 98% testing accuracy. It has generated a total of 3.9 million parameters during the training process. Its depth is just four. This model and all the subsequent models have been trained for ten epochs. The first one took 10 seconds and remaining nine epochs took 2 seconds. A total of 28 seconds are taken for the training of the LCC model. LCC model with SMOTE achieved 99.39% validation accuracy and 98% test accuracy. It has generated a total of 3.9 million parameters; its depth is 4 and takes 28 seconds for training. LCC model with class weights got 99.39% validation accuracy and 98% test accuracy. It has generated a total of 3.9 million parameters; its depth is 4 and takes 28 seconds for training. LCC model with data augmentation achieved 97.87% validation accuracy and 98% test accuracy. It has generated a total of 3.9 million parameters; its depth is 4 and takes 28 seconds for training. MobileNetV2 obtained 88.48% validation accuracy and 98% test accuracy. It has produced 3.5 million parameters. The depth of the model is 105 layers and took around 63 seconds. InceptionV3 achieved 94.84% validation and 95% test accuracy. It has generated 23.9 M parameters and has 189 layers. It took a total of 60 seconds for training. Xception achieved 94.84% validation and 95% test accuracy. It has produced 22.9 million parameters, has depth of 81 layers, and took 137 seconds for training. Ensemble model has been created from three models that are MIX. It achieved 94.24% validation accuracy and 94% test

TABLE 8.6

Results Comparison of LCC Model, Pretrained Models and Ensemble Models

Model	ValAcc (%)	Test Acc (%)	Para-Meters (Million)	Depth	Total Time (Sec)
LCC model	98.78	98	3.9	4	28
LCC with SMOTE	99.39	98	3.9	4	28
LCC with weighted class	99.39	98	3.9	4	28
LCC with data augmentation	97.87	98	3.9	4	28
MobileNetV2	88.48	88	3.5	105	63
InceptionV3	94.84	95	23.9	189	60
Xception	94.84	95	22.9	81	137
Ensemble (MIX)	94.24	94	50.3	375	82
VGG16	87.57	88	138.4	16	88
ResNet50V2	96.66	97	25.6	103	148
VGG19	87.87	88	143.7	19	82
Ensemble (VR)	93.93	94	164	119	91

accuracy. It has produced 50.3 million parameters, has a depth of 375 layers, and takes 82 seconds. VGG16 model has got 87.57% validation and 88% test accuracy. It has generated 138.4 million parameters, has depth of 16 layers, and took 88 seconds. ResNet50V2 performed better than all the other pretrained models. It has achieved 96.66% validation and 97% test accuracy. It has generated 25.6 million parameters and has 103 layers and it took the longest time of 148 seconds for training. VGG19 model has obtained 87.87% validation and 88% test accuracy. It has produced 143.7 million parameters, 19 layers deep, took 82 seconds time for training. Ensemble model (VR) is created from VGG16 and ResNet50V2 which has achieved 93.93% validation and 94% test accuracy. It has produced 164 million parameters and is 119 layers deep. It took 91 seconds for training time.

Few models achieved higher testing accuracy while few others have resulted in higher validation accuracy. The models that achieved higher testing accuracy while lower validation accuracy are InceptionV3, Xception, VGG16, ResNet50V2, VGG19 and ensemble of VGG16 and ResNet50V2 having 95%, 95%, 88%, 97%, 88%, 94% testing accuracy and 94.84%, 94.84%, 87.57%, 96.66%, 87.87%, 93.93% validation accuracy, respectively. As shown in the table, there is an identical testing accuracy for the SMOTE, weighted class and data augmentation methods. While validating the model, it is found that SMOTE and weighted class approach performs better than the performance obtained from the training of the LCC model on the original imbalanced data and data augmentation method. Therefore, it can be concluded from the experiments that the results obtained from SMOTE and class weighted approaches are better than the results of the model trained with original imbalanced dataset, and model trained with augmented data.

The LCC model graph is presented in Figure 8.7a. The graphs for LCC model with class balanced data are presented in Figure 8.7b–d for SMOTE, weighted class approach, data augmentation respectively. Pretrained model graphs for MobileNetV2, InceptionV3, Xception, ensemble of the previous three models, VGG16, ResNet50V2, VGG19 and ensemble of VGG16 and ResNet50V2 are shown in Figure 8.7e–l, respectively. Graphs for pretrained models show overfitting of data and hence there is a gap between training and validation results. The LCC model does not overfit and both the training and validation results indicate smooth learning with no fluctuations and irregular peaks. Although ensemble models do not overfit but their accuracy, sensitivity and specificity are relatively less than the LCC model. Therefore, it is clear from the graphs that LCC model is learning in the right manner and does not overfit.

The paper [10] proposed SVM with RU and SMOTE technique which achieved 92.94% accuracy on the Shengjing and Beijing hospital and the LIDC datasets. The work [11] integrated SMOTE, feature selection and score fusion techniques and achieved accuracy of 89.4% on 94 early stage lung cancer patients. The authors in [12] developed ensemble of UNet, Random Forest, ResNet and XGBoost and trained it on 33 LIDC cases achieved 84% accuracy [15].

The three models are developed in [13], first one is pretrained AlexNet combined with SVM achieved 98.62% accuracy and 86.45% sensitivity. Second model is AlexNet combined with DeepkNN achieved 97.75% accuracy and 84.12% sensitivity. Third one is AlexNet with Softmax achieved 99.52% accuracy and 88.26% sensitivity. All the three models have been trained on 100 images having 50 cancerous and

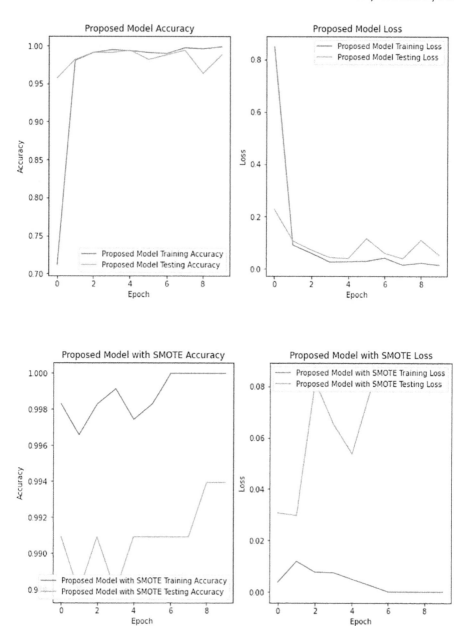

FIGURE 8.7   Lung cancer detection graphs.

(*Continued*)

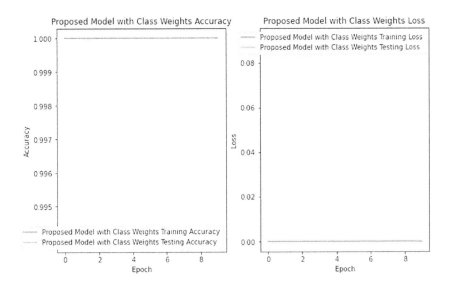

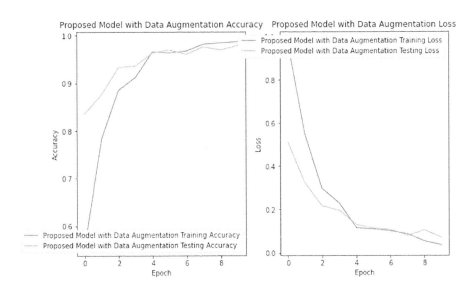

FIGURE 8.7 (*Continued*) Lung cancer detection graphs.

(*Continued*)

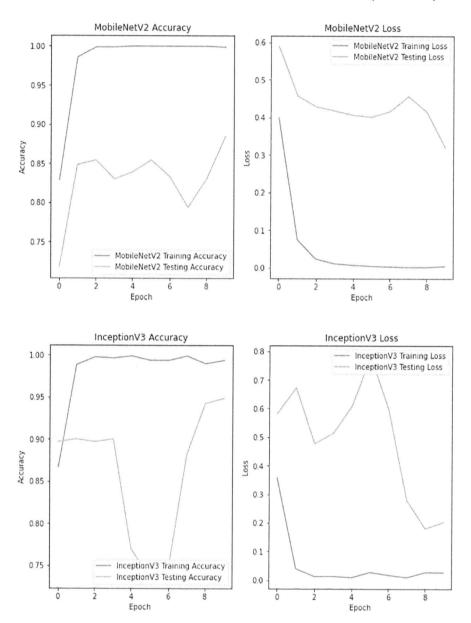

FIGURE 8.7 (*Continued*)   Lung cancer detection graphs.

(*Continued*)

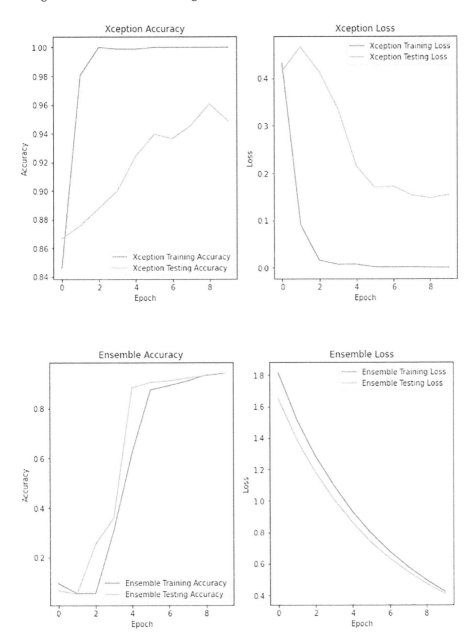

FIGURE 8.7 (*Continued*) Lung cancer detection graphs.

(*Continued*)

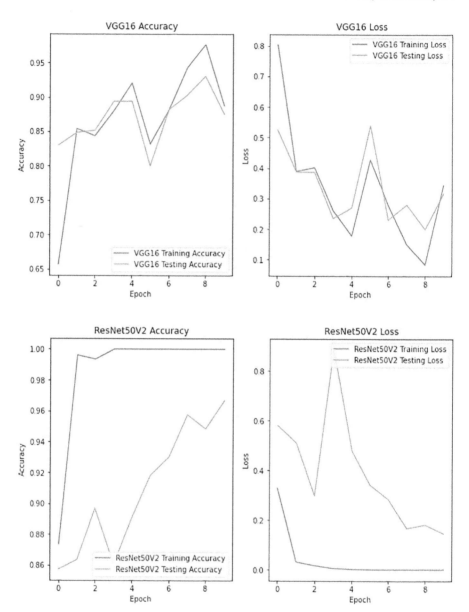

FIGURE 8.7 (*Continued*) Lung cancer detection graphs.

(*Continued*)

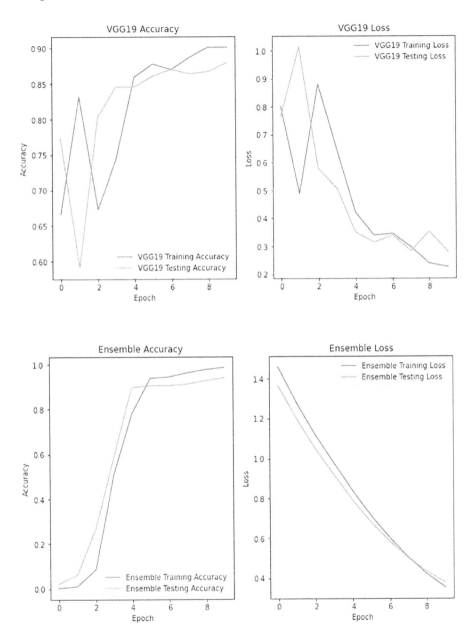

FIGURE 8.7 (*Continued*) Lung cancer detection graphs.

TABLE 8.7
Results Comparison with Existing Literature

Work	Procedure	Dataset	Results (%)
[10]	Proposed SVM with random undersampling and SMOTE	ShengJing Hospital, Beijing Xuanwu Hospital, and the LIDC	Acc – 92.94
[11]	Integrating SMOTE, feature selection and score fusion techniques	94 early stage lung cancer patients	Acc – 89.4
[12]	Ensemble of UNet + RandomForest and ResNet + XGBoost	33 cases of LIDC	Acc – 84
[13]	AlexNet + SVM	100 images having 50 cancer images and 50 normal images	Acc – 98.62 Sen – 86.45
	AlexNet + Deep kNN		Acc – 97.75 Sen – 84.12
	AlexNet + Softmax		Acc – 99.52 Sen – 88.26
LCC Model	**CNN Model**	**IQ-OTHNCCD**	**Acc – 98 Sen – 100**

50 non-cancerous. The proposed LCC model is based on CNN architecture trained on IQ-OTH dataset which has performed better than the previously described existing models and achieved accuracy of 98% and sensitivity of 100%. Although [13] achieved 99.52% accuracy but the sensitivity is low. The primary requisite of medical domain is to increase true positives and decrease false negatives which have been achieved in the LCC model. The comparison is presented in Table 8.7.

8.5 OBSERVATIONS

8.5.1 HYPERPARAMETERS TUNING

The Tuning of hyperparameters is an essential step of developing an efficient model. Hyperparameters are the values of the model supplied before the training process begins. These values can be set manually or automatically. In this work, both the approaches have been explored for the LCC task. Three automatic methods investigated are random search, hyperband tuner and Bayesian method. Early stopping through callbacks has also been examined to find out when training process will automatically stops based on the loss value. If the loss does not decrease for a 5 consecutive epochs, the training process stops. Manually modified hyperparameters are number of convolutional layers 3, 4, 5, number of filters 64, 128 and number of epochs 10, 20.

8.5.1.1 Hyperparameter Tuning – Automatic

Keras library provides hyperparameter tuners to automatically tune the values of the model. Automatic hyperparameter tuning process begins by first instantiating the tuner followed by running the built-in Tuner. The search method which runs the model with different values and eventually finds optimal values from its chosen values. Finally, print the performance of the model with the selected hyperparameter values.

Random Search: This method searches the hyperparameter space to find the optimal values. Grid search method is a predecessor to random search which explores every possible combination of hyperparameter values. Random Search is an improvement over grid search to avoid searching every possible combination and randomly pick few for experimentation. The results might not be best but close to the best in random search. After searching for the hyperparameter combinations random search method runs the entire training and validation process. This leads to wastage of time for full training and validation on badly chosen values.

Hyperband Tuner: To overcome the random search problem of running full training and validation, hyperband tuner run the training for few epochs. Based on the results obtained after running all the combinations on few epochs, the optimal one is chosen. Later the entire training and validation process is performed on the optimal hyperparameters obtained from running model few epochs.

Bayesian Method: Both the random search and hyperband tuners search for the hyperparameter combinations randomly. Bayesian method begins by choosing first few random combinations and performs the training and assess the performance. Subsequently, determines the next combination of values based on the results obtained from the first few random combinations. Therefore, Bayesian method learns from the previous combinations of the hyperparameters and choose subsequent combinations.

The three automatic hyperparameter tuning methods are compared in Table 8.8. The methods are compared on three parameters accuracy, loss and time taken for the training process.

The minimum accuracy is achieved by hyperband, maximum loss by random search and maximum time taken by hyperband. The maximum accuracy, minimum loss, and time is achieved by Bayesian tuner. Graphically the automatic hyperparameter tuning methods are shown in Figure 8.8. It is seen that Bayesian performs better than random and hyperband with respect to accuracy, loss and time.

8.5.1.1.1 Early Stopping—Callbacks

It can be considered as a regularization method in which the number of epochs for training and validation are automatically controlled. The number of epochs is chosen for the training and validation process. If the value is large, it consumes more time

TABLE 8.8
Random Search, Hyperband, Bayesian

Hyperparameter Tuning Methods	Accuracy	Loss	Time (Sec)
Random search	47.58	104.55	679
Hyperband	47.27	103.12	1554
Bayesian	**48.18**	**97.73**	**384**

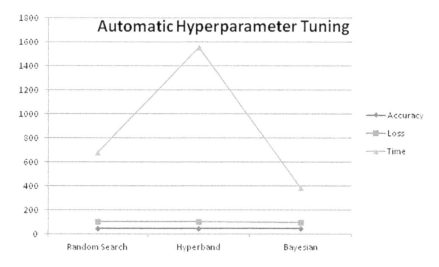

FIGURE 8.8   Comparison of the automatic hyperparameter techniques.

and might overfit and if the value is small, it might underfit. Therefore, the process of choosing hyperparameters can be automated using callbacks mechanism of keras library. This procedure of applying callbacks for choosing the number of epochs is called as early stopping.

In the method, there is a patience parameter which specifies how many epochs the model should wait before stopping the training early. When there is no improvement in the performance. The performance metrics that is monitored is 'loss'. The goal is to monitor the validation data and if the loss does not decrease for consecutive five epochs, the training process stops.

Table 8.9 shows the accuracy, sensitivity and specificity for three classes. Sen denotes sensitivity, spec denotes specificity and acc denotes accuracy. Class 0 is benign, class 1 is malignant and class 2 is normal. Among all the early stopping runs, forth run that stopped at epoch 8 performed better with respect to sensitivity and specificity of the 3 classes and accuracy. The table presents class wise sensitivity and specificity values.

The model was trained five times by specifying the upper limit of the epochs to be 20. First training process stopped after epoch 7 and gives 98% accuracy. Second time, the training process ended at epoch 13. Third one stopped at epoch 12. Both the previous cycles produced 98% accuracy. Fourth cycle took 8 epochs for training and achieved the highest accuracy of 99%.

Lastly, the fifth time the training process ended at epoch 11. Overall class wise sensitivity and specificity results indicate that eight epochs were adequate to generate better results compared to other cycles. However, it generates sub optimal value for class 0 specificity. Figure 8.9 shows the graph of five different runs of the LCC model for sensitivity and specificity related to class 0, 1, 2. The graph represent the class wise output values which show that early stopping I, II, III, and IV generated the lowest specificity output form class 0. For the other classes, the results are above 90%.

TABLE 8.9
Sensitivity, Specificity and Accuracy

Early Stopping-Epochs	Sensitivity (%)			Specificity (%)			(%)
	Class 0	Class 1	Class 2	Class 0	Class 1	Class 2	Acc
Early Stopping I -7	99.33	**100**	98.00	87.09	**100**	98.46	98
Early Stopping II – 13	99.33	99.37	97.50	83.87	**100**	97.69	98
Early Stopping III – 12	98.99	**100**	98.00	87.09	99.4	98.46	98
Early Stopping IV – 8	**100**	**100**	98	87.09	**100**	**100**	**99**
Early Stopping V – 11	99.33	90.32	**98.75**	**100**	98.5	96.92	98

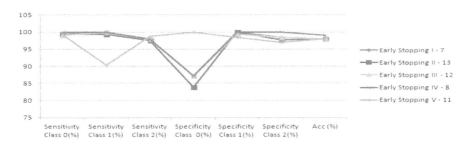

FIGURE 8.9   Early stopping.

8.5.1.2 Hyperparameter Tuning—Manual

8.5.1.2.1   Tuning—Convolutional Layers, Filters, Epochs

There are three hyperparameters that have been set manually for LCC model. They are the number of convolutional layers, filters and epochs. The chosen values for convolutional layers are 3, 4, 5, values for filters are 64, 128 and values for epochs are 10, 20. This gives a total of 12 (3*2*2) different model combinations. Each model has been assigned an acronym which has been given below.

- **C3F64E10:** Convolutional Layers 3, No of Filters 64, Epochs 10
- **C3F64E20:** Convolutional Layers 3, No of Filters 64, Epochs 20
- **C3F128E10:** Convolutional Layers 3, No of Filters 128, Epochs 10
- **C3F128E20:** Convolutional Layers 3, No of Filters 128, Epochs 20
- **C4F64E10:** Convolutional Layers 4, No of Filters 64, Epochs 10
- **C4F64E20:** Convolutional Layers 4, No of Filters 64, Epochs 20
- **C4F128E10:** Convolutional Layers 4, No of Filters 128, Epochs 10
- **C4F128E20:** Convolutional Layers 4, No of Filters 128, Epochs 20
- **C5F64E10:** Convolutional Layers 5, No of Filters 64, Epochs 10
- **C5F64E20:** Convolutional Layers 5, No of Filters 64, Epochs 20
- **C5F128E10:** Convolutional Layers 5, No of Filters 128, Epochs 10
- **C5F128E20:** Convolutional Layers 5, No of Filters 128, Epochs 20

The comparisons made among the resulting values obtained by tuning the hyperparameters manually are tabulated in Table 8.10.

TABLE 8.10

Comparison of Various Manual Configurations of Hyperparameters

Model	A	L	VA	VL	TA	Param	T
C3F64E10	**99.70**	**01.89**	**99.69**	**03.35**	**100**	996,163	20
C3F64E20	99.87	00.59	98	05.57	97.87	996,163	24
C3F128E10	99.61	04.41	98	06.56	98.18	2,139,715	31
C3F128E20	99.74	00.64	98	07.04	97.87	2,139,715	60
C4F64E10	100	00.22	96.96	15.00	97	312,195	18
C4F64E20	100	1.7e-04	98.18	06.52	98	312,195	24
C4F128E10	99.74	01.92	97.57	07.84	98	845,507	31
C4F128E20	99.87	00.54	97.87	12.59	98	845,507	61
C5F64E10	98.83	04.61	96.66	12.70	97	**185,283**	**15**
C5F64E20	99.74	01.07	97.57	08.79	98	**185,283**	26
C5F128E10	51.11	92.60	51.21	91.55	51	665,411	31
C5F128E20	99.87	00.51	94.24	23.04	94	665,411	61

Acronyms Used: **A** – Accuracy, **L** – Loss, **VA** – Validation Accuracy, **VL** – Validation Loss, **TA** – Testing Accuracy, **Param** – Parameter, **T** – Time in Seconds

The 12 models are compared on the performance metrics of accuracy, loss, validation accuracy, validation loss, testing accuracy, parameters, time in seconds. The first model with 3 convolutional layers, 64 filters and 10 epochs **C3F64E10** performed better than all the other models. The training accuracy is 99.70% and validation accuracy is 99.69% and the difference is just 0.01%. The model has achieved testing accuracy of 100%. Therefore, the most accurate hyperparameters is to have three layers of convolutions, 64 filters in each convolutional layer and training performed for ten epochs. In two other models with configurations **C4F64E10** and **C4F64E20**, 100% training accuracy is achieved however the validation accuracy is 96.96% and 98.18%. The difference between training and validation accuracy is 3.04% and 1.82% respectively. The higher the difference, the more is the overfitting. All the models except the first one show slight overfitting. Figure 8.10 is the graph of the 12 models performance. It is observed that epochs 20 took more time for training.

8.5.1.2.2 Train-Test Split Results

The training process has been conducted for several splits of training testing sets. The splits in percentages have been for 90%, 10% and 80%, 20% and 70%, 30% and 60%, 40% and 50%, 50% and 40%, 60% and 30%, 70% and 20%, 80% and 10%, 90% training testing, respectively, of each pair. Table 8.11 presents the accuracy, loss, validation accuracy, validation loss, test accuracy and time.

It is evident from the results that test accuracy and execution time are directly proportional to each other. When accuracy is high, the time taken is high too and the train set is higher than test set. Figure 8.11 depicts the graph of train-test splits performance results.

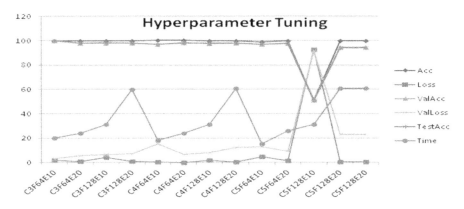

FIGURE 8.10 Manual Hyperparameter Tuning Graph.

TABLE 8.11
Train-Test Split

Split (%)	Acc	Loss	Val Acc	Val Loss	Test Acc	Time
90 – 10	99.70	01.39	100	02.24	100	27
80 – 20	99.89	00.47	97.72	08.33	98	20
70 – 30	99.61	01.45	98.18	08.73	98	20
60 – 40	99.54	02.30	96.81	07.75	97	20
50 – 50	98.91	04.12	95.44	23.74	95	13
40–60	99.77	03.00	96.05	12.61	96	12
30–70	100	00.20	94.66	17.89	95	11
20–80	100	00.02	91.00	41.93	91	11
10–90	100	00.07	79.14	123.36	79	11

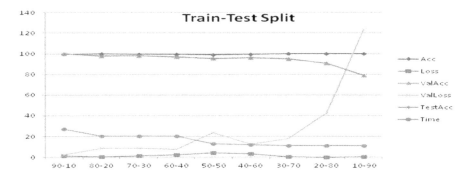

FIGURE 8.11 Train-test split results.

8.6 CONCLUSION

The CNN model called LCC has been developed. The model architecture has four layers, two convolutional and two dense layers. The IQ-OTH dataset consists of 1,097 lung CT images. It has three classes, benign (0), malignant (1) and normal (2). There are 120, 561, 416 images belonging to classes 0, 1, 2 respectively. The number of samples in corresponding to each class is not same therefore the dataset is imbalanced. The class imbalance issue is dealt with three different techniques, SMOTE, weighted class and data augmentation. During the training of LCC model, the original imbalanced dataset and balanced datasets are provided as input and the results are evaluated. SMOTE and weighted class methods performed better compared to data augmentation.

Furthermore, through transfer learning six different pretrained models have been fine tuned at their respective last layers and trained on the same dataset. An Ensemble model has also been developed from three pretrained models (MIX) and another ensemble model is developed from other two pretrained models (VR).

Finally, the comparison has been made among the prediction results of all the models. The LCC with SMOTE and weighted class approaches achieved higher results. It is also compared with existing work on the same task of LCC and outperformed the pretrained models. Lastly, hyperparameter tuning approaches, automatic and manual were explored along with callbacks. It is found out from the results that automatic hyperparameter tuning methods require more time and produce low performance whereas manual tuning gives better performance. The results obtained from early stopping indicate that there is no need to train the model for the all of the epochs, rather the training process can be automatically stopped when there is no progress made. Another observation is that different splits of train and test sets give different results. Larger train set takes more training time but yield better test accuracy and does not suffer from overfitting issue. On the other hand, larger test set takes shorter training time does not give good test results and also suffers from overfitting.

ACKNOWLEDGMENT

This work has been done under Visvesvaraya PhD Scheme for Electronics and IT (File Number: PhD-MLA-4(63)/2015–16) of Ministry of Electronics & Information Technology (MeitY), Government of India (GoI).

REFERENCES

[1] Alyasriy, Hamdalla, and A. H. Muayed. "The IQ-OTHNCCD lung cancer dataset." *Mendeley Data* 1.1 (2020): 1–13.

[2] Chawla, Nitesh V., et al. "SMOTE: Synthetic minority over-sampling technique." *Journal of artificial intelligence research* 16 (2002): 321–357.

[3] Mikołajczyk, Agnieszka, and Michał Grochowski. "Data augmentation for improving deep learning in image classification problem." *2018 International Interdisciplinary PhD Workshop (IIPhDW)*, IEEE, Swinoujscie, Poland, 2018.

[4] Sandler, Mark, et al. "Mobilenetv2: Inverted residuals and linear bottlenecks." *Proceedings of the IEEE Conference on Computer Vision and Pattern Recognition*, Salt Lake City, UT, USA, 2018.

[5] Szegedy, Christian, et al. "Rethinking the inception architecture for computer vision." *Proceedings of the IEEE Conference on Computer Vision and Pattern Recognition*, Las Vegas, NV, USA, 2016.

[6] Chollet, François. "Xception: Deep learning with depthwise separable convolutions." *Proceedings of the IEEE Conference on Computer Vision and Pattern Recognition*, Honolulu, HI, USA, 2017.

[7] Simonyan, Karen, and Andrew Zisserman. "Very deep convolutional networks for large-scale image recognition." *arXiv preprint arXiv:1409.1556* (2014).

[8] He, Kaiming, et al. "Deep residual learning for image recognition." *Proceedings of the IEEE Conference on Computer Vision and Pattern Recognition*, Las Vegas, NV, USA, 2016.

[9] Naseriparsa, Mehdi, and Mohammad Mansour Riahi Kashani. "Combination of PCA with SMOTE resampling to boost the prediction rate in lung cancer dataset." *arXiv preprint arXiv:1403.1949* (2014).

[10] Sui, Yuan, Ying Wei, and Dazhe Zhao. "Computer-aided lung nodule recognition by SVM classifier based on combination of random undersampling and SMOTE." *Computational and Mathematical Methods in Medicine* 2015 (2015).

[11] Yan, Shiju, et al. "Improving lung cancer prognosis assessment by incorporating synthetic minority oversampling technique and score fusion method." *Medical Physics* 43.6Part1 (2016): 2694–2703.

[12] Bhatia, Siddharth, Yash Sinha, and Lavika Goel. "Lung cancer detection: A deep learning approach." *Soft Computing for Problem Solving: SocProS 2017*, vol. 2. Singapore: Springer, 2019.

[13] Subramanian, R. Raja, et al. "Lung cancer prediction using deep learning framework." *International Journal of Control and Automation* 13.3 (2020): 154–160.

[14] Kumar, Vinod, et al. "Addressing binary classification over class imbalanced clinical datasets using computationally intelligent techniques." *Healthcare* 10.7 (2022).

[15] Keras Team. "Keras applications." *Keras*. io.[Online]. Available: https://keras. io/api/ applications (2019).

[16] Chaki, Jyotismita. "2 cancer data pre-processing techniques." *Current Applications of Deep Learning in Cancer Diagnostic*, Taylor and Francis, 19, 2023.

[17] Vidhya, C. S., M. Loganathan, and R. Meenatchi. "12 challenges and future scopes in current applications of deep." *Current Applications of Deep Learning in Cancer Diagnostics*, Taylor and Francis, London, 157, 2023.

[18] Nandipati, Bhagya Lakshmi, and Nagaraju Devarakonda. "Effective lung cancer diagnosis using multi-focus fusion of CT and PET images with deep learning strategies." *The Imaging Science Journal* 71 (2023): 1–17.

[19] Anisha, P. R., et al., eds. *Intelligent Systems and Machine Learning for Industry: Advancements, Challenges, and Practices*. CRC Press, New York, USA, 2022.

9 Water Quality Forecasting Using Deep Learning

A Study of the Brahmaputra Basin

P R Anisha, Rithika Badam, and
Vijaya Sindhoori Kaza
Stanley College of Engineering & Technology for Women

Poorvi Reddy Lakkadi
George Mason University School of Business

9.1 INTRODUCTION

The Brahmaputra basin covers an area of 580,000 square km, with China taking in 50.5%, India making up for 33.6%, Bangladesh accounting for 8.1%, and Bhutan for 7.8%. The distance spanned in India is 916 km (about 569.18 mi). The Indian states of West Bengal, Nagaland, Arunachal Pradesh, Meghalaya, Assam, and the whole of Sikkim are all included in the Brahmaputra basin. With a maximum length of 1,540 km on east-west and a maximum of 682 km north-south width, the basin has an asymmetrical shape. It is located between latitudes 23°N and 32°N and longitudes 82°E and 97°50'E. With a yield of 85 ha m/sq km, the Brahmaputra River is one of the greatest in the world. The enormous glacier mass just south of Konggyu Tsho Lake, a lake in the Himalayan Kailash Mountains at a height of 5,150 m, is where the Brahmaputra River originates. Subansiri, Kameng (Jiabharali), Manas, Buri-Dihing, Kopili, Sankosh, Dhansiri, Jaldhaka, Torsa, and Teesta are significant tributaries of the Brahmaputra River. The region of the Tibetan plateau inside the basin is covered in several glaciers and is between 3,000 and 5,000 m above sea level. The Brahmaputra catchment receives the most rain globally. Its hydropower potential has been estimated to reach 66,070 MW [1].

The Brahmaputra is the 15th longest river and the 9th largest by discharge in the world. Yarlung Tsangpo River is the name given to the river that originates in Tibet's Burang County, close to Mount Kailash, in the Manasarovar Lake region. The Brahmaputra is a significant river for agriculture and transportation in the area, measuring about 3,969 km (2,466 mi). Different regional languages have different names

DOI: 10.1201/9781032686363-9

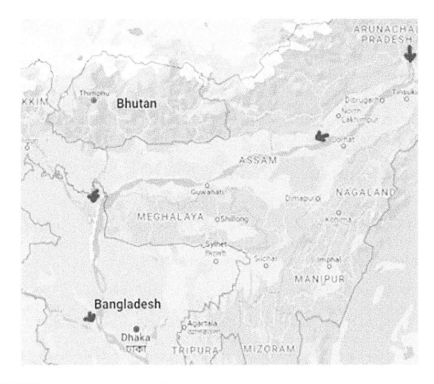

FIGURE 9.1 The Brahmaputra river basin.

for them. It is also popularly known as the crimson river of India and Tsangpo-Brahmaputra (when referring to the entire river, which includes the section that flows through the Tibet Autonomous Region) (Figure 9.1).

The river flows eastward for roughly 1,100 km (680 mi) between the Kailas Range to the north and the main Himalayan range to the south from its source. One of its tributaries, the Teesta River (or Tista), joins the Brahmaputra in Bangladesh. The basin divides into two waterways below the Tista. This river is a prime example of a braided river with a large meandering basin (651,334 km²) that frequently develops sand bars. With the uplift of the Himalayas and the growth of the Bengal foredeep, a large tectonic zone has formed in the Jamuna River. The placement of the major river systems in Bangladesh may be controlled structurally, according to theories put forth by several researchers. According to Morgan and McIntire (1959), a zone of "structural weakness" along the current course of the Ganga, Jamuna, and Padma Rivers is caused by either a deep fault or a subsiding trough. According to Scijmonsbergen (1999), these faults may induce width variations in the Jamuna and in upstream of the fracture, there has been more sedimentation [2].

One of the main factors contributing to the upper Brahmaputra catchment's snowmelt is an increase in temperature. The melting at its loftier watershed has a significant impact on the river's discharge [3]. The downstream discharge is then impacted by the river's flow. Floods and erosion are caused by the considerable increase in flow brought on by the significant retreat of snow. Considering the discharge, this river is distinguished by huge rates of discharge, high as well as erratic flows, quick channel aggradations, and quick basin denudation rates. As the Bengal Basin deepens due to erosion, the hydraulic radius will expand, allowing for a massive deposit of Himalayan ranges through effective conveyance. Brahmaputra River is essential to the survival of millions of Indian and Bangladeshi residents. 130million people are living in the delta, and more than 650,000 people reside on the riverine islands who depend on the yearly flood to replenish the floodplain soils with moisture and new sediments, which is essential for farming and aquaculture. Aus and Aman, the seasonal rice varieties, require floodwater to survive [4].

9.2   BACKGROUND

9.2.1   SIGNIFICANCE OF RIVER FLOWS OF THE BRAHMAPUTRA BASIN

Due to their ecological, socioeconomic, and geopolitical significance, the flow of the river in the Brahmaputra basin are of enormous significance. The flow of the river in the Brahmaputra basin are significant in the following ways:

a. **Ecological Importance**: Wetlands, floodplains, woodlands, and other different habitats are all supported by the Brahmaputra River and its tributaries. The ecological balance and provision of habitat for a wide range of plant and animal species depend on the river's flow. The region's total biodiversity benefits from these river flow. Apart from offering navigational aids, the Brahmaputra River is essential to maintaining the valley's flora and wildlife as well as the vegetation that supports it. During a study, the entire river system, which includes the states of Arunachal Pradesh and Assam, was subjected to a critical evaluation of the abiotic and biotic variables, their impact on the production process, fisheries structure and output, and changes through time. Rivers are "full of muscle, skin, and cartilage, which makes a clear case against pure engineering solutions," according to D'Souza. It is necessary to calculate the transaction cost between megawatts and protein. For many years, fish has been the primary protein source for people in this region and around the world [5].

b. **Agricultural Productivity**: One of the essential industries in strengthening the economy of a nation is agriculture. It significantly affects employment and food security, increasing the Gross Value Added (GVA). The Brahmaputra basin's water flows are essential for sustaining agricultural activity. Periodic flooding replenishes the rich soils in the floodplains by bringing sediments rich in nutrients. The irrigation provided by the river flows helps the area's agriculture be more productive. It encourages the growth of crops including rice, tea, and different vegetables. The agriculture industry dominates the Brahmaputra Valley's economy, contributing to more than 50% of the area's GDP and employing more than 70% of all workers. The land usage trends are observed to be stable and stagnant despite the favorable agroecological (soil-weather) conditions for agricultural expansion and growth. Studies of Land Use and Land Cover (LULC) changes are crucial for sustainable development and our relationship with the environment. But to get the most out of the riverine areas and prevent harm to the ecosystem, they must be used in the best possible way. Since the geography of the rivers is drastically changing, LULC is associated with erosion and deposition. Large rivers like the Brahmaputra experience natural erosion and sediment deposition processes that cannot be stopped. However, those who rely on agriculture and live in floodplains may find these changes to be quite important. The shape and size of the sandbars in the Brahmaputra River vary, and these vast sandbars can be used for a variety of activities. These sandbars' fertile soil offers the possibility of doing agricultural activities [6].

c. **Hydroelectric Power Generation**: The Brahmaputra River has particular significance to India for two reasons: first, the Brahmaputra Basin holds over 44% of India's total hydroelectric potential, the majority of which is yet untapped. Second, the river represents the backbone of the country's River Linking Project. The Brahmaputra River has tremendous hydroelectric potential, and the river's currents are essential for hydropower plants that produce electricity. Along the river and its tributaries, several dams and hydroelectric power plants have been built, supplying renewable energy and aiding in the region's economic growth. For the people and state governments of Northeast India, the recurrent summer floods along the Brahmaputra River and its tributaries pose a major issue. The local riverine communities have created a number of adaptation techniques to combat these destructive floods, but it is anticipated that climate change will make matters worse because melting Himalayan glaciers and modifications to the South Asian monsoon cause more severe floods to occur more frequently. In order to address India's expanding electricity needs, several more dams are being built in the Brahmaputra River basin concurrently. But despite the fact that these dams might shield populations downstream from floods, dam builders have chosen to prioritize hydroelectricity generating over flood control due to political and economic concerns. Additionally, severe energy poverty plagues Northeast India's rural areas, and hydroelectricity produced along the Brahmaputra is "evacuated" to far-off urban areas (Figure 9.2).

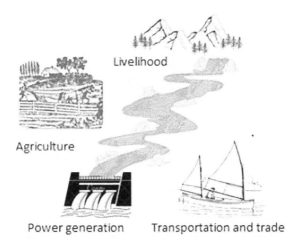

FIGURE 9.2   Significance of river flow.

d. **Transportation and Trade**: It is expected that climate change will make things worse because melting Himalayan glaciers and changes to the South Asian monsoon cause more severe floods to occur more frequently. Despite the fact that the local riverine communities have developed a number of adaptation strategies to deal with these destructive floods. To accommodate India's expanding power needs, many new dams are being built concurrently in the Brahmaputra River basin. But despite the fact that these dams might shield populations downstream from floods, dam builders have chosen to prioritize hydroelectricity generating over flood control due to political and economic concerns. Additionally, severe energy poverty exists in Northeast India's rural areas, and the hydroelectricity produced along the Brahmaputra is only distributed to far-off urban areas [7]. A crucial transit channel that promotes trade and commerce in the area is the Brahmaputra River. River flows make it possible to transport products and people, especially in distant places with poor road access. It promotes economic activities including fishing and river-based tourism as well as the transportation of goods like coal, tea, and lumber. For instance, the Siliguri Corridor connects the Northeast of India to the mainland despite being geographically distinct from the rest of India. Only through this corridor does any land trade connect the Northeast and the other regions of the nation, the huge and heavy materials needed for any industry's expansion can only be transported by rivers. Transporting goods by the river costs about half as expensive as doing so by road and about a third as expensive as doing so by rail and products are less likely to be stolen when they are transported by waterways [8].

e. **Flood Management and Water Resources**: The Basin's area's tributaries are all rain-fed and overflow with rainwater. The South West monsoon is primarily to blame for the precipitation here. Between May and September, precipitation occurs. Several flood waves occur in each of its tributaries according to the rainfall in the corresponding catchments. If the Brahmaputra and its tributary rivers flood simultaneously, it will be problematic and destructive. The management of water resources impacted by river flows in the Brahmaputra basin in both good and negative ways. Communities residing in flood-prone areas face hardships due to the recurring floods brought on by the monsoon rains. However, these floods rehydrate wetlands, replenish groundwater, and support the region's overall water balance. By using quick and short-term countermeasures such flow constriction by banks, anti-erosion techniques and river training operations, pro-siltation equipment sluices, and drainage development works, damage is as much as possible controlled [7].

The Brahmaputra basin's river flows have a major impact on a various factors, such as the region's ecology, agriculture, energy, transportation, and geopolitical dynamics. For sustainable development and the wellbeing of the inhabitants and ecosystems of the Brahmaputra basin, it is significant to comprehend and manage these fluxes [9, 10].

9.2.2 PROBLEM STATEMENT

In the Brahmaputra River basin, the prediction of water quality in all tributaries poses a significant challenge due to the lack of comprehensive and consistent data. The use of Deep Learning (DL) models, such as Long Short-Term Memory (LSTM) and Convolutional Neural Networks (CNN), aims to address this issue by analyzing the link between the parameters of water quality. The accurate prediction of these levels is crucial for assessing water contamination, evaluating water quality, implementing pollution control measures, and developing effective treatment procedures. However, the availability of fragmented and intermittent data, coupled with the complex dynamics of the river system, presents a considerable obstacle in achieving reliable and consistent forecasting capabilities. Therefore, there is a necessity to explore the potential of DL models in forecasting these levels and understanding the importance of predicting water quality, despite the challenges posed by data gaps and limited spatiotemporal coverage. This chapter details the significance of water quality forecasting while providing works studied on the same, additionally DL models like LSTM and CNN are trained for prediction of water quality of the rivers in Brahmaputra Basin.

9.3 IMPORTANCE OF WATER QUALITY FORECASTING

9.3.1 EVALUATION OF WATER QUALITY

To identify the quality and usefulness of a water body for varied reasons, such as drinking water, aquatic life support, or recreational activities, evaluating water quality requires assessing several physical, chemical, and biological factors. Below are some typical metrics and techniques for assessing water quality [11–13]:

a. **Physical Characteristics**:
   i. **Temperature**: Calculated with the aid of a thermometer to determine its impact on aquatic life and ecological functions.
   ii. **Turbidity**: A measurement of the water's cloudiness or clarity that influences light transmission and may reveal the presence of silt or pollutants.
   iii. **Color**: Determined visually or using spectrophotometry to detect any discoloration that could be brought on by pollution or naturally occurring contaminants.
b. **Chemometric Parameters**:
   i. **pH**: A pH meter is used to measure the acidity or alkalinity of water, which has an impact on aquatic life and chemical reactions.
   ii. **Dissolved Oxygen (DO)**: Used to measure the amount of oxygen available to aquatic life using an oxygen meter or a DO probe.
   iii. Analyzing nutrient concentrations is important because too much of some nutrients can lead to eutrophication and toxic algal blooms.
   iv. Testing for dangerous metals like lead, mercury, and arsenic, which can contaminate water supplies and provide health problems, is one type of heavy metals testing.

   c. **Biological Indices**:

     i. **Biotic Index**: Measuring the variety and quantity of indicator species, including macroinvertebrates, to determine the health of ecosystems and the quality of water.

     ii. **Microbial Contamination**: Checking for the presence of fecal coliforms, E. coli, or other indicator bacteria to assess the likelihood of contamination and if it is safe for drinking or other recreational activities.

   d. **Additional Parameters**:

     i. **Total Suspended Solids (TSS)**: determining the amount of suspended matter in a body of water, which can affect the movement of sediments, detail, and sunlight permeability.

     ii. The tests, Chemical Oxygen Demand (COD) and Biological Oxygen Demand (BOD), reveal the amount of oxygen required for the decomposition of organic materials, revealing the level of water pollution and the possibility of oxygen shortage.

When evaluating water quality, it is common to practice collecting water samples from various places, analyzing the samples in a lab, and then comparing the findings to specified regulatory criteria, guidelines, or thresholds. Continuous monitoring can also be accomplished by remote sensing or automated sensors [12].

9.3.2 DO LEVELS FOR WATER QUALITY ASSESSMENT

Water contamination can be indicated by the amount of dissolved oxygen (DO) when organic pollution and contaminants that consume oxygen are present. Here are a few ways that DO levels can reveal contamination [14]:

   a. **Oxygen Demand of Organic Waste**: Organic waste, such as sewage, agricultural runoff, or industrial effluents, provides food for bacteria and other microorganisms when it enters a body of water. These microorganisms deplete the water's dissolved oxygen as they eat the organic material. Consequently, a drop in DO levels may result from large quantities of organic contaminants. This drop in DO is referred to as the biochemical oxygen demand (BCOD), a measurement of the amount of oxygen required to break down organic materials. A higher load of organic pollution and contamination is observed through high BCOD readings.

   b. **Oxygen Depletion in Hypoxic Conditions**: Under some conditions, such as eutrophication or excessive algal development, aquatic plants or algae may reduce the oxygen content of the water at night or when they decay. Aquatic species may be in danger if this leads to hypoxic conditions, where the DO levels drop to dangerously low levels. With the expansion of algae and subsequent oxygen depletion, eutrophication frequently results from excessive nutrient inputs (such as nitrogen and phosphorus) from agricultural runoff or sewage.

   c. **Pollutants' Oxygen Consumption**: Some pollutants, including specific heavy metals or synthetic compounds, can devour dissolved oxygen when they enter the water. These contaminants can potentially interact with oxygen, lowering the levels of DO. The DO levels in adjacent water bodies can be impacted by industries that release chemicals that consume oxygen.

Monitoring and examining DO levels over time might yield vital knowledge regarding a water body's pollution state. Measured DO values are compared to established water quality criteria or guidelines to determine the degree of contamination, and the effect on aquatic organism health, and to forecast water quality for the next few years. Low levels of DO can point to the presence of pollution sources and assist pinpoint locations that need cleanup to improve the water's quality.

9.3.3 DO Levels for Water Quality Assessment

The levels of Dissolved oxygen contribute to water quality assessment in the following ways [15]:

1. **Protection of Public Health**: Human health is strongly impacted by water quality, especially when it comes to sources of drinking water. Accurate forecasting makes it possible to identify probable contamination incidents in advance and take prompt action to stop people from drinking contaminated water. Authorities can take appropriate action to safeguard the public's health and avoid waterborne infections by tracking and forecasting water quality.
2. **Environmental Protection**: Water quality forecasting aids in determining how different activities affect aquatic ecosystems. It enables the detection of probable pollution sources and the assessment of their impact on habitats, biodiversity, and the health of the entire ecosystem. It is possible to focus conservation efforts on high-risk locations and take steps to reduce environmental damage by precisely anticipating water quality.
3. **Effective Resource Management**: Accurate estimates of water quality help with effective water resource allocation and management. Understanding the suitability of water for various uses, like irrigation, industrial use, or leisure activities, is aided by this. Stakeholders can maximize water allocation, reduce waste, and ensure sustainable use of this finite resource by anticipating the quality of the water.
4. **Early Warning Systems**: The ability to create early warning systems for anticipated pollution incidents is made possible by water quality estimates. Predictive models can find patterns and trends that could result in declining water quality by using historical data and real-time monitoring. This enables authorities to send out alerts on time, put precautionary measures in place, and lessen the effects of pollution accidents.
5. **Regulatory Compliance**: Accurate water quality forecasts make it easier to follow regulations' rules and norms. Predictive models can be used by businesses and wastewater treatment facilities to evaluate the success of their pollution prevention strategies and confirm that the quality standards for their discharges are met. It makes it possible for regulatory agencies to efficiently monitor and enforce compliance.

6. **Economic Considerations**: Predicting water quality is crucial for industries that depend on sustainable and clean water sources. Based on anticipated water quality conditions, industries like fisheries, agriculture, tourism, and enterprises depending on the water can make educated judgments. In addition to ensuring the long-term sustainability of these industries, it aids in reducing the financial losses brought on by water-related disruptions.

In general, precise water quality forecasting facilitates informed decision-making, permits proactive management techniques, safeguards the environment and public health, and encourages the sustainable use of water resources. It is essential for guaranteeing the supply of clean, safe water for a variety of uses, which is advantageous for both ecosystem health and human well-being.

9.3.4 CHALLENGES

Predicting water quality can be difficult due to the many difficulties and variables at play. Here are some typical difficulties encountered when predicting water quality [16–18]:

a. **Data Availability and Quality**: Due to the many variables affecting water quality, obtaining thorough and precise data for water quality prediction is difficult. Pollutant concentrations, turbidity, dissolved oxygen, pH, and other variables can all change dramatically across time and space. Collecting sufficient historical data from various locations with a wide range of parameters is crucial for developing reliable prediction models. The availability and quality of the data may be constrained, and data collecting can be costly and time-consuming.

b. **Spatial and Temporal Variability**: Water quality parameters can exhibit substantial spatial and temporal variability. For example, river flow, tidal patterns, weather conditions, and human activities can all influence water quality. This variability requires capturing data at different locations and time points to adequately represent the range of conditions. However, monitoring stations may be limited in number, and data collection frequency may be irregular, making it challenging to capture the full extent of spatial and temporal variations.

c. **Nonlinear Relationships**: Water quality is often governed by complex interactions and nonlinear relationships among various parameters. Traditional linear models may not effectively capture these complex relationships, leading to inaccurate predictions. Advanced machine learning techniques, such as artificial neural networks, support vector machines (SVMs), and decision trees, are commonly used to forecast the nonlinear behavior of water quality measurements and identify intricate relationships.

d. **Data Preprocessing and Feature Selection**: Water quality datasets often suffer from issues such as missing values, outliers, and noise. Preprocessing the data to handle these issues and ensure data quality is essential for accurate predictions. Additionally, selecting relevant features from a multitude of potential variables can be challenging. Dimensionality reduction techniques and domain knowledge are often employed to identify and select the most informative features for water quality prediction.

e. **Limited Understanding of Underlying Processes**: While scientists have made significant progress in understanding water quality processes, certain aspects remain poorly understood or highly complex. Emerging pollutants, such as pharmaceuticals or microplastics, and their impacts on water quality present ongoing challenges. Additionally, complex chemical reactions and interactions among different pollutants and environmental factors further complicate accurate prediction. Ongoing research is necessary to improve our understanding of these processes and refine prediction models.

f. **Generalization to New Locations**: Models trained on data from specific locations may not generalize well to new locations due to variations in local factors and characteristics. Factors such as geological features, land use patterns, and pollution sources can differ significantly between regions. When developing prediction models, it is crucial to consider local conditions, geography, and potential sources of pollution to ensure accurate predictions for new areas. Incorporating site-specific data and local expertise can help improve the generalizability of the models.

g. **Predicting Rare Events**: Some water quality issues, such as extreme events like floods, contamination incidents, or harmful algal blooms, are relatively rare occurrences. Predicting these events accurately is challenging due to the scarcity of relevant data points. Imbalanced datasets, where rare events are underrepresented, pose difficulties for traditional machine learning algorithms. Specialized techniques, such as anomaly detection algorithms or ensemble models, can be employed to address the prediction of rare events by identifying patterns associated with such occurrences.

By addressing these challenges, researchers and practitioners can improve water quality prediction models and enhance our ability to monitor and manage water resources effectively. Collaboration among experts from different disciplines and advancements in data collection methods, sensor technologies, and machine learning algorithms are crucial in overcoming these challenges and developing robust water quality prediction systems.

9.4 DEEP LEARNING FOR WATER QUALITY PREDICTION

Utilizing their advanced mechanisms in examining intricate patterns and relationships in large datasets, DL algorithms have demonstrated positive results in predicting water quality. DL models can learn from past data on water quality and create precise forecasts. Here are some DL techniques frequently employed for predicting water quality [17,18]:

i. **Convolutional Neural Networks (CNNs)**: CNNs are usually used for modeling in image analysis, but they may also be utilized to analyze spatial data, such as water quality maps or satellite images. CNNs can extract pertinent characteristics from the input data and generate predictions based on spatial patterns.

ii. **Recurrent neural networks (RNNs)**: RNNs are useful for time-series data, such as for water quality forecasting. RNNs can discover patterns in sequential data and capturing temporal dependencies. Popular RNN variations that effectively describe long-term relationships and generate precise predictions for water quality parameters over time include Gated Recurrent Unit (GRU) and LSTM.

iii. **Deep Belief Networks (DBNs)**: DBNs are generative models that create hierarchical representations from data through unsupervised learning. They are made up of several layers of autoencoders or limited Boltzmann machines. By learning the underlying patterns and features in water quality datasets, DBNs have been utilized to forecast water quality, improving prediction accuracy.

iv. **Generative Adversarial Networks (GANs)**: GANs are composed of a discriminator and a generator that compete with one another. To produce synthetic water quality data that closely mimics real data, GANs have been employed in water quality prediction. The robustness and generalizability of the prediction models can be increased by adding this synthetic data to the training set.

v. **Hybrid Models**: By combining DL techniques with other conventional models like SVMs or Random Forests, hybrid models can take advantage of the advantages of both methodologies. While classical models can offer interpretability and efficiently handle limited datasets, DL models can extract high-level features.

It is crucial to remember that training big, high-quality datasets for DL models for predicting water quality is necessary. To guarantee the precision and dependability of forecasts, data preprocessing is essential. This includes handling missing data and identifying outliers. To assess the effectiveness and generalizability of DL models, model evaluation and validation are also required. By successfully capturing intricate patterns and dependencies in water quality data, DL approaches have the potential to enhance water quality prediction. They offer a potent tool for researchers and managers of water resources to produce forecasts that are more precise and timelier, aiding in effective management of water quality decisions [19].

9.4.1 Potential of DL Models in Water Quality Prediction

DL models have shown substantial developments in forecasting water quality. Complex nonlinear correlations between water quality measures can be captured by DL models. Numerous elements, such as the environment, sources of pollutants, and hydrological processes, have an impact on water quality. DL models are excellent at figuring out complex interactions and patterns in the data, which enables them to efficiently capture and take advantage of these nonlinear relationships. Without manual feature engineering, DL models may automatically extract pertinent features from raw data. This ability helps predict water quality, where it can be difficult to pinpoint the most traits. Improved prediction accuracy may result from the DL models learning hierarchical representations of data and extracting features at various levels of abstraction. Diurnal rhythms, seasonal fluctuations, and long-term trends are only a few examples of temporal elements that have an impact on the dynamic process of water quality. For capturing temporal dependencies in time series data, DL models like RNNs or temporal convolutional networks (TCNs) are a great choice. More precise forecasts can be made thanks to these models' ability to reflect the temporal dynamics and long-term interdependence of water quality factors. When spatial data is available, such as measurements from various sample locations or information from remote sensing platforms, DL models can make use of it. Particularly skilled at processing geographically distributed data and extracting spatial information are CNNs. The accuracy of estimates of water quality can be increased by DL models' ability to account for regional heterogeneity and spatial correlations. DL models have proven scalable and generalizable across various periods and geographical regions. DL models may generalize well to unseen data once trained on a sample dataset. This capacity for generalization offers a potent tool for projecting predictions beyond the range of facts at hand, assisting in resource allocation and decision-making. Additionally, DL models help in early detection and real-time water quality monitoring. DL models can provide accurate forecasts and alerts by continuously analyzing incoming data, enabling proactive management of water resources and reducing potential dangers. These systems may be essential for protecting the environment, ensuring public health, and improving water treatment procedures [20].

DL models have a lot of potential, but it's crucial to remember that their performance depends on good data, wise model choice, thorough training, and careful validation. Their efficiency in managing and predicting water quality is further increased by integration with domain expertise and complementing monitoring techniques [21].

9.4.2 Related Works

A study by D. Venkata Vara Prasad and Lokeswari entitled "Analysis and Prediction of Water Quality Using Deep Learning and Auto Deep Learning Techniques" Focus is placed on the use of DL and auto DL approaches for assessing and forecasting water quality by Y. Venkataramana, P. Senthil Kumar, G. Prasannamedha, S. Harshana, S. Jahnavi Srividya, K. Harrinei, and Sravya Indraganti. In brief, their work addresses the importance of water quality monitoring and the challenges associated with traditional methods. It highlights the potential of DL and auto-DL as advanced techniques for water quality analysis and prediction. The authors propose the use of DL models, such as CNNs and RNNs, to effectively capture and analyze water quality data. These models can learn complex patterns and relationships in the data, enabling accurate prediction of water quality parameters. Additionally, they introduced Auto Deep Learning, an automated technique for architecture search and hyperparameter optimization in DL models. By leveraging these advanced approaches, one can enhance their understanding of water quality dynamics and make informed decisions for water resource management and environmental conservation [1, 2, 4].

"Prediction of Water Level and Water Quality Using a CNN-LSTM Combined Deep Learning Approach" by Sang-Soo Baek, Jongcheol Pyo, and Jong Ahn Chun emphasizes the use of a hybrid DL technique that employs CNN and LSTM to forecast both water quality and level. The authors discuss how crucial it is to accurately anticipate water quality and level in a variety of environmental monitoring and management applications. The complex spatiotemporal patterns and correlations in the data can be difficult for traditional prediction tools to capture. The authors suggest a hybrid deep-learning strategy that makes use of the models in order to get around these drawbacks. The outcomes of the studies show how well the combined CNN-LSTM strategy performs in predicting water level and water quality. The model shows improved performance compared to traditional methods, indicating its potential for real-world applications in water resource management, flood forecasting, and environmental monitoring [22].

The authors M Vijay Anand, Chennareddy Sohitha, Galla Neha Saraswathi, and GV Lavanya have focused on water quality prediction using CNN (Convolutional Neural Network) in their paper, Water quality prediction using CNN. The paper addresses the significance of water quality prediction for effective water resource management and environmental conservation. Traditional methods of water quality prediction often rely on statistical techniques and empirical models, which may have limitations in capturing complex patterns and relationships in the data. In this paper, the authors propose the use of CNN, a DL technique, to enhance the accuracy of water quality prediction. CNN is well-known for its ability to extract spatial features from data, making it suitable for analyzing water quality data collected from various locations. The paper presents a comprehensive methodology for data collection, preprocessing, and model training using the CNN architecture. The authors highlight the importance of selecting relevant input features for the CNN model. The model shows improved accuracy compared to traditional prediction methods, indicating its potential for real-world applications. Overall, this paper emphasizes the application of CNN in water quality prediction. By leveraging the spatial feature extraction capabilities of CNN, researchers, and practitioners can enhance their understanding of water quality dynamics and make informed decisions for water resource management and environmental protection [23].

The paper titled "Short-term Water Quality Variable Prediction Using a Hybrid CNN-LSTM Deep Learning Model" by Rahim Barzegar, Mohammad Taghi Aalami, and Jan Adamowski focuses on using a hybrid CNN-LSTM DL model to predict water quality factors over the short term. In order to manage water resources effectively and monitor the environment, the study emphasizes the significance of accurate and timely forecast of water quality factors. Complex temporal and spatial patterns in the data are typically difficult to capture using traditional approaches for water quality prediction. In order to overcome these difficulties, the authors of this research suggest a hybrid model that combines the advantages of CNN and LSTM models. Data on water quality obtained from various places are used to extract spatial features using the CNN component of the model. As a result, the spatial relationships and patterns in the data may be captured by the model. The findings of the trials show that the hybrid CNN-LSTM model is capable of making precise predictions of short-term water quality indicators. The model surpasses conventional prediction techniques, demonstrating its promise for practical applications in environmental monitoring and water resource management.

9.5 WATER QUALITY FORECASTING IN BRAHMAPUTRA BASIN

The water quality in the Brahmaputra River's tributaries, specifically in the states of India, is examined in this chapter. The Brahmaputra River is a vital water resource for millions in Bangladesh and India. We investigate the efficiency of cutting-edge models to forecast and classify water quality into three ranges: good, medium and poor. CNNs have been popular in several disciplines, including computer vision, and have demonstrated to be quite successful at analyzing spatial data, such as photographs. CNNs can extract pertinent spatial information from the Brahmaputra River tributary data in the context of water quality prediction. CNNs may recognize patterns and relationships that lead to variations in data by processing the incoming data through several convolutional layers. On the other hand, the LSTM family of RNNs excels in processing sequential data. LSTM models capture the temporal dependencies and produce precise forecasts since water quality parameters are frequently influenced by temporal factors, such as seasonality and daily changes. LSTM models can successfully simulate the dynamic nature of water quality levels by keeping track of previous data. CNNs are excellent at catching spatial patterns while LSTM models are excellent at capturing temporal dependencies and considering the impact of things like river metabolic pulses on water quality [24].

By using convolutional filters on the input data, CNNs are excellent at extracting spatial characteristics, enabling them to find patterns and correlations between various tributaries and their quality levels. CNN can determine effect of these variables on dissolved oxygen solubility with variables like water temperature, sedimentation patterns, and geographic characteristics. A more thorough understanding of water quality patterns throughout the entire river system is made possible by this spatial study. LSTM models are excellent at identifying temporal dependencies in sequential data. The dynamic character of the water quality levels can be efficiently modeled by LSTM models by keeping track of previous observations and taking the order of data points into account. This makes it possible for the model to account for how river metabolic pulses, changes in water flow rates, and other time-varying factors affect water quality [25].

The focus of this chapter will be on the significance of forecasting and categorizing water quality into different categories, and we will go into specifics on how the LSTM and CNN models forecast water quality for its tributaries. The incorporation of DL models like CNN and LSTM offers interesting avenues, despite the difficulties associated with water quality prediction, such as the incomplete and sporadic nature of the data. We may use the capability of these models to enhance water quality assessment, pollution management, and treatment methods by taking advantage of the expanding availability of Earth's surface and hydrometeorological data. This chapter will examine the importance of predicting water quality, focusing on the function and potency of CNN and LSTM models in this area.

The data from Table 9.1 is collected from CPCB, The Central Pollution Control Board, a statutory organization in India under the Ministry of Environment, Forest, and Climate Change. The attributes include the primary factors affecting the water quality like Dissolved Oxygen (mg/L), Temperature (°C), Conductivity (µmho/Cm), pH, Bio-Chemical Oxygen Demand (mg/L), Nitrate (mg/L) and Total Coliform (MPN/100 mL) for tributaries of Brahmaputra Basin in India. After gathering historical water quality data from various monitoring stations or sensors, data preprocessing steps are applied. Clean and preprocess the collected data. This step involves handling missing values,

TABLE 9.1
Water Quality Parameters Data

Station Code	Location	State	T(°C)	DO	pH	EC	BCOD	Nitrate	Coliform
1030	DIBRUGARH	ASSAM	25	9	7.6	218	2.6	1	2,100
1262	NIMATIGHAT	ASSAM	28	8.4	7.7	209	2.8	1.4	910
1526	DHENUKHAPAHAR	ASSAM	32	7.8	7.8	169	2.7	1.2	2,000
1031	PANDU	ASSAM	31	9.2	7.6	170	2.4	1.4	2,100
1299	JOGIJHOGA NEAR BRIDGE	ASSAM	30	7.6	7.6	184	2.5	1.4	2,100
2069	PANBAZAR, GUWAHATI	ASSAM	30	9.2	7.5	188	2.8	1.6	2,100
2064	GUWAHATI, ASSAM	ASSAM	30	9.2	7.8	183	2.6	1.4	2,100
2067	SUALKUCHI, DIST. KAMRUP	ASSAM	26	9.5	7.8	186	2.8	1.6	2,000
2066	DHUBRI, ASSAM	ASSAM	33	7.5	7.8	228	2.5	1	1,500
3781	BOGIBEEL BRIDGE, BOGIBEEL	ASSAM	25	8.2	7.8	179	2.8	1.3	1,500
4004	BISWANATH GHAT	ASSAM	28	7.6	7.6	213	2.5	1	1,500

outlier detection and removal, data normalization, and feature selection or extraction. To create training, validation, and testing sets, divide the preprocessed data. The validation set is used for hyperparameter tweaking, the testing set is used to assess the model's performance, and the training set is used to train the model. Train the model using the training set. During training, the model learns to extract relevant spatial features from the input data and predict water quality parameters. Evaluate the trained model using the validation set. Measure its performance using appropriate evaluation metrics such as mean squared error (MSE) and root mean squared error (RMSE). Assess the performance of the trained model using the testing set, which represents unseen data. Compare the predicted water quality values with the actual measurements to evaluate the model's generalization ability and reliability. Once the CNN model is trained and evaluated, it can be used for water quality forecasting. Providing new input data to the trained model and will generate predictions for the desired water quality parameters.

9.5.1 CONVOLUTIONAL NEURAL NETWORKS (CNN)

CNNs have become an effective tool for processing and analyzing geographical data, particularly in computer vision. Although originally designed for image recognition tasks, CNNs have found use in several fields, including environmental sciences and the prediction of water quality. A CNN is built to efficiently capture spatial patterns and hierarchies in the input data. It has several layers, including fully connected, pooling, and convolutional layers. Convolutional layers extract regional features by applying filters to input data and find patterns at various spatial scales. These filters can be compared to feature detectors, which pick out details in the data. CNNs can analyze spatial data linked to its attributes' levels

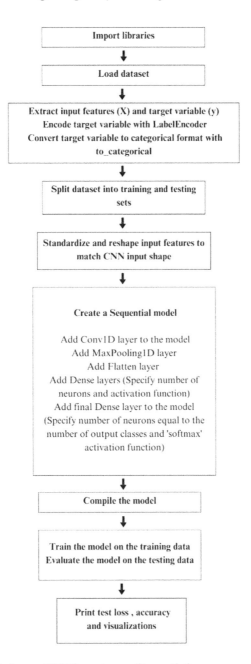

FIGURE 9.3 Work flow or CNN for water quality prediction.

in the context of water quality prediction for the Brahmaputra River's tributaries. Typically, factors like water temperature, pH levels, nutrient concentrations, and geographic information would be the input to the CNN. The CNN can determine the geographical patterns and relationships that contribute to fluctuations in the levels by processing this information through the convolutional layers. By seeing these trends, CNN can provide light on the variables affecting water quality and assist in identifying regions more vulnerable to contamination or call for focused intervention. CNNs aid in the development of a more thorough understanding of the physical and chemical concentrations in its tributaries by utilizing their capacity to record spatial patterns and hierarchies (Figure 9.3).

CNNs are majorly based on the Local receptive fields. CNNs are very good at capturing spatial patterns and structures in the data since this enables the network to concentrate on features and their spatial correlations. Convolutional layers in CNNs use convolutional filters to process the incoming data. These filters, often referred to as kernels, move across the input while adding and multiplying elements one at a time to create a feature map. CNNs can automatically extract pertinent features from the input data by learning the best values for the filters during training. This could increase the network's ability to generalize to various spatial scales and increase computing efficiency.

CNNs are made to take in input data that has hierarchical representations. The network learns more complicated and abstract information as it advances through various convolutional and pooling layers. Higher layers learn more complex spatial correlations whereas lower layers catch simpler patterns like edges and textures. CNNs can recognize complex geographical correlations and trends in water quality data due to this hierarchical representation. Through CNN, researchers and stakeholders can better understand the dynamics of the parameters and decide on strategies for pollution prevention and water treatment.

The variance of Training vs. Validation for loss and accuracy of the CNN model is shown in Figures 9.4 and 9.5.

The first plot shows the training and validation loss over each epoch, while the second plot displays the training and validation accuracy. These visualizations make it easier to comprehend how the model's performance varies as it is trained.

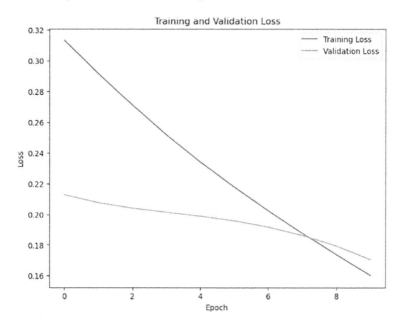

FIGURE 9.4   Variation of training vs validation for CNN.

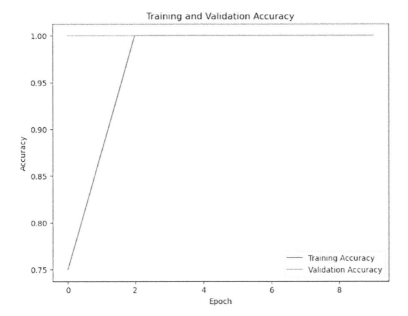

FIGURE 9.5 Variation of training vs validation accuracy for CNN.

9.5.2 LONG SHORT-TERM MEMORY MODEL

RNNs using LSTM architectures are used to model sequential data. In contrast to conventional feedforward neural networks, LSTM networks can detect dependencies and patterns in the data that span various time steps. This makes them especially suitable for time series analysis, where the temporal correlations and sequence of the observations are critical. Memory cells are used by LSTMs to store and access data across lengthy sequences. With the help of these memory cells, the network can recall prior observations and selectively ignore or update data based on how pertinent it is to the current prediction task. With this feature, LSTMs can accurately describe complicated temporal dynamics and long-term dependencies in the data. They use gate mechanisms like the input gate, forget gate, and output gate to control the information flow throughout the network. The input gate determines how much fresh information should be stored in the memory cell, whereas the forget gate controls how much of the old information is maintained there. The information flow from the memory cell to the following time step is controlled by the output gate. These gate mechanisms allow LSTMs to process and update data selectively, facilitating accurate predictions and reducing the vanishing gradient problem that standard RNNs frequently experience. LSTMs can capture the temporal dependencies and variations that affect levels of water quality in the context of water quality prediction. It can be strongly impacted by elements including seasonal fluctuations, daily cycles, and recurring events.

By considering the sequential nature of the data, LSTMs can efficiently predict these patterns and produce precise projections. LSTMs can capture the dynamics of water parameter levels in its tributaries and account for elements like river metabolic pulses and variations in water flow rates by preserving a memory of previous measurements. When analyzing data on water quality, which may include missing values or erratic sampling intervals, the ability of LSTMs to handle variable-length sequences is essential. The network can handle sequences of various durations and learn from them, accommodating the patchy temporal and spatial coverage frequently encountered in datasets on water quality (Figure 9.6).

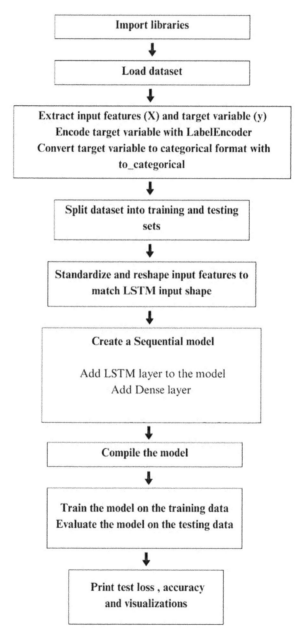

FIGURE 9.6   Work flow of LSTM for water quality prediction.

Because of their adaptability, LSTMs can handle real-world data situations where complete and continuous information might not always be accessible. LSTMs can also handle multivariate time series data, in which one range of parameter levels are influenced by several other factors, including water temperature, pH, and nutrient concentrations. To fully understand the dynamics of water quality, these variables can be employed as input features in LSTMs to capture the complex interactions and correlations between the many factors. By utilizing the advantages of LSTMs in modelling temporal relationships, managing variable-length sequences, and analyzing multivariate data, researchers may precisely estimate and forecast water quality levels. The predictive capacity can be further increased and a more thorough understanding of the dynamics of water quality can be provided by combining LSTMs and other techniques, such as CNNs. Researchers and stakeholders can better comprehend the temporal dynamics of water quality by utilizing the capabilities of LSTMs allowing them to make wise decisions regarding pollution prevention, water treatment, and resource management. For working relating to the prediction of water quality, LSTMs are an invaluable tool because of their capacity to manage long-term dependencies, and irregular sample intervals, and give uncertainty estimation.

The variance of Training vs. Validation for loss and accuracy of the LSTM model is shown in Figures 9.7 and 9.8.

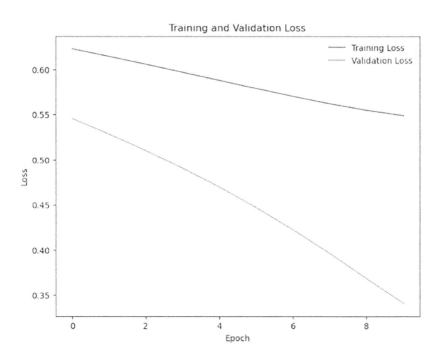

FIGURE 9.7   Variation of training vs validation for LSTM.

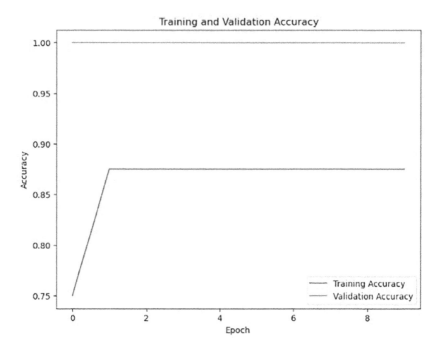

FIGURE 9.8 Variation of training vs validation accuracy for LSTM.

9.6 CONCLUSION

In conclusion, millions of people in the area rely on the Brahmaputra River for their livelihoods and general well-being. In many areas, such as transportation, irrigation, and food production, the river's flow is crucial. To use this vast river system sustainably, water quality must be maintained. When assessing water quality, pollution management methods, and treatment techniques, the assessment and forecast of water quality serve as a crucial metric. To comprehend river metabolic pulses and execute efficient management techniques, the predictions must be accurate and reliable. However, due to the complex dynamics and spatial-temporal fluctuations in water quality data, projecting the levels with accuracy offers several issues.

LSTM and CNN are the two DL models that have demonstrated significant promise in resolving these issues and improving the predictions. CNNs are excellent at identifying spatial patterns and extracting important characteristics from the data, but LSTMs excel at modelling temporal dependencies and managing sequential data. By combining the benefits of CNNs with LSTMs, we can provide predictions of water quality in the Brahmaputra River's tributaries that are more accurate and comprehensive. Through our research and analysis, we have demonstrated the effectiveness of CNN and LSTM models in forecasting. It has been demonstrated how well the CNN models can extract spatial characteristics and establish relationships between variables like water temperature, Biochemical Oxygen Demand (BCOD), and solubility.

However, the long-term trends and temporal dependencies that have a considerable impact on prediction have been captured by LSTM models. By merging spatial and temporal data, the integration of CNN and LSTM models has significantly improved prediction accuracy. The results of this study demonstrate the significance of the attributes as a key determinant of water quality and the consequences for pollution prevention and treatment techniques. The ability to make informed decisions and take proactive steps to protect ecosystems and sustain water quality depends on accurate estimates of water quality levels. Additionally, the use of CNN and LSTM models in water quality prediction offers up new avenues for comprehending the intricate dynamics of rivers and creating long-term management plans. To improve the precision and thoroughness of the models, future studies might investigate the integration of additional data sources and variables, such as nutrient concentrations and pH levels. It's vital to recognize the wider ramifications of this research in addition to the encouraging outcomes from using CNN and LSTM models for prediction. For the control of water quality, the preservation of ecosystems, and human health, accurate water parameter projections are important. The Brahmaputra River's tributaries' water quality levels may be accurately predicted, allowing stakeholders to make decisions about pollution prevention techniques, water treatment methods, and resource management. The knowledge gleaned from this study can aid in the creation of thorough systems for monitoring water quality as well as decision-support tools for managers of water resources and policymakers.

REFERENCES

[1] Haq, K.P. Rasheed Abdul, and V. P. Harigovindan. "Water quality prediction for smart aquaculture using hybrid deep learning models." *IEEE Access* 10, 18–27, 2022.
[2] Yang, Yurong, Qingyu Xiong, Chao Wu, Qinghong Zou, Yang Yu, Hualing Yi, and Min Gao. "A study on water quality prediction by a hybrid CNN-LSTM model with attention mechanism." *Environmental Science and Pollution Research* 28, no. 39, 2021.
[3] Reddy, C. Kishor Kumar, C. H. Rupa, and B. Vijaya Babu. "SLGAS: supervised learning using gain ratio as attribute selection measure to nowcast snow/no-snow." *International Review on Computers and Software*, 2015.
[4] Barzegar, Rahim, Mohammad Taghi Aalami, and Jan Adamowski. "Short-term water quality variable prediction using a hybrid CNN-LSTM deep learning model." *Stochastic Environmental Research and Risk Assessment* 34, no. 2, 2020.
[5] Baek, Sang-Soo, JongcheolPyo, and Jong Ahn Chun. "Prediction of water level and water quality using a CNN-LSTM combined deep learning approach." *Water* 12, no. 12, 2020.
[6] Khullar, Sakshi, and Nanhey Singh. "Water quality assessment of a river using deep learning Bi-LSTM methodology: forecasting and validation." *Environmental Science and Pollution Research* 29, no. 9, 2022.
[7] Wan, Xin, Xiaoyong Li, Xinzhi Wang, Xiaohui Yi, Yinzhong Zhao, Xinzhong He, Renren Wu, and Mingzhi Huang. "Water quality prediction model using Gaussian process regression based on deep learning for carbon neutrality in papermaking wastewater treatment system." *Environmental Research* 211, 2022.
[8] Sha, Jian, Xue Li, Man Zhang, and Zhong-Liang Wang. "Comparison of forecasting models for real-time monitoring of water quality parameters based on hybrid deep learning neural networks." *Water* 13, no. 11, 2021.

[9] Anisha, P.R., Reddy, C.K.K. and Nguyen, N.G., "Blockchain technology: a boon at the pandemic times-a solution for global economy upliftment with AI and IoT", In *Blockchain Security in Cloud Computing*, pp.227–252, 2022.

[10] Kogekar, Aishwarya Premlal, Rashmiranjan Nayak, and Umesh Chandra Pati. "A CNN-BiLSTM-SVR based deep hybrid model for water quality forecasting of the river Ganga." In *2021 IEEE 18th India Council International Conference (INDICON)*, pp. 1–6. IEEE, Guwahati India, 2021.

[11] Sakshi, Khullar, and Singh Nanhey. "Water quality assessment of a river using deep learning BI-LSTM methodology: forecasting and validation." *Environmental Science and Pollution Research* 29, no. 9, 2022.

[12] Wu, Junhao, and Zhaocai Wang. "A hybrid model for water quality prediction based on an artificial neural network, wavelet transform, and long short-term memory." *Water* 14, no. 4, 2022.

[13] Prasad, LV Narasimha, P. Shankar Murthy, and C. Kishor Kumar Reddy. "Analysis of magnitude for earthquake detection using primary waves and secondary waves." In *2013 International Conference on Human Computer Interactions (ICHCI)*, pp. 1–6. Chennai, IEEE, 2013.

[14] Yan, Jianzhuo, Qingcai Gao, Yongchuan Yu, Lihong Chen, Zhe Xu, and Jianhui Chen. "Combining knowledge graph with deep adversarial network for water quality prediction." *Environmental Science and Pollution Research* 30, no. 4, 2023.

[15] Ni, Qingjian, Xuehan Cao, Chaoqun Tan, Wenqiang Peng, and Xuying Kang. "An improved graph convolutional network with feature and temporal attention for multivariate water quality prediction." *Environmental Science and Pollution Research* 30, no. 5, 2023.

[16] Anisha, P. R., et al. "Early diagnosis of breast cancer prediction using random forest classifier." *IOP Conference Series: Materials Science and Engineering*, IOP Publishing, Guntur, India, 2021.

[17] Zhang, Lei, Zhiqiang Jiang, Shanshan He, Jiefeng Duan, Pengfei Wang, and Ting Zhou. "Study on water quality prediction of urban reservoir by coupled CEEMDAN decomposition and LSTM neural network model." *Water Resources Management* 36, no. 10, 2022.

[18] Lopez, Ann Laverene, N. A. Haripriya, Kavya Raveendran, Sandra Baby, and C. V. Priya. "Water quality prediction system using LSTM NN and IoT." In *2021 IEEE International Power and Renewable Energy Conference (IPRECON)*, pp. 1–6. IEEE, Karunagappally, India, 2021.

[19] Choi, Heelak, Sang-Ik Suh, Su-Hee Kim, EunJin Han, and Seo Jin Ki. "Assessing the Performance of Deep Learning Algorithms for Short-Term Surface Water Quality Prediction." *Sustainability* 13, no. 19, 2021.

[20] Bi, Jing, Luyao Zhang, Haitao Yuan, and Jia Zhang. "Multi-indicator Water Quality Prediction with Attention-assisted Bidirectional LSTM and Encoder-Decoder." *Information Sciences*, 2023.

[21] Allugunti, Viswanatha Reddy, C. Kishor Kumar Reddy, N. M. Elango, and P. R. Anisha. "Prediction of diabetes using Internet of Things (IoT) and decision trees: SLDPS." In *Intelligent Data Engineering and Analytics: Frontiers in Intelligent Computing: Theory and Applications (FICTA 2020)*, vol. 2, pp. 453–461. Springer, Singapore, 2021.

[22] Joseph, Ferdin Joe John. "Iot based aquarium water quality monitoring and predictive analytics using parameter optimized stack lstm." In *2022 6th International Conference on Information Technology (InCIT)*, pp. 342–346. IEEE, Nonthaburi, Thailand, 2022.

[23] Prasad, D. Venkata Vara, Lokeswari Y. Venkataramana, P. Senthil Kumar, G. Prasannamedha, S. Harshana, S. Jahnavi Srividya, K. Harrinei, and SravyaIndraganti. "Analysis and prediction of water quality using deep learning and auto deep learning techniques." *Science of the Total Environment* 821, 2022.

[24] Khan, Md Saikat Islam, Nazrul Islam, Jia Uddin, Sifatul Islam, and Mostofa Kamal Nasir. "Water quality prediction and classification based on principal component regression and gradient boosting classifier approach." *Journal of King Saud University-Computer and Information Sciences* 34, no. 8, 2022.

[25] Liu, Yibei, Peishun Liu, Xuefang Wang, Xueqing Zhang, and Zifei Qin. "A study on water quality prediction by a hybrid dual channel CNN-LSTM model with attention mechanism." In *International Conference on Smart Transportation and City Engineering*, vol. 12050, pp. 797–804, Chongqing, China, 2021.

10 Multimodal Fusion Techniques for Enhanced Fake News Detection
A Robustly Optimized BERT and Vision Transformer Approach

Sumaya Abdul Rahman, V Sai Deepa Reddy, and Aayesha Qureshi
Stanley College of Engineering & Technology for Women

Srinath Doss
Botho University

10.1 INTRODUCTION

Misinformation is prevalent on social media platforms and manually distinguishing between genuine information from disinformation is challenging and near impossible with the amount of user-generated content across all platforms. Fact-checking and third-party filtering are inadequate at dissipating fake news proliferation. Fake news creates irrational fears and panic, causes societal shifts, and has the power to influence major decisions about where our society is heading in terms of culture and our trust in governance, news outlets, etc. Research in models and architectures to detect fake news is of paramount importance to dissipate it from spreading like wildfire and causing chaos.

The community has a crucial role in the dynamics of the disinformation spread. Research in [1] reveals that fake news is spread furiously compared to true news in the community as fake news has a higher emotional appeal which leads to higher engagement and resharing. Community dynamics are incentivized by individuals and organizations to spread information. Several classification tasks like rumor detection, sentiment analysis, fact-checking, and stance detection though like fake news detection, the features that are extracted and utilized to classify differ. In study [2], the factors behind the proliferation of misinformation on social media platforms were investigated. Through a comprehensive analysis, the authors identify several

DOI: 10.1201/9781032686363-10

key factors, including the emotional content of fake news, source credibility, user engagement, and network structure. To take any action regarding fake content it needs to be detected first.

There has been research that utilizes the textual aspects of fake news using machine learning, deep neural network, and transformer-based models used to classify the textual content. As most of the content with high engagement has other modalities like images and audio along with text, hence extracting insights from them is essential for fake news detection. The reliability of the model increases considerably when combining other modalities into the final detection models. A combination of modalities is used to deceive the user or mislead them into an action that exposes their security vulnerabilities. As in a graphic image of the aftermath of a war used to share misinformation of a current political dispute that asks for donations for its behalf, such content spreads fast and puts many vulnerable users' data at risk when they click on the links these misleading posts have.

These findings provide valuable insights into understanding the mechanisms behind the dissemination of fake news and can help inform strategies to minimize its impact.

Though the majority of work is done for binary fake news classification, there is a nuanced interpretation of news content to different classes like true, satire/parody, misleading content, manipulated content, false connections, and imposter content. The Fakeddit dataset covers various domains and samples are distributed among various classes of fake news. This study experiments the approach with this dataset.

This study introduced the premise of fake news detection and importance of research in multimodal approaches for handling disinformation, with specific focus on reddit social media platform. Literature survey is covered in Section 10.2, it covers the research conducted with regards to using unimodal approaches utilizing the text or image modalities of the content and multimodal approaches that vary in the architectures but clearly have produced better results than unimodal approaches.

The methodologies are covered in Section 10.3, unimodal models Roberta and Vision Transformer (ViT) were trained for text and image respectively and multimodal model that fused the text and image features extracted from Roberta and ViT respectively. This study compares the various fusion techniques and implements attention-based fusion as attention to specific features may prove it to be more useful than direct fusion techniques. The resulting metric used to evaluate the models was accuracy in predicting fake news in reddit tweets and the metrics are presented in Section 10.4, and the conclusion the study arrived at are explained in Section 10.5 along with the various other avenues for research in extension to this study are explored.

10.2   LITERATURE SURVEY

Fake news has plagued society by infiltrating several aspects of the information consumed by users. Spread across news reporting and social media, the major formats through which information regarding everything is consumed. As the perception or opinion of someone regarding any topic of discussion is at risk of getting polarized or misinterpreted by just a few fake news contents they consume. In politics, the authenticity of the elections, in religion, the values the holy book represents, in international affairs, the stability of the relationships is at risk, in technological domains, the stock market price and economy are famously affected by disinformation's rapid infiltration in the platforms. Fake news can disrupt society and lead to severe panic, though efforts have been made [3], there is more research effort required. Hence, there is a dire need for models that can detect fake content on the internet with high accuracy and explainability capable of moderating the abundant content produced each minute.

Machine learning algorithms like Support Vector Machine (SVM), Naive Bayes, and Logistic Regression have been used for fake news detection [4], and have performed consistently well. Deep neural network-based models like Convolutional Neural Networks (CNNs) in [5], Recurrent Neural Networks (RNN), and Long-Short term models (LSTM) in [4,6] are also used for fake news classification tasks.

Neural networks are superior in capturing complex relationships and modeling sequential and temporal contexts and hence perform better at intricate classification tasks like fake news detection. As the transformer-based models like Bidirectional Encoder Representations from Transformers (BERT) and sentence-BERT in [7] and [8] comparison of several transformer-based models like BERT, BERT without LSTM, Robustly Optimized BERT Approach (RoBERTa), ALBERT, and a hybrid model of BERT and BERT+ALBERT, but ultimately RoBERTa demonstrated superior performance compared to other models because of its ability to effectively handle large batches of text data.

By utilizing masked language modeling during training, RoBERTa achieved a better understanding of language in general and showed improved accuracy when applied to specific tasks. Furthermore, the use of these large batches made it easier to train the model in parallel across multiple processors or machines, enhancing its efficiency and scalability. In simpler terms, RoBERTa's success can be attributed to its efficient utilization of large batches and the parallel training process, leading to enhanced language comprehension and task performance. The notable benchmark datasets used for this task are FakeNewsNet and BuzzFeedNews. The models used to beat the state-of-art fake news detection have been accompanied by more modalities or components of the news to achieve better results [9].

FakeNewsNet dataset which has both image and text components has been used to extract image-based features and patterns pertaining to fake news [10]. The application of deep learning techniques for assessing the authenticity of visual content along with a proposed visual veracity analysis framework that performed better at extracting the features to detect fake news [11]. Other techniques were explored like the data mining approach in [12]. Utilizing the image components to detect is a crucial step to moving forward with multimodal fake news detection. The multimodal approach performs better at fine-grained classification tasks than the unimodal approaches explored in [13, 14].

Most of the prior research on identifying misinformation focused on utilizing features related to text and user metadata. Specifically, these studies extracted textual characteristics by employing CNNs to detect misinformation in [15,16,17]. The research being conducted to identify and classify the information using multiple modalities has proven to bring more accurate results like in [18] which experimented with combining text and image features for fake news detection. Modalities present currently are text, image, video, network, and speech. Several researchers have utilized and used multiple modalities to extract features to do the task, like [7] has used text and speech modalities to identify bias, [18–20] have combined the text and image features by fusing them to perform tasks: identifying deception, fake news, and fauxtography respectively.

The increase in cyberbullying and hate speech needed models to perform better and images and speech modalities have been used more fiercely in data related to these. [21,22] used the combination of text and image modalities for tasks related to cyberbullying using machine learning models like SVM, NB, LR, and CNN. Apart from these modalities of dialogue, user-based features can be extracted from user profiles like in [23]. Network-based features can be extracted from the dissemination of posts or tweets on graphs [24,25].

A multimodal model was proposed where the BERT model extracted the textual features and VGG for image features extraction then followed by 16 layers of LSTM and mean pooling layer to classify the news as fake or not, FakeNewsNet dataset [26] was used and the F1 score of 79.55% was achieved in [27]. Twitter and Weibo datasets are benchmark datasets used for various proposed architectures for multimodal fake news detection. Li et al. [28] proposed the Entity-Oriented MultiModal Alignment and Fusion Network (EMAF); it is made up of cross-modal alignment and fusion forwarded to a classifier. Accuracies obtained using EMAF are 97.4% and 80.5%, respectively, for Twitter and Weibo datasets.

Model architecture that derives event-invariant features, the Event Adversarial Neural Networks (EANN) model was proposed in [29] in which simple concatenation is used to combine the features, the accuracies produced were 71.5% and 82.7% for Twitter and Weibo datasets respectively. Singhal et al. [30] proposed a multimodal model, SpotFake, it fuses the features by concatenating the text features extracted from BERT and image features from VGG and feeding it to a fully connected neural network to classify the content. It achieved 77.7% and 89.2% accuracies on Twitter and Weibo datasets, respectively.

Work in [31] proposed a Multigrained Multi-modal Fusion Network (MMFN) which utilizes a transformer-based architecture. This network incorporates a multimodal module that integrates both fine-grained features and coarse-grained features that have been encoded by the CLIP encoder. It performed better than [29,30] with accuracies of 93.5% and 92.3% for Twitter and Weibo datasets, it can be inferred that the transformer-based architectures which are modified to weigh in features that are most useful can perform much better. The progressive fusion network (MPFN) introduced in [32] integrates the representational data from each modality at various stages by employing a visual feature extractor rooted in the transformer framework. MPFN effectively fuses text and image features through a mixer, establishing strong connections between modalities and achieving superior performance.

The paper [33] introduces the Adaptive Water Strider Algorithm (A-WSA) for optimal feature selection and weight factor optimization in a multimodal fake news detection model. A-WSA is utilized to attain optimal features derived from both image and text data, and to optimize the weight factor for feature fusion. The proposed A-WSA approach demonstrates effectiveness in utilizing multi-modal data for automated fake news classification. Although most of the focus on fake news is binary classification approach, studies like [34] focus on the heterogeneous graph that contains nodes and proposed a model that resulted in F1 scores of 88.5% (2_way_label), 85.8% (3_way_label), and 83.2% (6_way_label).

Another major study [35] focuses on addressing the issue of misinformation spread on social media platforms through CrossModal Misinformation (CMM). They contrast CMM with Asymmetric Multimodal Misinformation (AMM) and highlight the unimodal bias that arises in training and evaluation processes. To tackle this, they introduce FIGMENTS, an evaluation benchmark for CMM that excludes AMM and employs modality balancing. They also propose CHASMA, a method for generating synthetic training data, and show that incorporating CHASMA improves performance on FIGMENTS, using the Fakeddit dataset.

This study focuses on employing attention in all aspects of building a multimodal model for Fake News Detection on Fakeddit dataset. Unlike neural networks and simple machine learning models, transformers' self-attention aspect has the power to provide interpretability and produce rich contextual representations that focus on the relevant aspects. Hence, Roberta model for text and ViT for image were trained as unimodal approaches to classify the respective modalities. This study explores if without complicating the architecture of the model just by the fusion technique chosen the performance would vary or not. Attention aspect is integrated into the fusion of the features extracted from the transformer-based models. It results in a simple architecture of Roberta and ViT producing features that are fused using attention mechanism by calculating weights that helps the final classification layers to focus on the relevant features the most to give out accurate classification.

10.3 METHODOLOGY

10.3.1 Dataset

The Fakeddit dataset is a recently introduced collection of data that utilizes multiple modes of information to detect fake news. The dataset contains over 1 million samples. The data was collected from the social news aggregation and discussion website Reddit, covering various categories of fake news, such as fake news articles, manipulated images, and misleading headlines.

The dataset provides a diverse range of topics and genres, hence it is a valuable dataset for researchers dealing with fake news detection. The dataset also includes various statistical measures, such as the average sentence length, word count, and number of images per sample, which can be used to analyze the dataset's characteristics and tailor detection methods accordingly. Vocab size considered is 90,000 as our dataset has 90,435 unique words and the sentence length considered is 15 as it's the average and encompasses most of the samples except a few hundred in a 6.5 lakhs size dataset.

By referring to Figure 10.1, we can observe the 80:20 ratio distribution of the Fakeddit dataset between the train and test split for training our models. We are using two features from the dataset: "clean_title" and "2_way_label", 0 represents the Real news and 1 represents the Fake news.

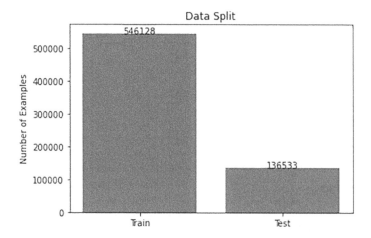

FIGURE 10.1   Dataset distribution into train and test sets.

Furthermore, Figure 10.2 provides insights into the distribution of sentence lengths within the Fakeddit dataset. Analyzing the sentence length distribution can help in understanding the text complexity and structuring appropriate models for fake news detection.

10.3.2   RoBERTa

RoBERTa is a transformer-based model that excels at capturing complex linguistic patterns and semantic representations in textual data. It achieves this by leveraging the power of self-attention mechanisms, which enable it to model to detect distant connections and contextual associations within the input text. Additionally, RoBERTa benefits from its extensive pretraining on diverse text corpora, enabling it to learn a broad understanding of language. RoBERTa was chosen for multimodal fusion fake news detection due to its exceptional text understanding capabilities, extensive pretraining on diverse corpora in natural language processing tasks, and its open-source availability. With its transformer-based architecture and ability to capture complex linguistic patterns and semantic representations, RoBERTa is well-suited for the purpose of fake news detection. Its pretraining ensures a broad understanding of language, making it adaptable to the diverse nature of news articles encountered in fake news detection. By leveraging RoBERTa's advanced capabilities, we aim to improve the accuracy and effectiveness of fake news detection in our research.

10.3.2.1   Roberta Preprocessing

We perform text tokenization and preprocessing using the Hugging face transformers library and the Roberta tokenizer. The tokenizer breaks down the text to individual tokens. The paper uses the 'roberta-base' pre-trained tokenizer.

Figure 10.3 provides an outline of the pre-processing tasks included in training the RoBERTa model. To begin with, we use the 'clean_title' attribute from the

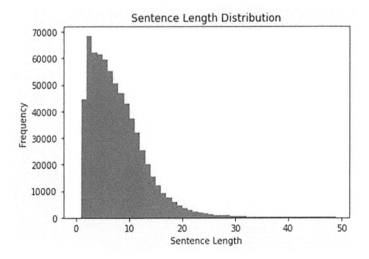

FIGURE 10.2 Sentence length distribution of samples in dataset.

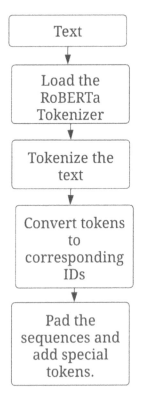

FIGURE 10.3 Pre-processing flowchart for RoBERTa model training.

fakeddit dataset and it contains the text data. The tokenizer method tokenizes each text entry in the 'clean_title' column. Tokenization breaks the text into individual texts, taking into account language-specific rules and tokenization conventions used by the RoBERTa model.

To further process the text data, we convert the tokens into their corresponding token IDs. Each unique token is assigned a numerical ID based on RoBERTa's tokenizer's vocabulary. To ensure consistent input lengths, the sequences of token IDs need to be padded or truncated to a fixed length. Any sequences longer than 15 are truncated, while shorter sequences are padded with zeros. Padding is done at the end of the sequences and then finally we add special tokens. Special tokens, such as the [CLS] (classification) and [SEP] (separator) tokens, are required to mark the beginning and separation of sentences in the input data.

Each sequence in 'input_ids' is modified by adding the [CLS] token positioned at the start and the [SEP] token positioned at the end. Using list comprehension. The [CLS] and [SEP] tokens help the model understand the start and end of the input sequence during training and inference.

10.3.2.2 Roberta Architecture

The architecture utilizes a pre-trained RoBERTa model to encode the input text using tokenization and attention mechanisms. It provides a way to extract RoBERTa features for each text entry in the fakeddit dataset, which can be further utilized for tasks such as fake news detection.

First, the pre-trained Roberta model is loaded. Two input layers, input_ids and attention_mask, are defined and they represent the input tokens and attention masks for the RoBERTa model. The RoBERTa model is called with the input layers as arguments to obtain the output features. The dictionary {"input_ids": input_ids, "attention_mask": attention_mask} is passed to the RoBERTa model. The [0] indexing is used to extract the output features from the RoBERTa model. We iterate through the fakeddit dataset (assuming it is a DataFrame) to process each text entry.

For each entry, the text is tokenized using the tokenizer.encode_plus() function. The tokens are padded to maximum length of 15 using the max_length parameter. The input IDs and attention mask are extracted from the encoded text. The RoBERTa features are obtained by calling the roberta_features_model with the input IDs and attention mask. The obtained features are appended to the roberta_features list.

Finally, the list of feature arrays, roberta_features, is converted to a Numpy array.

10.3.3 VISION TRANSFORMERS

In our pursuit of multimodal fake news detection, we have opted to employ the ViT as a cornerstone of our fusion technique. ViT's selection arises from its exceptional capabilities in computer vision tasks, setting it apart from alternative approaches. By harnessing transformer-based architectures, ViT integrates self-attention mechanisms that adeptly capture long-range dependencies within images and facilitate comprehensive modeling of contextual information.

ViT's scalability enables efficient processing and learning on extensive multimodal datasets, while its cross-modality fusion potential provides a robust framework for integrating visual information with other modalities. By leveraging ViT's attention mechanisms, contextual understanding, scalability, and cross-modality fusion, our objective is to advance the detection of fake news by enhancing our understanding across multiple modalities.

10.3.3.1   ViT Preprocessing

The preprocessing steps for ViTs involved several components to prepare the data for training the model. First, the dataset used for training was stored in a buffer of size 512. Figure 10.4 provides a visual representation of the pre-processing steps involved in training the ViT model. The training data was processed in batches of size 256 to facilitate parallelization and optimize the training procedure.

The image size was set to 72×72 pixels to maintain a reasonable resolution while considering computational constraints. Furthermore, the images were divided into patches of size 6×6 pixels. This division resulted in a total of (IMAGE_SIZE // PATCH_SIZE) ** 2 patches, which formed the input representation for the ViT model.

Layer normalization was employed with an epsilon value of 1e-6 to ensure stable training and facilitate faster convergence. The model consisted of eight transformer layers, allowing for the capture of complex dependencies in the data. Attention mechanisms were employed with four attention heads, enabling the model to attend to different aspects and relationships within the data. The projection dimension was set to 64, while the transformer units were defined as [128, 64]. The model also featured a multi-layer perceptron (MLP) head with units defined as [2,048, 1,024], enabling the model to learn higher-level representations and make more accurate predictions.

To further improvise the robustness and capabilities of the ViT model, a data augmentation pipeline was constructed using the Keras Sequential API. This pipeline included operations such as data normalization, resizing the images to a size of 72×72 pixels, random horizontal flipping, small rotations, and random zooming with height and width factors of 0.2. These augmentation techniques introduced variations in the training data, thereby mitigating the risk of overfitting and enhancing the model's capability to handle unseen data.

Finally, the normalization layer of the data augmentation pipeline adapted to the mean and variance of the training data (x_train). This step ensured that the input data was appropriately normalized, aligning it with the statistical properties of the training set.

10.3.3.2   ViT Architecture

We explore two variations of the ViT model: a vanilla version and a modified version that incorporates Shifted Patch Tokenization and Locality Self Attention (LSA). The goal is to analyze the impact of attention mechanisms on fusion techniques. The ShiftedPatchTokenization layer is applied to the augmented images. This layer extracts patches from the images and performs cropping, shifting, and padding operations. The patches are then flattened and linearly projected using a dense layer. Layer normalization is applied to the flattened patches to enhance their representation.

The PatchEncoder layer follows, which encodes the patches by incorporating position embeddings. The position embeddings are generated using an embedding

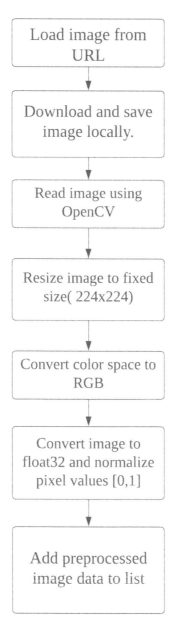

FIGURE 10.4 Pre-processing flowchart ViT model training.

layer based on the number of patches and the projection dimension. The core of the architecture consists of multiple Transformer blocks. Each block consists of a layer normalization step, followed by a multi-head attention mechanism. In the vanilla version, the standard MultiHeadAttention layer is used, while in the modified version, the MultiHeadAttentionLSA layer is employed, which includes a trainable temperature term. The attention mechanism calculates attention scores between the patches and applies softmax normalization. The resulting attention output is obtained by weighted summation of the values.

Skip connections are incorporated between the attention output and the encoded patches to facilitate information flow. Layer normalization is then applied to the skip connection output, followed by a MLP module. The MLP applies a series of dense layers with Relu activation and dropout, contributing to feature extraction and transformation.

Finally, the encoded patches are layer-normalized, flattened, and subjected to dropout regularization. The resulting features are fed into another MLP module with dense layers and dropout. The final output of the MLP is passed through a dense layer with the required number of output classes representing the classification logits. The optimizer utilizes a learning rate of 0.001 and a weight decay of 0.0001. The model is trained for 50 epochs. By utilizing this architecture, we aim to investigate the performance of different fusion techniques in the context of attention mechanisms. The vanilla ViT serves as a baseline, while the modified version with Shifted Patch Tokenization and LSA provides insights into the impact of these enhancements on fusion performance.

We construct a new model, known as the "feature_extractor," using the Keras library. This model is designed to extract features from the ViT model. By specifying the inputs as the same inputs used for the ViT model and setting the outputs to the layer immediately preceding the final layer in the ViT model, where we can effectively capture the features generated by the ViT model. Each sample in the dataset is associated with a 1,024-dimensional feature vector, which encode learned high-level representations of the corresponding input image.

10.3.4 FUSION TECHNIQUES

10.3.4.1 Concatenation

To fuse the features from the ViTs and RoBERTa models, concatenation was performed. The ViT features are first flattened to have a shape of (n, 1,024). This flattening operation reshapes the feature tensor to a two-dimensional matrix, where each row corresponds to an individual input sample, and each column represents a distinct feature dimension. Figure 10.5 provides a visual representation of the concatenation process for multimodal fusion.

Next, the RoBERTa features are reshaped to have a shape of (n, 15 * 768). This transformation collapses the second and third dimensions of the RoBERTa features, combining the 15 time steps with the 768 feature dimensions into a single dimension. Finally, the flattened ViT features and reshaped RoBERTa features are concatenated along the feature dimension (axis = −1). This concatenation operation results in a fused feature representation where the ViT features and RoBERTa features are combined into a single feature vector for each input sample. The shape of the final fused feature representation is (n, 1,024 + 15 * 768).

The fused feature representation obtained through concatenation allows for the incorporation of both visual and textual information, capturing the combined knowledge from the ViT and RoBERTa models. This joint representation was utilized for classification that requires multimodal input.

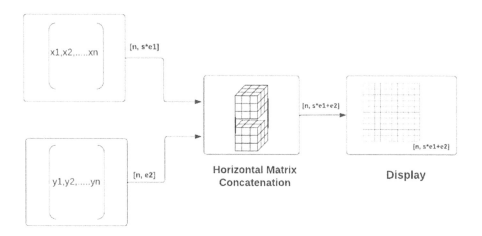

FIGURE 10.5 Concatenation process for multimodal fusion.

10.3.4.2 Addition

In multimodal fusion using the add function as shown in Figure 10.6, the features from the text and image modalities are combined by element-wise addition. After applying RoBERTa to the text data, the resulting text features have a shape of (n, 15, 768). This means you have n samples, each with a sentence length of 15 and a feature dimension of 768. Image Features: Using ViTs on the image data, the extracted image features have a shape of (n, 1,024). This represents n samples with a feature dimension of 1,024.

Since the text and image features have different shapes, they need to be aligned before fusion. In this case, alignment is necessary to synchronize the sequence length of text features with the sample count of image features

To align the text features with the image features, the text features of shape (n, 15, 768) are broadcasted along the sample dimension (n) to match the number of samples in the image features. Broadcasting was used to replicate the text features along the sample dimension, resulting in text features of shape (n, 15, 768).Once the features were aligned, the add function was applied to combine them. Element-wise addition was performed, where each corresponding element in the text and image features was added together. The text features of shape (n, 15, 768) and the image features of shape (n, 1,024) are added element-wise. The result was a fused feature representation with a shape of (n, 15, 1,792).

The outcome of the fusion process using the add function was a fused feature representation with a shape of (n, 15, 1,792). This fused representation contains combined information from both the text and image modalities. Each element in the fused features is the sum of the corresponding elements in the text and image features, resulting in a combined representation that captures information from both modalities

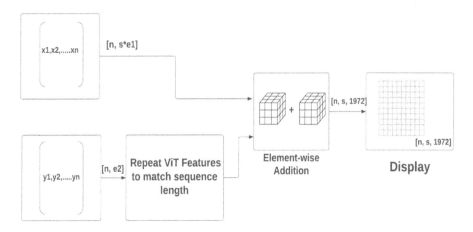

FIGURE 10.6   Addition process for multimodal fusion.

10.3.4.3   Maximum

To combine the RoBERTa and ViT features effectively, we employed a maximum fusing process. First, we repeated the ViT features 15 times along the second axis to align with the sequence length of the RoBERTa features, resulting in a ViT feature tensor with the shape (n, 15, 1,024).Next, we performed an element-wise maximum comparison between the RoBERTa features and the repeated ViT features. As shown in Figure 10.7, this process captured the maximum value for each corresponding element, resulting in a fused feature tensor with the shape (n, 15, 768).

Optionally, as an alternative approach, we considered obtaining a single representation for each sample by applying the maximum operation along the second axis (the sequence length axis). This would have yielded a final fused feature tensor with the shape (n, 768), where each sample would be represented by a single embedding vector combining the information from both RoBERTa and ViT features.

However, after careful consideration, we decided to proceed with the fused feature tensor of shape (n, 15, 768) rather than obtaining a single representation. This choice was made to retain the sequence-level information from both models, allowing for a more detailed analysis and interpretation of our data.

By following this fusing process, we successfully integrated the information from RoBERTa and ViT features, creating a fused feature tensor that encapsulates the combined knowledge from both models. This approach allowed us to capture a richer and more comprehensive representation of our data for further analysis and interpretation.

10.3.4.4   Cross-Modal Attention

In this paper, we use a cross-modal attention mechanism for fusing features from different models, specifically RoBERTa and ViT, to effectively classify fake news in

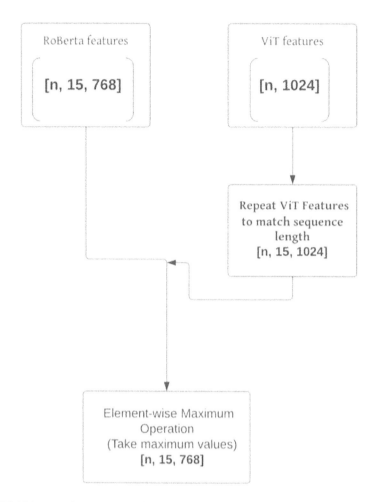

FIGURE 10.7   Maximum process for multimodal fusion.

a multimodal setting. The attention mechanism is crucial in combining these features to generate a final fused feature representation denoted as F. We provide a detailed explanation of the fusion process below.

Given the RoBERTa features, denoted as Fr with a shape of (n, 15, 768), and the ViT features, denoted as Fv with a shape of (n, 1,024), we outline the steps involved in the fusion process using the attention mechanism as shown in Figure 10.8.

Query, Key, and Value Calculation:

To begin, we employ linear transformations to the input features *Fr* and *Fv*. This yields the query *Q*, key *K*, and value *V* representations. The linear transformations are defined as follows:

$$Query: Q = Linear(Fr) \rightarrow shape\ (n,\ 15,\ 768)$$

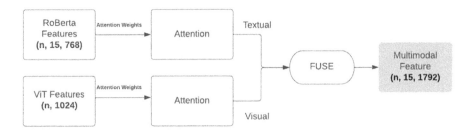

FIGURE 10.8   Cross-modal attention process for multimodal fusion.

$$Key: \ K \ = \ Linear\,(Fr) \ -> \ shape \ (n, \ 15, \ 768)$$

$$Value: \ V \ = \ Linear\,(Fv) \ -> \ shape \ (n, \ 1024)$$

Attention Score Calculation:

The attention scores between the query and key features are calculated by taking the dot product between Q and the transpose of K. We achieve this by performing matrix multiplication and transposing the key features along the last two dimensions. The attention scores are calculated as follows:

$$AttentionScores: S = Q \ K^{\wedge}T -> shape(n,15,15)$$

Attention Weight Calculation:

After capturing the attention scores, we normalize them using the softmax function. This normalization ensures that the scores reflect valid attention weights that collectively sum up to 1. The calculation of attention weights is as follows:

$$Attention \ Weights: \ A \ = \ softmax(S) \ -> \ shape \ (n, \ 15, \ 15)$$

Weighted Sum Calculation:

To capture the relevant information from both RoBERTa and ViT features, we compute the weighted sum of the value features V using the attention weights A. This operation is performed as follows:

$$Weighted \ Sum: \ W \ = \ A{\cdot}V \ -> \ shape \ (n, \ 15, \ 1792)$$

The weighted sum W results in a tensor with a shape of (n, 15, 1,792), where n represents the batch size, 15 denotes the number of time steps, and 1,792 represents the combined feature dimension obtained from RoBERTa and ViT features.

Fused Feature Representation:

The resulting tensor W represents the fused feature representation denoted as F. It has a shape of (n, 15, 1,792), capturing the combined information from RoBERTa and ViT. By utilizing this cross-modal attention approach, we can effectively integrate information from RoBERTa and ViT features to enhance the classification of fake news in a multimodal setting.

We assess the effectiveness of this approach by performing experiments on the provided datasets and evaluating the classification performance. The experimental results showcase the superior performance of our proposed fusion method compared to individual models. The attention mechanism allows the model to focus on relevant information by assigning different weights to different parts of the input features. By computing attention scores between the query and key features, we can identify the importance and relevance of each feature in the domain of fake news detection. It enables the model to allocate more attention to the most informative and discriminative features for fake news classification.

Overall, the attention mechanism in our method plays a critical role in extracting relevant features, highlighting the discriminative aspects of the input data, and effectively fusing multimodal information. This mechanism enables our model to gain an understanding of the complex nature of fake news, leading to more accurate and reliable detection results in a multimodal context.

10.3.5 MULTIMODAL MODEL

In the research paper, the features are given to a neural network model for classification. Figure 10.9 demonstrates the Flow diagram of the model. First, the necessary libraries and modules are imported, including TensorFlow, Keras, and sklearn. The neural network architecture is defined using the Sequential model from Keras. It consists of densely connected layers with ReLU activation functions. Batch normalization layers and dropout layers are added to enhance the model's generalization and prevent overfitting.

The final layer uses a sigmoid activation. The model is compiled with the Adam optimizer, a learning rate of 1e-4, binary cross-entropy loss function, and accuracy as the evaluation metric.

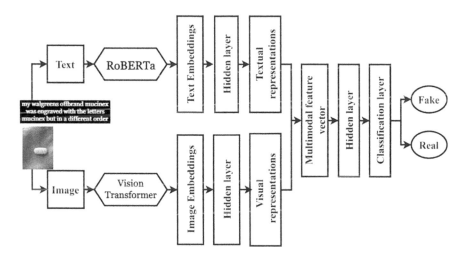

FIGURE 10.9 Architectural flow diagram of the multimodal fake news detection.

The model is then trained using the fit function. The training data, train_features, and train_labels are passed to the model along with the number of epochs and a validation split of 0.2 for monitoring the performance of the model is analyzed during the training process. Afterward, the model is tested on the evaluation dataset using the evaluate function, which computes the test loss and accuracy. Finally, the test accuracy is evaluated.

10.4   RESULTS

The evaluation metrics used to analyze the various approaches are the accuracy, precision, recall and F1 score.

Table 10.1 compares the singular modality approach using text and image and multimodal approach combining text and image modalities to identify fake news. The unimodal approach of fake news detection for text resulted in better performance than image, this significant difference could be accounted for the fact images alone do not mislead users but their correlation to the text is the deceiving aspect of the tweets. Multimodal model performance is substantially higher than unimodal models, with attention fusion technique producing the highest accuracy.

Table 10.2 presents the results of multimodal model approaches that vary in the fusion technique used to combine the individual modalities features before feeding them into classification layers. Among all the four techniques, attention performed the best, and maximum performed close to it. The fusion techniques investigated in this study include Concatenate, Addition, Maximum, and Attention fusion. These techniques

TABLE 10.1
Results of All Approaches for Fake News Detection

Approach	Models	Accuracy (Test)
Unimodal-Text	RoBERTa	0.8574
Unimodal-Image	Vision Transformer (ViT)	0.8041
Multimodal- Text + Image	RoBERTa + ViT (Attention)	0.9205

TABLE 10.2
Results of Different Fusion Techniques for (RoBERTa + ViT) Multimodal Model

Combination Methods	Accuracy (Validation)	Accuracy (Test)
Concatenate	0.8672	0.8672
Addition	0.8664	0.8668
Maximum	0.9021	0.9029
Attention	0.9194	0.9205

aim to combine the outputs of the base models, enhancing the overall performance of the multimodal fake news detection system. To evaluate the effectiveness of each fusion technique, we report the accuracy scores obtained on both the validation and test datasets.

The accuracy scores serve as a key performance metric to measure the reliability of the multimodal fake news detection system. They indicate the percentage of correctly classified instances among all the instances in the respective datasets. Higher accuracy scores suggest better performance in accurately identifying fake news articles.

The results acquired from the experiments indicate that the Attention fusion technique achieved the highest accuracy scores. On the validation dataset, the Attention fusion technique attained an accuracy score of 0.9194, while on the test dataset, it achieved a slightly higher accuracy score of 0.9205. This suggests that the Attention fusion technique effectively combines the information from the base models, resulting in improved fake news detection performance.

The Maximum fusion technique also demonstrated competitive performance, achieving accuracy scores of 0.9021 on the validation dataset and 0.9029 on the test dataset. This fusion technique calculates the maximum value from the outputs of the base models, thereby leveraging the strengths of each model.

On the other hand, the Concatenate and Addition fusion techniques yielded slightly lower accuracy scores compared to the Attention and Maximum techniques. The Concatenate fusion technique achieved an accuracy score of 0.8672 on both the validation and test datasets. Similarly, the Addition fusion technique obtained accuracy scores of 0.8664 and 0.8668 on the validation and test datasets, respectively.

Overall, the results indicate that the attention-based fusion technique outperformed the other fusion methods, demonstrating its effectiveness in integrating the base models' outputs for improved fake news detection. The findings of this study provide valuable insights into the selection and use of machine learning models for multimodal fake news detection systems, highlighting the significance of attention-based fusion approaches in enhancing performance and Table 10.3 showcases the confusion matrix produced for this model.

The evaluation metrics used to compare the various fusion techniques are compared in Table 10.4. Among these techniques, attention-based fusion achieved the highest performance across all metrics. Concatenation and addition techniques achieved slightly lower scores, with concatenation obtaining a precision of 0.8543, recall of 0.8632, F1 score of 0.8571, and accuracy of 0.8672, and addition obtaining a precision of 0.8574, recall of 0.8692, F1 score of 0.8637, and accuracy of 0.8668.

TABLE 10.3
Confusion Matrix of Multimodal Model
(RoBERTa + ViT + Attention Fusion)

	Positive	Negative
Positive	70,089	5,003
Negative	6,368	55,070

TABLE 10.4

Evaluation Metrics of Multimodal Model (RoBERTa + ViT + Attention Fusion)

	Precision	Recall	F1 Score	Accuracy
Concatenation	0.8543	0.8632	0.8571	0.8672
Addition	0.8574	0.8692	0.8637	0.8668
Maximum	0.8928	0.8975	0.8935	0.9029
Attention	0.9168	0.9333	0.925	0.9205

TABLE 10.5

Accuracies of Other Multimodal Fake News Detection Approaches Compared to the Best-Performing Approach in this Study

Algorithmic Approach	Accuracy (Validation)	Accuracy (Test)
BERT + EfficientNet (Maximum)	0.8334	0.8318
BERT + ResNet50 (Addition)	0.8551	0.8551
BERT + ResNet50 (Concatenate)	0.8564	0.8568
InferSent + VGG16 (Maximum)	0.8655	0.8655
BERT + VGG16 (Maximum)	0.8694	0.8699
BERT + ResNet5 (Maximum)	0.8929	0.8909
RoBERTa + ViT (Maximum)	0.9021	0.9029
RoBERTa + ViT (Attention)	0.9194	0.9205

Attention-based fusion technique has proven to be effective for integrating text and image features, providing superior performance compared to other fusion techniques.

Table 10.5 presents a comparison of accuracies among different multimodal fake news detection approaches, including the proposed RoBERTa + ViT model with attention in our study. The results demonstrate that our approach outperformed the other algorithms, achieving an impressive accuracy of 92.05% on the test data. Notably, the BERT + ResNet5 algorithm obtained the second-highest accuracy of 89.09%. These findings underscore the effectiveness of our proposed model in accurately detecting multimodal fake news and Figure 10.10 presents the visualization to compare the accuracies of the approaches in Table 10.5.

10.5   CONCLUSION

In this study, the experimenting with different fusion techniques keeping the pre-processing and models as constant has produced results that are interpreted as follows. With regards to the computational expenses' attention was the most computationally expensive fusion technique compared to other three techniques. Attention performed significantly better than concatenate and addition fusion techniques but close to maximum approach in terms of accuracy. Among concatenate and addition, both of which use simple operations unlike attention have not performed better than

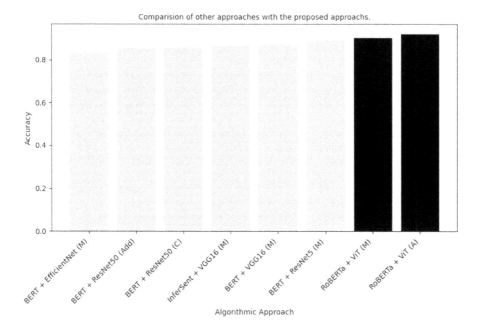

FIGURE 10.10 Bar-plot comparing the accuracies of other approaches (gray) and approach proposed in this study (black). (M-Maximum, Add-Addition, C-Concatenate, A-Attention).

maximum, despite concatenate approach providing a more comprehensive representation by including all the features. Maximum and Attention techniques have proven to be more effective at the fusion for multimodal fake news detection as they both focus on focusing on the most prominent or salient features among all the features produced by the models individually. Hence, techniques that can extract the most important features and assign higher weights to the features which influence the outcome the most among the final features are to be focused upon.

REFERENCES

[1] Vosoughi, S., D. Roy, and S. Aral, "The spread of true and false news online: The role of community structure." *Proceedings of the National Academy of Sciences*, 117(6), 2722–2728, 2018.

[2] Liu, Y., Y. Huang, D. Hu, J. Zhao, and S. Li, "What makes fake news spread? Identifying key factors influencing the spread of fake news on social media", *Telematics and Informatics*, 49, 101384, 2020.

[3] Dreyfuss, E. and Lapowsky, I. "Facebook is changing news feed (again) to stop fake news." *Wired*, 2019.

[4] Abdullah-All-Tanvir, Ehesas Mia Mahir, Saima Akhter, and Mohammad Rezwanul Huq. "Detecting fake news using machine learning and deep learning algorithms", *7th International Conference on Smart Computing & Communications (ICSCC),* Sarawak, Malaysia, 2019.

[5] Alonso-Bartolome, Santiago and Isabel Segura-Bedmar. "Multimodal fake news detection", *arXiv:2112.04831v1 [cs.CL]*, 2019

[6] Liu, Yang and Yi-fang Brook Wu, "Early detection of fake news on social media through propagation path classification with recurrent and convolutional networks", *ThirtySecond AAAI Conference on Artificial Intelligence, (AAAI–18)*, New Orleans, LA, AAAI Press, pp. 354–361, 2018.

[7] Shaar, Shaden, Nikolay Babulkov, Giovanni Da San Martino, and Preslav Nakov. "That is a known lie: Detecting previously fact-checked claims", *58th Annual Meeting of the Association for Computational Linguistics, ACL'20*, Seattle, Washington, USA, pp. 3607–3618, 2020.

[8] Joy, Sajib Kumar Saha, Dibyo Fabian Dofadar, Riyo Hayat Khan, and Md. Sabbir Ahmed, Rafeed Rahman. Dhaka, Bangladesh, "A comparative study on COVID-19 fake news detection using different transformer based models", *arXiv:2208.01355v1 [cs.CL]*, 2022.

[9] Lan, Zhenzhong, Mingda Chen, Sebastian Goodman, Kevin Gimpel, Piyush Sharma, and Radu Soricut. "Albert: A lite BERT for self-supervised learning of language representations", *International Conference on Learning Representations (ICLR)*, West Indies, 2020.

[10] Shu, K. et al., "FakeNewsNet: A data repository with news content, social context, and spatiotemporal information for studying fake news on social media", *IEEE/ACM International Conference on Advances in Social Networks Analysis and Mining (ASONAM)*, Istanbul, Turkey, 2018.

[11] Nguyen, D. T. et al. "Visual veracity analysis for fake news detection", *IEEE International Conference on Big Data (Big Data)*, Milan, Italy, 2019.

[12] Sun, W. et al., "Fake news detection on social media: A data mining perspective", *26th International Conference on World Wide Web*, Perth, Australia, 2017.

[13] Singh, V. K., Ghosh, I., and Sonagara, D, "Detecting fake news stories via multimodal analysis". *Journal of the Association for Information Science and Technology*, 72, 3–17, 2021.

[14] Kaliyar, R. K., Kumar, P., Kumar, M., Narkhede, M., Namboodiri, S., and Mishra, S, "DeepNet: An efficient neural network for fake news detection using news-user engagements", *5th International Conference on Computing, Communication and Security (ICCCS)*, Patna, Bihar, India, pp. 1–6, 2020.

[15] Nguyen, D. T., Bui, Q. H., Le, N. H., & Nguyen, V. H, "Multimodal deep learning for fake news detection", *International Conference on Advanced Technologies for Communications*, Hanoi City, Vietnam, 2022.

[16] Kaliyar, R. K., A. Goswami, P. Narang, and S. Sinha, "Fndnet - a deep convolutional neural network for fake news detection," *Cognitive Systems Research*, 61(C), 32–44, 2020.

[17] Tian, L., X. Zhang, Y. Wang, and H. Liu, "Early detection of rumours on twitter via stance transfer learning," In *Advances in Information Retrieval*, J. M. Jose, E. Yilmaz, J. Magalhaes, P. Castells, N. Ferro, M. J. ˜ Silva, and F. Martins (Eds.). Cham: Springer International Publishing, pp. 575–588, 2020.

[18] Nakamura, K., S. Levy, and W. Y. Wang. "Fakeddit: A new multimodal benchmark dataset for fine-grained fake news detection", *12th Language Resources and Evaluation Conference*, Italy, pp. 6149–6157, 2020.

[19] Volkova, Svitlana, Ellyn Ayton, Dustin L Arendt, Zhuanyi Huang, and Brian Hutchinson, "Explaining multimodal deceptive news prediction models." In *Proceedings of the International AAAI Conference on Web and Social Media*, USA, vol. 13, pp. 659–662, Munich, Germany, 2019.

[20] Wang, Yuping, Fatemeh Tahmasbi, Jeremy Blackburn, Barry Bradlyn, Emiliano De Cristofaro, David Magerman, Savvas Zannettou, and Gianluca Stringhini, "Understanding the use of fauxtography on social media", *Proceedings of the International AAAI Conference on Web and Social Media*, Australia, vol. 15, pp. 776–786, 2021.

[21] Weber, Derek and Frank Neumann, "Who's in the gang? Revealing coordinating communities in social media", *IEEE/ACM International Conference on Advances in Social Networks Analysis and Mining (ASONAM)*, Australia, pp. 89–93, IEEE, 2020.

[22] Hosseinmardi, Homa, Sabrina Arredondo Mattson, Rahat Ibn Rafiq, Richard Han, Qin Lv, and Shivakant Mishra, "Detection of cyberbullying incidents on the Instagram social network". *arXiv:1503.03909*, 2015.

[23] Castillo, C., Mendoza, M., and B. Poblete, "Information credibility on twitter," In *Proceedings of the 20th International Conference on World Wide Web, ser. WWW '11*. New York, NY: Association for Computing Machinery, pp. 675–684, 2011.

[24] Ma, J., W. Gao, and K.-F. Wong, "Rumor detection on twitter with tree structured recursive neural networks," *56th Annual Meeting of the Association for Computational Linguistics*, Melbourne, Australia, vol. 1, pp. 1980–1989, 2018.

[25] Zhou, X. and R. Zafarani, "Network-based fake news detection: A pattern-driven approach," *IEEE/ACM International Conference on Advances in Social Networks Analysis and Mining12*, 2019.

[26] Han, X., Li, P., Yao, H., and Qian, K. "FakeNewsNet-multimodal: A multimodal dataset for fake news detection", *IEEE International Conference on Big Data*, West Indies, 2021.

[27] Giachanou, A., Zhang, G., and Rosso, P, "Multimodal multi-image fake news detection", *IEEE 7th International Conference on Data Science and Advanced Analytics (DSAA)*, Sydney, Australia, pp. 647–654, 2020.

[28] Li, P., Sun, X., Yu, H., Tian, Y., Yao, F., and Xu, G. "Entity oriented multi-modal alignment and fusion network for fake news detection", *IEEE Transactions on Multimedia*, pp. 1–1, 2021. doi:10.1109/TMM.2021.3098988.

[29] Wang, Yaqing, Fenglong Ma, Zhiwei Jin, Ye Yuan, Guangxu Xun, Kishlay Jha, Lu Su, and Jing Gao, "EANN: Event adversarial neural networks for multi-modal fake news detection", Vol 109, *KDD*, China, pp 849–857, 2018.

[30] Singhal, Shivangi, Rajiv Ratn Shah, Tanmoy Chakraborty, Ponnurangam Kumaraguru, and Shin'ichi Satoh, "SpotFake: A multi-modal framework for fake news detection", Vol 110, *IEEE BigMM*, India, pp. 39–47, 2019.

[31] Zhou, Yangming, Yuzhou Yang, Qichao Ying, Zhenxing Qian, and Xinpeng Zhang, "Multi-modal fake news detection on social media via multi-grained information fusion", *arXiv:2304.00827v1 [cs.CV]*, 2023.

[32] Jing, Jing, Hongchen Wu, Jie Sun, Xiaochang Fang, and Huaxiang Zhang, "Multimodal fake news detection via progressive fusion networks," *Information Processing & Management*, 60(1), 2023.

[33] Kishore, Vikash and Mukesh Kumar, "Enhanced multimodal fake news detection with optimal feature fusion and modified Bi-LSTM architecture", *Cybernetics and Systems*, 2023.

[34] Kang, Z., Y. Cao, Y. Shang, T. Liang, H. Tang, and L. Tong, "Fake news detection with heterogenous deep graph convolutional network", In K. Karlapalem, H. Cheng, N. Ramakrishnan, R. K. Agrawal, P. K. Reddy, J. Srivastava, and T. Chakraborty (Eds.), *Advances in Knowledge Discovery and Data Mining* (pp. 408–420). Cham: Springer International Publishing, 2021.

[35] Papadopoulos, Stefanos-Iordanis, Christos Koutlis, Symeon Papadopoulos, and Panagiotis C. Petrantonakis, "Figments and misalignments: A framework for fine-grained crossmodal misinformation detection", *arXiv:2304.14133v1 [cs.CV]* 27, 2023.

Index

accuracy 202
agriculture 43, 44
applications 43
Artificial Intelligence 3, 41, 77
   decision trees 169
   multilayer perceptrons 156
   random forest 156, 169
   support vector machines 156, 169
automotive sector 43, 44

big data analytics 3, 94

case studies 137
cloud computing 3, 32, 157
cyber physical systems 41

energy sector 43

fake news detection 230

green technologies 15

healthcare 43, 44
health monitoring system 156

Industrial Internet of Things 2, 76
   advancements 82, 83, 84
   data storage 91, 92
   potential of IIOT 81
   technologies 90, 93
Industry 5.0 2, 108
Internet of things 2, 77, 156, 157
logistics 43, 44

loss 199
lung cancer 177
   CT images 178
   PET images 179

machine learning 41, 77
   decision trees 169
   multilayer perceptrons 156
   neural networks 169
   random forest 156, 169
   support vector machines 156, 169

neural networks 169

performance metrics 202
potential benefits 109

renewable energy 107
retail 43, 44

smart grid 142
smart health monitoring systems 158
   devices 159
supply chain management 49
sustainability 27
3D Printing 3, 77

water quality forecasting 206
   background 208
   challenges 214
   deep learning models 215
   importance 211

Milton Keynes UK
Ingram Content Group UK Ltd.
UKHW031130141024
449569UK00006B/308